THE OTHER END
OF THE LEASH

ALSO BY PATRICIA B. McCONNELL

Beginning Family Dog Training
The Cautious Canine: How to Help Dogs Conquer Their Fears
I'll Be Home Soon! How to Prevent and Treat Separation Anxiety
How to Be Leader of the Pack, and Have Your Dog Love You for It!

BOOKS AND BOOKLETS WITH OTHER AUTHORS
Puppy Primer (with Brenda Scidmore)
*Feeling Outnumbered? How to Manage and Enjoy
Your Multi-Dog Household* (with Karen B. London)

THE OTHER END OF THE LEASH

Why We Do What We Do Around Dogs

PATRICIA B. MCCONNELL, PH.D.

BALLANTINE BOOKS
New York

To my Mom and Dad

NOTES FROM THE AUTHOR

All of the people and dogs that are described in this book are based on real people and real dogs. But family problems are very intimate things, whether they relate to dogs or people or both, so in order to protect people's privacy I have changed the names of all the dogs (except mine) and all the clients that I mention in this book. In some cases, I changed the breed of the dog or the sex of the client. Many of my clients will no doubt relate to some of the cases that I describe, because so many of the problems that I see are shared by hundreds, if not thousands, of dog owners. If you think you recognize yourself or your own dog, know that you're not alone—I probably saw dozens or hundreds of people and dogs with the same issues. Unless, by chance, you're bursting with pride about being mentioned in the book—in that case, *of course* it's about you!

A word of caution and supportive advice: if you have a serious or potentially serious behavioral problem with your dog, don't hesitate to find good, professional assistance. There's actually very little that's intuitive about handling and training a dog, especially one with a serious behavioral problem, and there's no substitute for getting a helpful coach who can help you one-on-one. You wouldn't try to learn basketball just by reading a book, so if you need to play the game, do what any parent would do for their child, and find a good, knowledgeable coach. Don't be embarrassed, as people often are about coming to see me for help with their dog. I don't know anyone who finds it humiliating to take his car to a mechanic. But as with mechanics, there's a huge range of expertise and ethics out there. Be sure to find someone who is well-versed in using positive reinforcement and who is just as kind to you as they are to your dog. See the References in the back of the book for more direction about how to locate qualified assistance. And don't hesitate to talk to your vet about your dog's health. Sometimes behavioral problems derive from physical ones.

And finally, a note to the readers: Rather than using "he" exclusively or awkwardly using "he and she" when I refer to generic dogs, I have alternated between "he" and "she" throughout the book. It's just simpler, and in writing and dog training, simpler is almost always a good thing.

CONTENTS

ACKNOWLEDGMENTS

This book was cultivated with my mother's love of dogs and my father's love of literature. I am filled with gratitude for all that my father, G. Clarke Bean, was able to give me, and for all that my mother, Pamela Bean, continues to provide.

My academic mentors Jeffrey Baylis and Charles Snowdon are still a source of inspiration and support. I will forever be indebted to them both for all that they have taught me, and for their ability to combine critical thinking with their deep love for animals and their curiosity about them. I am also grateful to the Department of Zoology at the University of Wisconsin–Madison, for its support during my Ph.D. research and at present for my course, "The Biology and Philosophy of Human/Animal Relationships."

I don't know what I did to deserve every author's dream agent, but the wisdom and support of Jennifer Gates, of Zachary, Shuster and Harmsworth, has meant more to me than I can ever say. I am equally grateful to my editor, Leslie Meredith, whose belief in the book has always been stalwart, and who was invaluable at many stages of the writing. Sloppy kisses to her dog, Dylan, with a promise of doggie treats coming when he least expects it. My sincere thanks also to Maureen O'Neal and all at Ballantine for their support and hard work.

This book never could have been written without the staff at Dog's Best Friend, Ltd. Without the dedication and professionalism of Jackie Boland, Karen London, Aimee Moore, and Denise Swedlund, I never would have been able to leave the office and write at home every morning for such a long time. I am also grateful to all of the Dog's Best Friend, Ltd. dog training class instructors and volunteers, who skillfully and lovingly educate the animals at both ends of the leash almost every week of the year.

Much of the good in this book is due to the thoughtful comments of a group of friends and colleagues. Jeffrey Baylis, Jackie Boland, Ann Lindsey, Karen London, Beth Miller, Aimee Moore, Denise Swedlund, and Charles Snowdon provided thoughtful feedback that substantially improved the book. I am also grateful to Frans de Waal for reviewing some of the sections on chimpanzee and bonobo behavior, and to Steven Suomi for our discussions about personality in primates. I was lucky to have the interest and support of several people at the Vilas County Zoo in Madison, Wisconsin, and thank Mary Schmidt and Jim Hubing especially, for providing opportunities for me to schmooze with their chimps and with Mukah the orangutan.

I could never have finished the book on deadline without the support and help of dear friends during my dog Luke's battle with soft tissue sarcoma. Dmitri Bilgere, Jackie Boland, Harriet Irwin, Patrick Mommaerts, and Renee Ravetta generously assisted the daily transporting of Luke to the University of Wisconsin–Madison Veterinary Medical Teaching Hospital for radiation treatments. I am also grateful to four very special veterinarians, John Dally of the River Valley Veterinary Clinic, Christine Burgess of the University of Wisconsin Veterinary Medical Teaching Hospital, Kim Conley of the Silver Springs Animal Wellness Center, and Chris Bessent, DVM and Chinese Medicine Specialist, for all their skill and support during that challenging time.

All my Vermont Valley Vixen friends should know how special our monthly brunches are to me—I am everlastingly grateful that I live nestled in a countryside brimming with beauty and good friends. My dear friends Dave and Julie Egger, Dmitri Bilgere, Karen Bloom, Karen Lasker, Beth Miller, and Patrick Mommaerts all were important in their own ways, and I am a lucky woman to have them as friends. I'm equally lucky to have two profoundly supportive and amazing sisters Wendy Barker and Liza Piatt who, even though we live far apart, are always close to my heart.

I am indebted to Mary Vinson and the Coulee Region Humane Society in La Crosse, Wisconsin, for their generous permission to use photos from the book *Tails from the Heart* by Susan Fox with photos by Cathy Acherman. I thank Frans de Waal for his generosity in allowing the use of his photographs of chimpanzees from the books *Chimpanzee Politics* and *Peacemaking Among Primates*. Karen London also deserves grateful thanks for her photographic contributions to the photo section of this book. Zachary Sauer's research assistance was greatly appreciated and deserves thanks as well.

Special thanks to Dr. Cecelia Soares, a veterinarian and marriage and family therapist who graciously shared the phrase "The Other End of the Leash," which is also the name of her consulting business. Dr. Soares offers seminars and consultations to veterinarians and their staff members on communication and other topics related to the human side of veterinary practice. She can be reached at 925-932-0607 or 800-883-2181.

The thousands of dogs and their owners with whom I have worked have taught me more than I can express—thanks for letting me learn and grow along with you. I give grateful thanks to a list of amazingly talented dog trainers and behaviorists who, over the years, have provided skill and inspiration to me and thousands of others: Carol Benjamin, Sheila Booth, William Campbell, Jean Donaldson, Donna Duford, Job Michael Evans, Ian Dunbar, Trish King, Karen Pryor, Pam Reid, Terry Ryan, Pia Silvani, Sue Sternberg, and Barbara Wodehouse. I list those names with absolute assurance that I will remember yet one more absolutely essential person— the day after the book is released. Whoever you are—thanks (and my apologies). Kudos and warm wishes to Doug McConnell and Larry Meiller, my favorite co-hosts of all time. I also thank Ricky Aaron, who has taught me virtually nothing about dogs, because he made me laugh when he called me up and begged me to mention his name.

My friend and colleague Nancy Raffetto deserves her own special thanks, for having the vision and the courage to join with me in opening up Dog's Best Friend Training, Ltd., in 1988, at a time when Applied Animal Behaviorists were practically unknown. Looking back, I'm still amazed that two Ph.D.s, knowing virtually nothing about business but a lot about behavior, managed to launch what is now a thriving enterprise. Thanks for riding the whitewater with me, I could never have done it alone.

Acknowledgments and admiration to all at the magazine *The BARk* ("the *New Yorker* of dog magazines) for their support of my writing and their exquisite efforts to combine beautiful writing and great art with a passion for dogs and their humans.

My sweetest and most extravagant thanks go to my dear friend Jim Billings, whose friendship, support, and wise advice have been like food and water to me over the last year and a half.

And finally, I declare my love and admiration for Luke, Tulip, Pip, and Lassie—four remarkable individuals who have enhanced and enriched my life beyond description.

INTRODUCTION

It was twilight, so it was hard to tell exactly what the two dark lumps on the road were. Cruising at seventy miles an hour on the interstate, tucked between a station wagon and a semi, I was contentedly driving home from a herding dog trial. But as the black shapes got closer, my state of serenity shifted. They were dogs. Live dogs, at least for the moment. Straight out of a Walt Disney movie, an old Golden Retriever and an adolescent Heeler mix were trotting in and out of the highway, oblivious to the danger. Years ago I had watched a dog hit head-on by a car, and I'd give a lot to get the image out of my mind. It seemed inevitable that it was going to happen again.

I pulled off the road and parked behind another truck. Friends from the trial who were driving ahead of me had also seen the dogs. We exchanged terrified looks and ran back toward the dogs on our bank of the stream of traffic, the dogs across the lanes as if across a flooding river. They looked friendly, used to people, perhaps even happy to see something with legs instead of tires. Traffic was moving fast across all four lanes. Visibility was poor. The traffic noise was deafening; there was no way the dogs could have heard us speak to them. At just the wrong time, the dogs started ambling across the road to us. We threw out our arms like traffic cops and lunged forward to stop them. They stopped, a second before a Miller Beer truck would have hit them. For a moment we stood there frozen, terrified. The responsibility *of doing just the right thing, of somehow interfering in a way that would save their lives rather than ensure their deaths weighed like a stone in our bellies.*

We "called" to them at a break in the traffic, bending over in a play bow and turning our bodies away to encourage them to come to us. Then we would turn and stop them like traffic cops when the cars in the next lane loomed over the hill, coming so fast, I was sure they'd be killed. This silent dance of life and death continued, our bodies turning back and forth, our only means of communicating through the noise of the traffic. It all seemed to happen at the speed of light, the dogs oblivious to the danger, moving forward toward us, then stopping, then backing up as we moved our own bodies to thread them through the traffic.

But that, plus a lot of good luck, was enough. Just by shifting forward with our arms out, we could stop the dogs, and by shifting backward and turning away, we could get them to move toward us. No leash, no collars, no control but the effect of our bodies, communicating "come" and "stop" with the turn of a torso. I still don't understand how they made it. But they did. I will forever be grateful for the responsiveness of a dog to the right visual signals.

All dogs are brilliant at perceiving the slightest movement that we make, and they assume that each tiny motion has meaning. So do we humans, if you think about it. Remember that minuscule turn of the head that caught your attention when you were dating? Think about how little someone's lips have to move to change a sweet smile into a smirk. How far does an eyebrow have to rise to change the message we read from the face it's on—a tenth of an inch?

You'd think that we would automatically generalize this common knowledge to our interactions with our dogs. But we don't. We are often oblivious to how we're moving around our dogs. It seems to be very human not to know what we're doing with our body, unconscious of where our hands are or that we just tilted our head. We radiate random signals like some crazed semaphore flag, while our dogs watch in confusion, their eyes rolling around in circles like cartoon dogs.

These visual signals, like all the rest of our actions, have a profound influence on what our dogs do. Who dogs are and how they behave are partly defined by who we humans are and how we ourselves behave. Domestic dogs, by definition, share their lives with another species: us. And so this is a book for dog lovers, but it's not only a book about dogs. It's also a book about people. It's a book about how we're the same as our dogs and how we're different from them.

Our species shares so much with dogs. If you look across the vast range of all animal life, from beetles to bears, humans and dogs are more alike than we are different. Like dogs, we make milk for our young and raise them in a pack. Our babies have lots to learn while growing up; we hunt cooperatively; we play silly games even as adults; we snore; we scratch and blink and yawn on sunny afternoons. Look at what Pam Brown, a New Zealand poet, had to say about people and dogs in the book *Bond for Life*:

> Humankind is drawn to dogs because they are so like ourselves—bumbling, affectionate, confused, easily disappointed, eager to be amused, grateful for kindness and the least attention.

These similarities allow the members of two different species to live together intimately, sharing food, recreation, and even bearing young together.[1] Lots of animals live closely linked to others, but our level of connection with dogs is profound. Most of us exercise with our dogs, play with our dogs, eat at the same time as our dogs (and sometimes the same food), and sleep with our dogs. Some of us still depend on our dogs for our work. Sheep ranchers in Wyoming and dairy farmers in Wisconsin need their dogs as much as or more than they do machinery or high-tech feeding systems. We know that dogs enrich the lives of many of us, providing comfort and joy to millions around the world. Studies even show that they decrease the probability of a second heart attack. We don't put up

---

1. That may sound extreme, but ask any breeder who's paced the floor waiting for puppies how closely connected she felt to her dog and how clingy her dog gets right before delivery.

with shedding and barking and carrying pooper-scoopers on walks for nothing.

And look what we've done for dogs. *Canis lupus familiaris,* the domestic dog, is now one of the most successful mammals on earth, thanks to hitching his star to ours. It's been estimated that there are about four hundred million dogs in the world. Many American dogs are eating organic food, going to canine chiropractors and doggy day-care centers, and chewing on millions of dollars a year in toys. Now that's a successful species.

But we also have our differences. We humans don't relish rolling in cow pies. Nor do we, for the most part, eat the placentas of our newborns. We don't greet one another, thank heaven, by sniffing one another's rumps. While dogs live in a world of scents, we think of ourselves as chemically illiterate. Partly because of those differences, humans and dogs often miscommunicate, and the consequences range from mildly irritating to life-threatening. Some of this miscommunication stems from an owner's not understanding dog behavior and how animals learn, and I encourage all dog lovers to read lots of good books about dog training. Training dogs turns out not to be intuitively obvious, and the more you learn, the easier and more fun it will be.

Some of this miscommunication, though, results not just from ignorance about how to train a dog but from fundamental differences between the behavior of two species. After all, dogs aren't the only animal in the relationship. We humans at the other end of the leash are animals, too, with our own biological baggage of behavior that came along on our evolutionary train ride. We don't come to dog training as blank slates, any more than dogs do. Dogs and dog lovers alike have been shaped by our separate evolutionary backgrounds, and what each of us bring to the relationship starts with the heritage of our natural history. Although our similarities create a bond that's remarkable, we are each speaking our own native "language," and a lot gets lost in the translation.

Dogs are canids, the taxonomic family that includes wolves, foxes, and coyotes. Genetically dogs are wolves, pure and simple. Wolves and dogs share so much of their DNA that they are almost impossible to distinguish genetically. Wolves and dogs interbreed freely, and their offspring are just as fertile as their parents.[2] By studying wolf behavior, we learned what it means when our dogs flatten their ears or lick our faces. Wolves and dogs communicate to members of their pack with the same set of postures that convey submission, confidence, or threat. If you saw either a wolf or a dog standing still and erect, growling deeply, and looking directly into your eyes, you'd correctly conclude that the same message was being sent from each of them. So dogs, in one sense, are wolves, and there's much to learn about a dog by studying a wolf and its pack.

But in another sense, a very important one, dogs aren't wolves at all. Domestic dogs are not as shy as wolves, they are less aggressive than wolves, they are less likely to roam, and they are far more trainable. You don't see a lot of people herding sheep with wolf/dog hybrids. Take it from me as a biologist and a sheep farmer, it wouldn't be pretty. Dogs actually behave most like juvenile wolves, Peter Pan wolves who never grew up, and in Chapter 5 we'll talk about how that might have occurred. Regrettably, in the last several decades, popular conceptions of wolves and dogs have oversimplified their similarities. Perhaps that is what motivated Raymond and Lorna Coppinger, in their book *Dogs,* to emphasize the differences between dogs and wolves. They say in their introduction: "Dogs may well be closely related to wolves but that does not mean they behave like wolves. People are closely related to chimps but that doesn't make us a subspecies of chimpanzee, nor does it mean we behave like chimps."

I'm reminded of the saying about describing a glass as either half full or half empty. Each observation is correct; it just emphasizes a different perspective. My own bias is that *both* perspectives are essential, and so I'd argue that it's valuable to look at what's shared *and* what's different between wolves and dogs. And that is true of our own behavior as well. We *do* behave like chimps in many ways, and of course, in other ways we don't.

For years scientists have found it valuable to "compare and contrast" human behavior with that of other primates. From popular books like

2. Breeding dogs to wolves can cause a host of biological problems and is a practice that I strongly discourage.

The Naked Ape and *The Third Chimpanzee* to academic ones like *Tools, Language, and Cognition in Human Evolution,* scientists have been looking at humans as primates for many decades. It's a key issue in the fields of physical anthropology, cultural anthropology, ethology, and comparative psychology. And it's not just academia: the Oubi tribe of the Ivory Coast saw humans and chimpanzees as the descendants of two brothers, which would make us cousins. It's not at all a bad biological analogy, given that we humans and chimps share about 98 percent of our genes. In a lovely irony the tribe envisioned the "handsome" brother as being the father of humanity but the "smart" brother as the father of chimps.

We have much to gain by looking at ourselves as the touchy, playful, and drama-loving primates that we are. We may be an animal like no other, with intellectual abilities that are nothing less than amazing, but we are still bound by many of the laws of nature. Our species and species close to us like chimpanzees, bonobos,[3] gorillas, and baboons have inherent tendencies to behave in certain ways. Chimpanzees and bonobos don't build stadiums, use Post-it notes, or write books about themselves, but for all our differences, we are more alike than not. For instance, there are striking similarities among the postures and gestures of chimpanzees, bonobos, and humans, each of whom relate to their kin with kisses, embraces, and even hand-holding.

I don't mean to diminish our unique status as human beings by recalling our primate heritage. We *are* unique, so much so that it is reasonable to talk about "humans and animals" instead of "humans and other animals." Whether you believe that it's God-given or driven by natural selection (or both), we are so different from all other animals that we deserve to be in our own category. But as different as we are, we are still linked with other animals in important ways. The more we learn about biology, the more we discover how close to other species we really are. We

---

3. There are two species of primates that used to be called chimps. Common chimpanzees (*Pan troglodytes*) are the larger of the two and are the best known; this is the species that Jane Goodall studied. As is convention, I'll refer to them as "chimpanzees." The other species, sometimes called the pygmy chimpanzee, is now called the bonobo (*Pan paniscus*). Bonobos are smaller, more likely to walk bipedally than chimps, and so sexual that much of their behavior can't be shown on TV nature shows. That's saying a lot, given what our species does on television.

are so closely related to chimpanzees, bonobos, and gorillas that some taxonomists have reclassified all of us into our own subfamily, the Homininae. Chimps, bonobos, and humans, the most closely related apes, are intelligent animals with complex social systems who have long periods of learning and development, who require a tremendous amount of parental investment, and who tend to behave in certain ways in certain contexts, even when we humans aren't aware of it. For example, all three species have a tendency to repeat notes when we're excited, to use loud noises to impress others, and to thrash around whatever is in our paw if we're frustrated. This behavior has no small effect on our interactions with dogs, who in spite of some barks and growls, mostly communicate visually, get quiet rather than noisy to impress others, and are too busy standing on their paws to do much else with them.

There are many examples of how this behavioral heritage can create trouble in our relationships with dogs. For example, we humans love to hug. It's called "ventral-ventral" contact in the primate literature, and chimps and bonobos love to do it, too. They hug their babies, and their babies hug them. Adolescent chimps hug each other, and so do adult chimps when they're reconciling from conflict. Gorilla mothers and their babies are great huggers. I'll never forget listening to biologist Amy Vedder telling how she entered a cabin with a baby gorilla huddling in terror in the back of the room.[4] Amy, who had observed gorillas for years, gave a perfect replica of the "belch" vocalization that gorillas give in greeting. The frightened, sick young gorilla crawled across the room, pulled himself up onto her chest, and threw his long arms around her torso. Just as a lost child would hug his mother, it was natural for the gorilla to hug Amy and for her to hug him back. The tendency to want to hug something that we love or care for is overwhelmingly strong. Try telling an adolescent girl, or any four-year-old, not to hug her beloved dog. Good luck.

But dogs don't hug. Imagine two dogs standing up on their hind legs, forelegs wrapped around each other, chests and muzzles pressed together.

4. A mostly unacknowledged heroine who, along with her husband, Bill Weber, deserves most of the credit for mountain gorilla conservation in Rwanda. You can read their compelling story in the book *In the Kingdom of Gorillas*.

You probably haven't seen that a lot at the dog park. Dogs are just as social as we are, veritable social butterflies who can't live a normal life without a lot of social interaction. But they don't hug. They may paw at another dog as an invitation to play, they may slap a paw over the shoulders of another dog as a display of social status, but they don't hug. And they often don't react kindly to those who do. Your own dog may benevolently put up with it, but I've seen hundreds of dogs who growled or bit when someone hugged them.

The reason that I've seen all those growling dogs is because I'm an Applied Animal Behaviorist, and I consult about serious behavior problems in companion animals. Both my scientific training[5] and my hands-on experiences with people and dogs have led to the perspective that I advance in this book. For my Ph.D. research I recorded and studied the sounds that animal handlers from a variety of cultural and linguistic backgrounds used to communicate to their working domestic animals. In one sense I was studying our own species as you would any other species of animal, objectively recording and analyzing the sounds made by the trainers, just as other scientists study the notes of a bird's song. That perspective, along with extensive training in the precise observation and description of behavior, has led me to pay attention as much to our own behavior as to that of our dogs. Teaching "The Biology and Philosophy of Human-Animal Relationships" at the University of Wisconsin–Madison and cohosting a national animal behavior and pet advice show, "Calling All Pets," continually remind me how essential our relationships with other animals are and, at the same time, how often our own primatelike tendencies cause us problems.

Just as important, my experiences as a dog trainer,[6] a breeder and trainer of working Border Collies, a competitor in herding dog trials, and a dog owner who makes no apology for being crazy in love with my dogs have continually reminded me how easy it is for us humans to miscommunicate to our dogs.

---

5. My Ph.D. is in zoology, my minor is in psychology, and my specialty is ethology, or the study of animal behavior.
6. I've taught dog training classes for more than twelve years.

Some of the stories in this book are about my own four dogs and the life we share together on a small farm in Wisconsin. The other stories are from consultations with concerned dog owners. I wasn't surprised when people started coming in with serious problems, often involving aggression in dogs. When you're a Certified Applied Animal Behaviorist who specializes in aggression, you are often the "last hope," and you hear some pretty dramatic stories and meet some pretty damaged dogs. I've lost count of the number of dogs who've come charging into my office, snarl-barking and lunging, leading with their teeth. I've worked for years in an environment in which one small mistake will get me badly hurt. Although I can never say that I've gotten used to it (every once in a while, I think, "What the hell am I doing making a living this way?"), I expected it. We can't live with animals with the equivalent of carpet knives in their mouths without running into occasional problems.

Although I expected to work with dogs who got in trouble with their teeth, I didn't expect to see so much emotional suffering. Almost every week I've seen one or two "Do-I-have-to-kill-my-dog?" cases, with heartbroken owners crying in the office while discussing whether to euthanize their best friend. It is true that an inspiring number of problem dogs can be rehabilitated or managed safely if the owners have the ability and the right environment. But no matter how hard some owners try, some dogs are so damaged that they present an unacceptable level of risk. Part of my job is to initiate difficult discussions about the ethical quandary of protecting members of your own species but not betraying an individual who feels like part of your family. Some of these cases could break your heart. They did mine.

What's striking about many of these cases is that they so often relate as much to our behavior as to that of the dogs. I don't say that in the sense that their owners weren't responsible or thoughtful enough about caring for and training their dogs. I mean it on a deeper level, on a level of how our natural tendencies as primates can elicit equally inherent responses in a dog, even though each party thinks that the other is communicating something that it's not. I'm reminded of those arguments that we get into with our own species, our voices and heart rate rising, until we realize that we and the person that we're arguing with are talking about two completely different things and that we actually don't disagree at all. I've already mentioned how our tendency to want to express love to a dog through hugging can get us both into trouble. Dogs often interpret hugs as aggressive actions, and so they defend themselves from this madness with the only means they have, their teeth. And there we were, just trying to tell them that we love them.

I see the same miscommunication on a daily basis when people greet dogs on the street. We primates greet with head-on approaches, extend our forepaws, and make direct, face-to-face contact. This tendency is so strong that passersby will reach and lean toward a tense, stiff-legged dog, even one who is quietly growling, even while the owner is saying, "Please *do not pet* my dog! He isn't good with strangers!" The world is full of hapless dog owners who ineffectually try to stop other humans from doing something that comes naturally. Our hardwired way of greeting others is so strong that it can override clear signals that tell us to stop.

Not all of these translation troubles lead to serious problems. More often we simply confuse our dogs or undermine our own training efforts. We confuse our dogs by repeating words no matter what the dog is doing, because that's what chimps and humans tend to do when they get anxious or excited. We're oblivious to the visual signals that we're sending to our dogs while we're busy constructing long sentences, because speech is so very important to our species. We raise our voices for no reason and are far too quick to jerk a leash around if we get frustrated, because that's what bipedal apes tend to do.

Focusing on the behavior at our end of the leash isn't a new concept in dog training. Most professional dog trainers actually spend very little time working with other people's dogs: most of our time is spent training humans. Take it from me, we're not the easiest species on the block to train. Hang around after dog training class and listen to what the trainers are talking about. It isn't always your dog. As a matter of fact, one of the few things you can get a large group of dog trainers to agree on is that humans are a lot harder to train than dogs. But it's not because we're stupid, and it's not because we're not motivated. We're simply us, and just as dogs chew and bark, we tend to do things that are natural to us, even when they don't serve us well.

Good professional dog trainers are good partly because they understand dogs and how dogs learn. But they are also good because they are aware of their own behavior. They've learned to stop doing some of the things that are natural to our species but are misinterpreted by dogs. It may not come naturally, but to some extent, it's easy, and you can learn much of it in this book. Becoming aware of the ways that we behave around our dogs does take a certain amount of energy, a kind of mindfulness about what we're doing that we often lack. But once you start paying attention, once you focus your awareness on your own behavior instead of your dog's, you automatically become clearer and more sensible to your dog.

Just turning around and moving *away* from your dog can radically increase the chance that he'll come when you call. Learning a few easy moves can help you teach your dog to lie down and stay, no matter what's going on in the rest of the house. I don't mean to imply that it's easy to be a great dog trainer; it's not. I'm as proud of my ability to train a dog as I am of my Ph.D., and that's saying a lot. But whether you are a professional dog trainer or a family member with a beloved pet, you can improve the relationship between you and your dog by becoming more aware of your own behavior.

Every year several students come to see me at the university and ask how they can become an Applied Animal Behaviorist. Some of them tell me they are interested primarily because they love animals so much and work themselves up to confessing that they don't really like people much at all. But we humans are an integral part of the lives of domestic dogs, and we can't fully relate to a domestic dog without taking our own species into account. The more you love your dog, the more you need to understand human behavior. The good news, speaking as a biologist, is that our species is as fascinating as any other. I find myself just as enamored of *Homo sapiens* as I am of *Canis lupus familiaris,* because even when we humans are idiots, we're interesting ones. So I invite all of you to show our own species the same patience and compassion that we show dogs. After all, dogs seem to like us a lot, and I have the utmost respect for their opinion.

The similarities that we share, and the differences that confuse us, are a blessing and a curse in our relationship with dogs. An understanding of those similarities and differences was a blessing that evening on the highway. After the dogs successfully made it across the lanes of traffic, we held on to their collars with viselike grips, laughing and crying in adrenaline-charged relief. I used my car phone to call the vet clinic number on their tags. The clinic's vet happened to be driving back on the same highway from a crisis at a dairy farm, so he drove up in less than ten minutes. He had the dogs back home within the hour. Seems the young Heeler cross had seduced the elderly Golden into no-man's-land. I called the owner the next day, and we both cried, grieving over what might have happened, overjoyed at what really did.

The dogs are alive because we were lucky, because the goddess of dog love was looking over us, and because we knew how our behavior affected them. Pay attention to your own behavior. Believe me, your dog is.

1

MONKEY SEE, MONKEY DO

The Importance of Visual Signals
Between People and Dogs

Being an Applied Animal Behaviorist who works with aggressive dogs in my office is one thing. Working with them on a stage in front of a couple of hundred people is another. In a private consultation, all your attention is focused on the dog, but when you're doing a demonstration, your focus is divided between the dog and the audience. Important signals may last only a tenth of a second and be no bigger than a quarter of an inch, so you can get into trouble trying to attend to both an audience and a problem dog at the same time. There's a kind of Evel Knievel feeling about working with an aggressive dog up on a stage. You prepare meticulously to have all the odds in your favor. You get a good night's sleep, eat healthy food, and interview the dog owner extensively beforehand. You work with good, reliable people on whom you can count. And then you hit the ramp and hope you'll make it over the canyon.

The Mastiff I was working with at one seminar must have weighed more than 200 pounds, with a head the size of an oven. He had been lunging at strangers for the last several months, scaring his owners as much as their friends. Tossing treats steadily, I got closer and closer to him while I talked to the audience about what I was doing. Out of the corner of my eye, I saw that the Mastiff looked relaxed, anticipating another treat, breathing normally. I turned my attention to a question from the audience, as I continued tossing treats, and took one step closer. I was now only a few feet away.

1

Donna's eyes alerted me. I had glanced at Donna Duford, a wise and experienced professional dog trainer, and by the look on her face, I knew I was in trouble. The Mastiff was standing right beside me but had become chillingly still. I glanced in his direction, but looked directly into his eyes, although only for a microsecond—a mistake, and a stupid one at that. Direct eye contact with a nervous dog is a beginner's mistake that you either learn to avoid or you get out of the business.

The dog exploded like a freight train of teeth and muscle, lunging right at my face. His growl-barks shook the building. I did what every highly trained professional does in that circumstance. I backed up.

Little Movements Have Big Effects

If I had not made eye contact with the Mastiff, if my eyes had moved some fraction of an inch over to the left or right, he wouldn't have lunged. All that ballistic power would've sat, quietly watching, if I had changed the path of my gaze a quarter of an inch. A barely perceptible change in my behavior would have resulted in the stunningly obvious difference between a 200-pound dog sitting quietly or launching toward my face.

That story may be a bit dramatic, but the same impact of subtle movements underlies each and every one of your interactions with your dog. Dogs are brilliant at perceiving minute changes in our bodies and assume each tiny motion has meaning. Small movements that you make result in huge changes in your dog's behavior. If you learn anything from this book, learn that. The examples are endless. Standing straight with your shoulders squared rather than slumped can make the difference in whether your dog sits or not. Shifting your weight forward or backward, almost imperceptibly to a human, is a neon sign to a dog. Changes in the way that your body leans are so important that an incline of half an inch backward or forward can lure a frightened stray dog toward you or chase her away. Whether you breathe deeply or hold your breath can prevent a dogfight or cause one. I've worked with aggressive dogs every week for thirteen years, and I've seen repeatedly that sometimes tiny movements can defuse a dangerous situation—or create one.

When I asked a veterinary student what she had learned after spending two weeks with me, she said, "I never realized how important the details of my actions were—how tiny changes in things like shifting your weight can have huge effects on an animal's behavior." This information doesn't seem to be obvious to any of us. But how strange, given how important minuscule movements are within our own species. As I asked in the introduction, how far do you have to raise an eyebrow to change the message on your face? Go look in the mirror, right now if it's convenient. Raise the corners of your mouth just the slightest bit and see how much it changes the "look" on your face. Watch the face of one of your family members and think about how little it has to change to convey information. That information, what we learn about others by watching for small movements in their faces and bodies, is critical to our relationship with them. It is also deeply rooted in our primate heritage. Primate species vary tremendously, from a 4-ounce, sap-eating pygmy marmoset to a 500-pound, leaf-chomping gorilla. But all primates are intensely visual, and all rely on visual communication in social interactions. Baboons lift their eyebrows as a low-intensity threat. Common chimps pout their lips in disappointment. Rhesus macaque monkeys threaten with an open mouth and a direct stare. Both chimpanzees and bonobos reach out with their hand to reconcile after a spat. We primates use visual signals as a bedrock of our social communications, and so do dogs.

Our dogs are tuned to our body like precision instruments. While we're thinking about the words we're using, our dogs are watching us for the subtle visual signals they use to communicate to one another. Any article or book on wolves will describe dozens of visual signals that are key to the social interactions of pack members. In the book *Wolves of the World,* one of the world's authorities on wolf behavior, Erik Zimen, describes forty-five movements that wolves use in social interactions. By comparison he mentions vocalizations only three times. That doesn't mean

that whines and growls aren't critically important in the social relationships of wolves. They are. But the depth and breadth of visual signals—of
subtle head cocks, shifts in weight forward or backward, stiffening or relaxing of the body—are vast in wolves, and every interaction I've ever had
with a dog suggests that visual signals are equally integral to communication in dogs.

So here we have two species, humans and dogs, sharing the tendencies to be highly visual, highly social, and hardwired to pay attention to
how someone in our social group is moving, even if the movement is minuscule. What we don't seem to share is this: dogs are more aware of our
subtle movements than we are of our own. It makes sense if you think
about it. While both dogs and humans automatically attend to the visual
signals of our own species, dogs need to spend additional energy translating the signals of a foreigner. Besides, we are always expecting dogs to do
what we ask of them, so they have compelling reasons to try to translate
our movements and postures. But it's very much to our own advantage to
pay more attention to how we move around our dogs, and how they move
around us, because whether we mean to or not, we're always communicating with our bodies. Surely it'd be a good thing if we knew what we
were saying.

Once you learn to focus on the visual signals between you and your
dog, the impact of even tiny movements will become overwhelmingly obvious. It's really no different from any sport in which you train your body
to move certain ways when you ask it to. All athletes have to become
aware of what they are doing with their bodies. It's the same in dog training. Professional dog trainers are aware of exactly what they're doing with
their bodies while they're working with a dog. That's not true of most dog
owners, whose dogs minute by minute try to make sense of the stir-fry of
signals that radiate from their owners.

Dogs never seem to lose their keen awareness of our slightest movements. I taught my dogs to sit when I unintentionally brought my hands
together and clasped them at waist level. It seems that I made this motion,
without even knowing it, when I called my dogs to come and was getting
ready to ask them to do something else. Often I would first ask them

to "sit," so my dogs quickly learned that clasped hands were usually followed by a "sit" signal. Apparently they figured that they might as well save us both time and do it right away. Every dog owner illustrates this every day. Maybe your dog runs to the door when you reach for your jacket. Perhaps you've played chase with your dog, and now, each time you lean forward, your dog dashes away from you. Most people move their hand or finger when they ask their dog to sit, even if they're not aware of it. But your dog is, and your action is probably the cue that's most relevant to him.

When I started professionally training dogs and their humans, one of the first things that hit me was how the owners focused on the sounds that they made, while the dogs appeared to be watching them move. This observation compelled me and two undergraduate students, Jon Hensersky and Susan Murray, to do an experiment to see if dogs paid more attention to sound or vision when learning a simple exercise. The students taught twenty-four six-and-a-half-week-old puppies to "sit" to both a sound and a motion.[1] Each pup got four days of training to both signals given together, but on the fifth day the trainer only presented one signal at a time. In a randomized order the pup either saw the trainer's hand move or heard the beeplike "sit" signal. We wanted to see whether one type of signal, acoustic or visual, resulted in more correct responses. It did: twenty-three of the twenty-four puppies performed better to the hand motion than to the sound, while one puppy sat equally well to either. The Border Collies and Aussies, as you might predict, were stars at visual signals, getting a total of thirty-seven right out of forty possible (and only six out of forty right to acoustic signals). The Dalmatian litter sat to sixteen of twenty visual signals but only four of twenty acoustic ones. The Cavalier King Charles Spaniels showed the smallest difference between visual and acoustic signals, with eighteen right of twenty possible visual signals and ten of twenty acoustic ones. If you have a Beagle or a Miniature Schnauzer, you will not be shocked to learn that these puppies sat, in total, for thirty-two of the forty times that they saw the "sit" visual signal

1. Four each from a litter of Beagles, Cavalier King Charles Spaniels, Border Collies, Australian Shepherds, Miniature Schnauzers, and Dalmatians.

and exactly *zero* of the forty times that they heard the acoustic signal. That'll teach you to call your Beagle to come when she's chasing a rabbit in the woods.

I'm cautious about this experiment, because it's a difficult piece of research to pull off cleanly. Unless the motion and sound had been completely automated, I couldn't guarantee that they were presented for exactly the same duration. Since the students had previously given the pups treats from their other hand, did that predispose the pups to focus on a hand signal? How could we be sure that we were presenting an equal "amount," or intensity, of each signal? A larger sample size of puppies would have been better, and so forth. But the trainers were ignorant of the real hypothesis (I told them it related to genetics and sex). I videotaped the training sessions and found that the motion and the sound began and ended within a few hundredths of a second of each other, and we worked hard to get as clean a test as we could under the circumstances. Given the ease with which dogs learn visual signals, and the universal phenomenon of mammalian brains' selectively attending to certain stimuli over others, I suspect that the results are meaningful. Ironically people often enthuse over their dog's "amazing" ability to learn a hand signal, as though that were a particularly advanced behavior. In actuality your dog's response to your voice is the miracle!

Hey, Human! I'm Trying to Tell You Something!

Visual though primates may be, we humans often miss the signals that our dogs are sending us. For example, in my seminars I do a demonstration in which I pet and praise my Border Collie Pip for giving me a ball back. Pip is my sleeper Border Collie, who looks a bit like a goofy Labrador cross when in fact she's from pristine sheepdog lineage. But she loves balls like life itself, so to reward her for giving me the ball back, I coo to her and lavishly stroke her head. People watching respond to my efforts to praise Pip and seem to feel really good when

I'm done. They feel so good that they give me an A+ when I ask them to grade my efforts to make Pip glad that she gave me the ball. But I give myself a D, because although the audience enjoyed hearing my praise and seeing me pet her, Pip just wanted the ball. I repeat the exercise, this time telling the audience to pay careful attention to Pip's face. Her reaction is obvious once you focus your attention on her. She ignores my sweet words, squints her eyes, ducks her head away from my hand, and presses forward, staring like a laser at the ball. Pip is no different from most of our dogs, who love petting and praise in some contexts but not others. After all, even if you adore a good massage, do you want one in the middle of an important meeting or a close tennis match? Why on earth would a dog, even one who lives to be stroked, want petting in every possible context in her life? We wouldn't, no matter how much we love a good rubdown.

As soon as the audience has learned to focus on Pip's reactions rather than their own, they get it. Pip's avoidance of my hand and obvious impatience to get the ball back aren't subtle at all. But for some reason we humans tend not to pay attention to the visual signals that our dogs send us. Hundreds of clients who come to my office for help with their dogs have described their pet's aggression as having appeared "out of the blue." Yet I could plainly see, even as the owners were talking to me, that the dog was clearly communicating, "Stop petting me like that. I'm going to bite you if you don't stop."

It's become a cliché that we love dogs because they give us "unconditional positive regard." Anyone who knows how to interpret the visual signals of dogs knows how naive that is. If you want to get a good belly laugh out of a group of dog trainers, start talking about "unconditional positive regard" from dogs. It's a guaranteed knee-slapper. My Border Collie Cool Hand Luke—noble, loyal Luke, who once risked his life to save mine—has a look that can only be translated as a four-letter word. The word is not *love*. Luke adores me, I'm quite sure of it. But it doesn't mean that he adores me every second of his life, any more than you adore your favorite human every single second of yours.

I think some of us have convinced ourselves that our dogs love us constantly and relentlessly, simply because we're not very good at reading their nonverbal communications to us. But once you start spending your life with dogs, it becomes screamingly clear that love is only one of the emotions that they feel. Most of these signals are easy to pick up on, if we'd only take the time to look. Many of the visual signals that dogs send aren't restricted just to their own species: as early as 1872 Charles Darwin wrote about the universal expression of emotions in nonhuman animals, from disgust to fear to confident threats. We have to be careful not to overgeneralize and assume that every expression on a dog's face is equivalent to one on ours—a "grin" on a dog could be a sign of fear (although it also can be on a human)—but equally important is the ability to carefully observe the expression on our dog's face. Just as a professional tennis player can see the seam of the ball as it rushes toward her at 90 miles an hour, good professional dog trainers can see quick, subtle visual signals that are rich with information. Anyone can learn to do it; you just have to focus your attention.

Fieldwork in Your Living Room

My field is ethology, which is the science of understanding animal behavior as the interaction of evolution, genetics, learning, and the environment. Ethology is based on a foundation of good, solid observations. It's a rigorous field, involving all the high-tech instruments and mathematical analyses necessary for evaluating genetics, physiology, and neurobiology. But it starts with basic observations that anyone can learn to do: watch an animal and write down what it's doing. It sounds simple, because all you need is you, an animal, a pencil, and paper. No expensive machine with a long name is required. If no dog is handy, any moving animal will do (including your office mate, friend, or spouse). Just describe what the bird outside, the dog inside, or your colleague is doing. Be specific and clear. "My dog is walking around" is not specific and clear. "My dog is walking slowly at about one stride per second, head held parallel to the shoulder girdle, ears relaxed and drooped 40 degrees to the side but not pinned back . . ." is specific and clear. By the time you get it down on paper, the animal will long since have changed what it was doing. This simple exercise quickly leads to frustration, but it eventually elicits admiration for the complexity of behavior.

One of the demonstrations that I love to give in my seminars involves asking the audience to count out just one little second for me. While they chant "one one thousand" in unison, I leap, twist, flap my arms, smile, frown, laugh, and heaven only knows what else. If you videotaped it and analyzed it as an animal behaviorist does, you could record dozens of separate actions, all happening within the time span of a second. A second is an eternity to an animal behaviorist, because many actions can occur in less than a tenth of a second. Making good observations is tricky, because too much can happen at once for your brain to notice it all, much less get it down on paper. Because so many actions can occur simultaneously, one of the first things that ethology students learn is to focus their attention on specific actions or areas and ignore the rest until a later observation period. As you get more observant, you can take in more details at the same time, but when you first start, it pays to be selective. Honing your observational skills is directly related to having a better-behaved dog, because what you do around your dog should be related to what your dog is doing. Just because his movements are subtle doesn't mean that they're not important.

After years of working with dogs who'd bite me if I didn't read their body language right, I have a hierarchy of body parts to watch. When I first meet a dog, my primary attention is on the dog's center of gravity and his breathing. Is the dog leaning toward me, away from me, or standing square over all four paws? Is the dog frozen still, breathing normally, or breathing too fast with shallow breaths? At the same time, I'm looking at the dog's mouth and eyes, where there's a world of information, but being careful not to stare directly at him. Tails are also important, but not as important as what's on his face, and you simply can't take in everything at once. If there's a lot going on—say, the dog is barking/lunging at me or, worse, standing stiff and hard-eyed with the corners of his mouth pushed forward—I probably won't have a clue what's happening with his tail until a few seconds later.

We Practice at Sports, Don't We?

Some dog owners are brilliant at reading their dogs from the word go. They are the "naturals," the people who seem to attract animals like a magnet—Snow Whites in the woods with deer licking their cheeks and birds playing in their hair. And then there's the rest of us, me included, who simply need to learn about animals the old-fashioned way, by practicing. One way to practice is to watch and write down what you see. Artists and scientists know this: we don't *really* see something until we ask our minds to translate it into words or pictures. So become your own Jane Goodall. Take a sketchbook with you and your dog to the dog park (any paper with a solid backing will do) and start watching, describing, and sketching specific movements of your dog. Focus on which way her body leans and write it down and try to sketch a picture. Notice whether the corners of her mouth (the commissure) go forward or backward and write down when it happens and when it doesn't. Do her eyes look "hard" or "soft" when she's greeting another dog? How does her tail set change when she sees another dog? Is it the same change as when she sees a human? Focus on just one body part at a time; otherwise, your brain gets swamped and you can't really focus on a specific action. Try keeping your notes and sketches together in a journal and go back often to read what you wrote.

Alternatively you can try videotaping some dogs and playing the tape back in slow motion, over and over. You might be surprised at how much can happen in a brief period of time and how much you'll see once the action is slowed down. With practice your brain gets better at observing changes in behavior, and you'll develop what's called a "search image" for a specific posture. You'll be able to see subtle changes that happen so fast that your friends won't even notice. That will allow you to respond more quickly and more appropriately to your dog. Without doing anything else, you'll become a better dog trainer, and almost like magic, your dog will become better behaved.

Humans as Random Signal Generators

If humans are understandably a bit slow at responding to the visual signals that our dogs are sending, we are downright dense about the signals that we generate ourselves. Your dog, however, is a pro: he or she notices just about every move that you make. Here's an experiment that you can try, focusing on the signals that you give to your dog, whether you mean to or not. This one is really easy, because now you're the actor, and your dog is the observer. Your job is to identify the visual signals to which your dog has learned to respond. Take yourself and your dog to a quiet place, away from the hubbub of the rest of the family and other dogs. Stand relaxed but immobile and ask your dog to "sit" without moving anything but your lips. The first thing I notice when I do it is how hard it is to keep from moving. Did your head go down just a tiny bit when the dog approached? Did you raise your eyebrows a millimeter? All of those movements are easily seen by your dog and could possibly act as cues. Now sit down on the floor, stop moving as best you can, and ask the dog to sit. Now leave the room and ask the dog to sit when she can't see you (peek or ask a friend to see what she does).

Now ask your dog to sit in the way you usually do. Allow yourself to move freely; let your body do what it normally does. There's little doubt that you're going to move somehow. While you're playing this game, don't worry whether your dog sits or not, because I want you to pay attention to *your* behavior. Did you raise your hand or your finger? Did you step forward a bit? Tilt your head? After you've observed your own behavior, see if you can find a pattern to what movements your dog sits to and what he doesn't (beyond Fido's getting sick of your asking for a "sit" over and over!). Experiment with different movements and you'll probably discover that your dog is keyed in to specific actions, just as much as, or more than, your voice.

This won't work for all dogs. Some of them have learned to ignore your body and listen to your voice. The most common scenario that I see is people who are not only inconsistent within themselves but whose family members each have very different movements for the same message. Dad holds a hand out for "sit" the same way that Mom does for "stay." Painfully it's often the smartest and most willing dogs that suffer the most when the family is inconsistent. You can practically see smoke coming out of their ears while they desperately look for a predictable pattern from their humans.

The best way to discover the signals that you send to your dog is to have a friend videotape you. Few of us are truly aware of how we move our bodies when we're interacting socially, which is one of the reasons that seeing ourselves on video can be upsetting. "Who *is* that person?" we think, appalled that we close our eyes while we talk or have a habit of scratching our chins. But your dog knows, far better than you, exactly how and when you move every part of your body and is likely paying more attention to those motions than to your voice. Try taping the whole family and compare how each of you moves when you're signaling your dog. If you're like most, you'll start wondering how your dog has managed all these years without needing a straitjacket.

Once you become aware of your own actions, you've done half of what you need to do to help your dog understand you better. By continuing to be aware of how you move around your dog, you can consciously settle on clear, consistent visual signals that your dog can understand. I remember seeing a dear little spaniel whose owner's signals were so confusing that even I didn't know what she wanted her dog to do. This woman adored her dog, but her dog was exhausted from trying to understand her confusing stir-fry of signals. When the woman got up to leave, her dog sat down beside me and wouldn't budge. It wasn't because I'm special—lots of dog trainers can tell the same story. The poor dog had finally found someone who made sense to her, and she didn't want to lose the relief that comes with clarity. That sad, awkward moment changed later to joyful enthusiasm when my client began to regulate her body's movements when she "talked" to her dog. Now they're the best of friends, just as it should be.

Even If You Know What Signal You're Sending, It Might Mean Something Different to Your Dog

Yesterday I was working with Mitsy, a terrier mix who's so cute she should have her own Walt Disney movie. But her behavior isn't quite as endearing. She's fearful and will bark defensively at large men who approach fast and at elderly people who shuffle as they walk—a reaction that often indicates the potential for aggression. Walking around the neighborhood with her and her owner, I enlisted three dog-loving men to help us by throwing treats for her as they walked by. The goal was for her to learn that approaching unfamiliar men are not only safe, they are the bearers of yummy treats. Even though I'd explained what we needed them to do, each man took the treat in his hand and, instead of throwing it toward Mitsy, tried to walk right up to her, then bent forward toward her face, and reached out his hand to try to give her the treat. The third man I asked didn't just lean toward her, he sort of fell toward her. Perhaps I should have paid more attention to the fact that we were standing in front of a bar.

But with the exception of the barfly, what our helpers were doing was something natural to all of us humans. Although each of them had listened to my instructions that they should stop 10 feet away from the dog and throw the treat, and had nodded in agreement that that's what they'd do, each tried to walk right up to her and extend his hand toward her. I found myself physically blocking all three of them, knowing that if they got too close, Mitsy would get alarmed and learn exactly the wrong thing. ("Yup, I knew it. Men are indeed dangerous creatures.") As politely but quickly as possible, I moved in front of them to stop them, smiling like an idiot to counter my behavior. My line of work teaches you the art of benevolently pushing people around. Granted, it's a little more involved when the other person is doing a cartoon imitation of a spaghetti-legged drunk and ends up draped over you like a burlap bag while you try to calm Mitsy by saying "Goooooood girl, that's a goooooood girl" and simultaneously tell the owner out of the other corner of your mouth to *"Walk away calmly but briskly right now!"*

It is frustrating to animal behaviorists and dog trainers that the behavior of other people is so hard to influence, but it also makes sense. Because we're humans and not dogs, we don't intuitively know how dogs interpret our actions. Even when we are aware of what we're doing with our body, we're watching through a primate filter while they're tuned to the canine channel.

Greetings, Canine and Primate Style

Imagine walking down the street and seeing someone whom you know and are happy to see. What do you do? Most of us call out his name, maybe wave to get his attention, and move directly toward him. It's especially polite to look directly at his face as you get closer, walking straight toward him, looking right into his eyes and smiling. As you get close enough to touch, you might reach out your hand to shake his or wrap both arms around his chest in a warm hug. Perhaps you move your face directly to his and kiss his cheek. The ultimate in friendliness is to look deep into his eyes and kiss him directly on the mouth. Ummmm, so sweet and friendly. Not if you're a dog, it's not. That oh-so-polite primate approach is appallingly rude in canine society. You might as well urinate on a dog's head.

Direct head-on approaches can be threatening to dogs, especially shy ones meeting a person or dog whom they don't know. Watch two well-socialized but unfamiliar dogs greet at the park. The politest of dogs tend to approach from the side, perhaps even at 90 degrees. They avoid direct eye contact. On the other hand, two dogs standing face-on, staring into each other's eyes, are trouble—big trouble—and I see it sometimes in dog-to-dog aggression cases. Dogs may greet head-on on occasion, but it's not polite, and it leads to tension and sometimes aggression.[2] When we do primate-based, head-on, direct approaches to dogs, they often respond as if they are being threatened. I must have seen more than a thousand dogs who are comfortable if you greet them by standing sideways and letting them come to you but who will lunge and bark aggressively, and possibly bite, if you stride up straight toward them, stare directly into their eyes, and reach your hand over the top of their heads. Polite dogs not only avoid direct approaches, they don't greet unfamiliar dogs by slapping their paw over the head of the other dog.

Literally hundreds of clients have tearfully described scenarios similar to the one I recounted with Mitsy, as they walk down the street with a dog who is nervous around strangers. A stranger approaches, walking directly toward the dog. My client stops, clearly explains that the dog is shy and can't be trusted around strangers, and tells the person to *please* not pet the dog. The stranger, while saying something like "Why not?" or "Oh, but I like dogs," then bends face-to-face toward the dog and extends his or her hand over the dog's head. The dog either backs away in fear, learning yet again that people are social idiots, or barks, snaps, or bites.

Years of helping shy dogs to be comfortable around strangers is what taught me how powerful our hardwired greeting behavior really is. In the beginning stages of treatment for shy dogs, it's critical that people stop their approach long before the dog becomes uncomfortable. But the urge to go face-to-face with a dog and to reach out and touch her is so powerful that it's literally overwhelming to some people. We just can't seem to stop ourselves. That compelling need to reach out with our own paws didn't come out of the blue: reaching and petting behind the head is a common sign of affection in many primates, chimpanzees and humans included. "Reach out and touch someone" is more than just an advertising jingle; it's a reminder of how "reaching out" and "touching" are deeply rooted aspects of our social behavior.

---

2. If the dogs are great friends, then just like humans, they allow social freedoms that they would never accept from strangers, so sometimes you will see dogs who are fast friends break all the rules of canid greeting ceremonies.

I've worked with hundreds of cases like Mitsy's, and I've learned that it doesn't matter what I say, and it doesn't matter what the person I'm talking to says: the action of moving directly at a dog and extending a hand in greeting is so hardwired that you often have to physically stop people from doing it. The only solution is to use two people: one with the dog and the other beside the stranger, ready to move between the stranger and the dog if the stranger can't resist a typical primate greeting. I've learned to "body block" people politely, to ensure that they don't get too close, and to intercept extended hands from strangers by tossing a treat or a ball for them to catch.[3] Just as primates want to extend their hands in greeting, we humans can't seem to resist trying to catch something that's moving toward us. "Would you throw this treat for the dog?" I'll say, tossing it briskly toward the kindly man approaching on the sidewalk. Most people become so engaged with catching the object that they stop thinking about reaching toward the dog. You can train people, honest; it's just harder than it is with dogs.

Hugging

Reaching out your hand to a dog is one thing, but hugging is another. I mentioned in the introduction how strong our tendency to want to hug is and how perhaps it relates to our primate heritage. Thanks to the efforts of hundreds of animal behavior researchers, we know that most primates express affection with "ventral-ventral" contact (chest-to-chest and face-to-face), hugging one another and patting others behind the head or on the shoulders. Jane Goodall, in her best-selling book *In the Shadow of Man,* describes greetings between familiar chimps as including bowing, crouching toward the ground, holding hands, kissing, touching, *embracing,* and patting. Except for humans, chimpanzees and bonobos are the huggers of the animal kingdom, hugging one another when they are excited, happy, anxious, or downright terrified. Frans de Waal, in

---

3. Don't try this without coaching from an experienced professional if your dog has ever threatened a stranger.

Peacemaking Among Primates, describes exuberant chimps as kissing, embracing, and patting one another on the back when released into a large outdoor enclosure after a long winter in somewhat cramped, indoor winter quarters. But they are just as likely to cling to one another when they are nervous. The same chimps hugged to console one another after a nerve-racking fight that upset the entire troop. Chimps and bonobos are also kissing fools, kissing when excited, to reconcile after social tensions or fights, and to greet one another after absences. How many of us can't resist kissing our dog? Other primates like baboons and gorillas don't embrace as often as humans, chimpanzees, and bonobos, but baboons who are close friends will wrap their arms around each other in a display of mutual affection, and gorillas spend a lot of time in physical contact. In all ape species, mothers and young spend long periods in a mutual embrace, our young growing up belly-to-belly and face-to-face for much of their early years.

In my experience the individuals who most want to hug and pet soft living things are young adolescent girls and children between about three and five years of age. I've worked with dozens of families with sweet young girls who got growled at, snapped at, or bitten on the face (usually not badly, thank heavens) when they threw their arms around their dog. Like young female primates everywhere, they craved cuddling and touching. Yet while they were thinking warm, loving thoughts, their dog interpreted their hug as a rude, domineering threat display. Please don't think I'm defending a dog who snaps or bites; I'm not. All my dogs will tolerate typical primate behavior without as much as a blink. Not long ago a woman visiting my farm hugged Luke around the neck so hard that his eyes literally started to bug out before I could get her to stop. "Good boy, good boy," I crooned, as I sped to disengage him from her half nelson. He turned his head and looked miserable, but he didn't even try to get away. But not all dogs are so tolerant. Just like people, dogs come in a variety of personalities and have had a variety of learning experiences, and we can't expect all dogs to be as polite as we wish all humans would be (but often aren't).

The only time dogs "hug" each other is when the male clasps the female during sex or when a dog (male or female) mounts another dog in a dominance display or in play with familiar dogs. If one dog reaches a paw over the neck of another in the first seconds of their initial greeting, he's pushing the socially acceptable boundaries of canine good manners. A "paw over" is the precursor to what's called "standing over" in canine ethology, and it's done in the context of establishing the social hierarchy. I do see dogs use it in the first second or so of a greeting, but they're not necessarily polite ones. I suspect that in canid society it's as rude as it is for us to push someone aside to get out the door first. Of course, familiar dogs do it in play all the time, but only after they've made friends and have given visual signals that they'd like to play—just as football players do things to one another on the field that they'd never do off it.

The number of people who don't seem to be aware of how their behavior is interpreted by dogs is frightening. I recently watched David Letterman, my favorite late night TV show host, get bitten by a dog on his show. He leaned forward, staring directly into the dog's eyes, put his hands on either side of the dog's face, and pressed his face within inches of the dog's eyes. Completely by accident, he then stepped on the dog's tail. But it wasn't stepping on his tail that was the primary trigger, which was Letterman's interpretation. Even before the bite, I was watching in horror as his eyes moved closer and closer to the dog's eyes, my heart racing with the inevitability of what was about to happen. I was so concerned that he'd be bitten, I was literally bouncing up and down in bed, yelling at the television like an idiot, as if somehow he could hear me. To an untrained human, just being a human, looking directly into the dog's eyes was a kind, friendly thing to do. That's the way Letterman greets Julia Roberts, and that's the way we all greet people we really like. In dog society that would be a scene from a sci-fi horror movie. You just couldn't be more rude to a dog unless you walked up and bit him. The most amazing aspect of Letterman's experience is that the dog didn't bite him sooner. Lest you get smug, remember that Letterman was just being a human—what else would he be?

The next time you see a dog you'd like to greet, stop a few feet away, stand sideways rather than straight on, and avoid looking directly into her eyes. Wait for the dog to come all the way to you. If she doesn't, she doesn't want to be petted. So don't pet her. It's not really that much to ask. Do you want every stranger you see on the street to handle your body? If the dog approaches you with a relaxed rather than a stiff body, let the dog sniff your hand, careful to hold your hand low, under rather than over her head. Always pet unfamiliar dogs on the chest or under their chin. Don't reach over their heads to pet them. What would you think if an unfamiliar animal the size of King Kong waltzed up and reached over and behind your head with its huge paw?

And hugging? Ah, hugging. I'm human, too, and the fact of the matter is, sometimes I just can't resist, and I stretch my arms around Cool Hand Luke or pony-sized Great Pyrenees Tulip to indulge myself. My dogs tolerate it because we're not strangers, because they're willing to put up with all kinds of foolishness to get my attention, because I don't do it when they're agitated, because they've been conditioned to associate it with pleasurable things like massages, and because they are relatively submissive to people and probably figure that they don't have much choice. Besides, they know who can get to the meat in the freezer.

There's no doubt that the Mastiff on stage could've bitten me if he'd wanted to. Dogs have faster reaction times than people, and even though I backed up, I'm sure he could've connected long before my brain told my body to move. But lucky for me, he just wanted me out of his space, and I was able to turn the incident into a useful part of the seminar. The audience and I had a great discussion about the importance of visual signals. I stayed relatively close to the Mastiff (I didn't want him to learn that lunging at people made them go away, but neither could he learn anything useful if I was too close) and eventually was able to get the Mastiff comfortable with me right beside him again. His owners learned a lot about how to manage and treat a huge dog who was dangerous around strangers. And I went to sleep that night grateful that my foolish mistake hadn't resulted in anything more than my feeling like an idiot. Sometimes I think that the primary purpose of dogs is to keep humans humble. Any dog trainer will tell you that they seem to be doing a great job of it.

2

TRANSLATING PRIMATE TO CANINE

How Your Body "Talks" to Your Dog and How to Make Sure It Says What You Want

My client Mary arrived home on the first snowy day of winter, bundled up against the cold with her new down jacket. The warm, balmy weather, unusual for late November, had quickly changed into a winter blizzard, and to keep out the wind, she had pulled her parka's hood up tight around her head. She looked forward to an enthusiastic greeting from her Saint Bernard, who always met her at the door, wagging his entire body from the shoulders back. Baron was behind the door, barking with excitement as Mary used the key to let herself in. But as soon as she entered the house, Baron's face was overcome with shocked surprise. He looked up at her in stunned silence for a moment, and then, with eyes round as pancakes, he bellowed out two woofs before he ran into the bathroom, leaped into the tub, and cowered.

Sure that something was horribly wrong with her dog, Mary ran after him and called his name repeatedly. When she found him in the tub, she reached out to help him and caused him to scramble in terror out of the bathtub, knocking her over in the process, until he found solace in the closet. Mary tried for almost ten minutes to get him out, desperately worried about her dog's bizarre behavior. But all 200 pounds were wedged in the closet and had no intention of budging, not even for the treats she used to try to lure him out. Finally she gave up and sat down on her bed, discouraged. By now she was hot, so she unzipped her hooded parka and threw it on the bed. She walked out of the room to get some water, and when she did, Baron trotted out of the closet after her. Surprised when she heard him behind her, she turned and said his name quietly. Baron, soft and sweet now, slurped her face with his huge, pink tongue.

As we talked later in the office about it, Mary realized that Baron had first come to her in early summer and had only met people in his puppyhood who were wearing no more than a light jacket. He'd never seen anyone with a parka hood clasped around her head. For that matter he'd never met anyone with a hat on. He'd been a normal, friendly puppy, although perhaps a bit quiet around strangers. His first barks were to the UPS man who delivered a large package. It all started to make sense to Mary when I left the room and put on a big, hooded jacket. When I returned, Baron froze in his tracks when he saw me, until I took the jacket off. You could almost hear him sigh with relief.

Silhouettes

I don't think dogs understand the concept of "removable parts" as we do. If someone comes to your house with a new hat on, you don't assume that they've morphed into some outer-space alien. But dogs do, at least a lot of them. Some dogs will bark their heads off when their beloved owner comes into the house with a large hat on or go big-eyed when surprised by someone with a backpack (or a mail carrier with a bag of mail). If you think about it, why should dogs understand how our silhouette changes randomly? We know that dogs pay a lot of attention to shapes. Many a dog in my office has started barking at a silhouette of a black cat on the wall. Even more dogs go crazy over the life-size painting of the face of Bo Peep, my first Great Pyrenees. Two dark, round circles (her eyes) within a doggie-shaped white oval are enough to create a barking fest that could raise the dead. The dogs usually bark when you least expect it. They look up, who knows why, all of us settled in cozily until *BARR RARR RARR RARR* rattles the walls and slops our teacups like an earthquake. It's just an image, but it's an image of the things that mean "dog" to another dog.

So what are dogs to think when they see us coming with huge, round, threatening eyes (sunglasses) and weird, menacing growths on our head (hats) and appallingly dangerous extensions growing out of our hands or our hips (canes, packages)? There's no reason that dogs, intelligent though they might be, should understand that our silhouettes, that oh-so-important visual signal that they use all the time to identify what's approaching, are mutable and not fixed. Shy dogs are especially put off by hats, huge coats, or packages, so if you have a dog who seems wary of all the strange forms in which humans come, help him out by wearing a hat around the house for a couple of weeks. Get him used to your coming into the house with a backpack or whatever it is that seems to bother him. Most dogs eventually learn to ignore our insectlike ability to change life-forms, but some of them need a little help. Come to think of it, I've seen a few outfits that I wanted to bark at myself.

Calling Your Canine to Come

A few years ago my Border Collie Luke and I were in the fresh green grass of a Wisconsin hillside, both of us learning how to work as a team to split a small flock of sheep into two parts. Called a "shed," it's the triple lutz of sheepherding, requiring split-second timing and a level of control and wisdom from both dog and handler usually seen in Olympic pairs skating. With the flock between the human and the dog, the handler calls the dog in to split off some of the sheep and then asks the dog to focus on one group and move it away from the others. As much a novice as I, Luke kept picking up the wrong group of sheep, in spite of my clear arm signal, until a wise handler made it simple with just one observation. "Be sure that your feet and your face are pointed toward the sheep you want your dog to pick up." Voilà. Problem solved. Pointy primate that I am, I was pointing with my paw toward the sheep I wanted Luke to drive away. I probably turned my head and looked at Luke in some hapless attempt to influence what he did next. Meanwhile, Luke was watching where my feet and face were directed, and it was always toward the wrong group of sheep. It hadn't occurred to me to pay attention to my feet and face, and I had been busy pointing for all I was worth toward the sheep I wanted him to follow. But Luke's not a primate, he's a dog, and like all dogs, he tends to go in the direction that I'm facing, not where I'm pointing. (Ever seen a dog lift up his leg and point with his paw?)

This ethological observation leads to a practical tip to get your dog to come when called. The best way to get a dog to come to you is to turn away from him and move in the opposite direction (which is actually "toward you" from the standpoint of the dog). This is so unnatural to us humans that I sometimes have to take clients by their sleeve and pull them away from their dogs to prevent them from moving forward. Dogs want to go the way that you're going, and to a dog that's the way that your face and feet are pointing. We primates want to stand facing our dog and talk about it. Look at how we move to close the distance between ourselves and other primates—we walk right at them. But that can be an inhibiting signal to a dog. To your dog you can look just like a traffic cop stopping traffic when you move directly toward him. So if you're calling "Come" and walking forward, your voice says, "Come over here," while your body says, "Stay there." Besides, if you're moving toward your dog, why shouldn't your dog stop and politely wait for you to finish your approach? The most subtle of "approaches" can have a profound effect on a dog. Even leaning your body forward just a bit can stop a sensitive dog in his tracks.

The best way that I know to visually "call" a dog to come is to bend down as if in a doggie play bow, turn *away* from your dog, and clap. Your version of a play bow is the closest signal there is in canine language to encourage your dog to come to you. After all, dogs have no signal among themselves that means "come over here right away." If you look at domestic dogs and wolves, there's nothing described in the literature that means "come right now." I tell people to think of it as a circus trick, not something that we can automatically expect of a good dog. Good dogs don't arrive knowing to trot over when you call "Come" with your voice and yet say "Stop" with your body. Besides, humans don't have a "come" signal either. Do you throw your magazine down and leap across the room when your spouse calls your name? Haven't you ever said "Just a minute" when someone tried to get your attention? Surely our dogs say that to us all the time. "Just a minute, I think I smell squirrel!" "Just a minute, I smell food. I'll be right with you." Is there a reason that your dog should naturally be more accomplished at obedience than you are?

There's nothing I can tell you in one short chapter that will guarantee that your dog will come every time you call. I taught my own dogs to come when "called" by starting when they weren't too distracted by something else. (Good teachers always help their students by starting at a reasonable level of difficulty.) I called with a clear, consistent signal like "Tulip, come!" while I clapped my hands, bent forward a bit in a play bow, turned my body sideways, and started to move away. The microsecond that my Great Pyrenees, Tulip, moved toward me, I started cooing "Good girl! Good girl!" and ran away faster. That action lured her in my direction and at the same time rewarded her with one of her favorite activities—a good chase game. Dogs may love treats and petting, but they love a good run, too, and it seems to be a wonderful reward for coming when called. (If your dog becomes too excited and starts getting nippy as he nears you, stop your run before he catches up to you, turn toward him, play bow, and give him a treat.)

So Tulip, who loves to chase things, learned that if I called her and she stopped what she was doing and moved toward me, she got to play her favorite game. Often I'd throw a ball or treats behind me as she arrived, adding on yet another fun chase game to sweeten the pot. Years of playing this game paid off recently, when Tulip was hot on the heels of a red fox who came tearing out of the barn. Tulip instantly stopped her chase when I yelled "*No!*" and came running when I called "Come!" I am still fluffed with pride and gratitude. Tulip, who is the size of a small sheep and can run like a deer, was stretched out at full speed, about 3 feet from the fox, both of them ricocheting through the trees up the hill. It's her job to protect the farm from uninvited coyotes and foxes, but there's a hole in the fence, and I didn't want her leaving the farm. Getting a Border Collie to stop a chase is one thing. Getting a Pyrenees to stop in the middle of doing her job is another. Great Pyrenees like Tulip don't exactly dominate the obedience ring: they were bred to spend their lives with the sheep, guarding them from predators, and they are famous for their independence. They are, in some ways, the anti–Border Collie. Border Collies, bred to work in harmony with a human handler, turn simple "sit" signals into an exercise of obsessive precision. ("Sit? OK, I can do that. Would you like me to sit like this, forward a little bit or maybe back an inch or two? I could try balancing on my tail; would that be good?") Great Pyrenees, on the other hand, will consider your request, but to a Pyrenees it's always a request.

I must have played "come" with Tulip five times a day when she was an adolescent. I called "Come" in a happy but clear voice, made my behavior conducive to her coming by turning and moving away from her, and rewarded her with a chase game and then either threw a ball or a treat when she caught up to me. The pièce de résistance with Tulip was to take advantage of having more than one dog. A couple of times a week, I'd call all the dogs to come and give treats to the first three dogs who showed up. Since at first Tulip was always the farthest away when I called, and the slowest to respond, she kept coming in fourth. "Oh, too bad, Tulip," I'd say. "I'm out of treats! Guess you'll just have to get here sooner next time." She did, not because she understood what I was saying but because she learned that a quick response paid off.

Will turning away from your dog rather than facing forward get your dog to come when you call her off a running squirrel? Don't count on it, but if you remember to turn away from your dog when you call her to come and reward her with a chase, a ball, or a treat, she'll come more than she used to, guaranteed. (I find it most useful in this circumstance to also teach a dog to stop first to "no.")

I was thinking of all this while I walked my Border Collies at the local dog park recently. We walked for an hour, the dogs 10 to 40 feet ahead of me, at their comfortable ground-eating canid trot. In keeping with dog park etiquette, I called my dogs back closer to me each time that I saw a group of people and other dogs approaching. It was crowded that day, and I must have called them back thirty times. They listened and responded every time, but I wondered what they must have thought of my repeatedly calling them and then walking right back toward where they had already been. Poor dogs; they must think we're crazy.

Take the Space

Sheep and sheepherding dogs taught me that any of us humans can control the behavior of a dog by simply controlling the space around him. Border Collies do the equivalent all the time: they control other animals, no matter what the species, by taking charge of the space around them just by their movements. Herding dogs can't put leashes and collars on their sheep or cattle, and so they have to control them some other way. They control other animals by blocking the way that they *don't* want them to go and leaving them easy access to the way that they *do* want them to go. It's much like being a goalie in a soccer game, where your job is to protect a particular space, not to control the behavior of the ball. If you can replicate this, and learn to manage the space *around* your dog, you can stop relying on a leash or a collar to get your dog to do what you want. Equally important, you can stop having to lunge toward your dog to grab his collar. I see far too many dogs who snap or bite when their owners reach toward their collars, often because the dogs have learned to associate it with being jerked around, choked, or pulled away from something interesting.

I use visual signals for space management all the time now when I'm with my dogs. Say I've put Tulip on a "stay," and she starts to get up and investigate the corn bread crumbs that I've dropped on my kitchen floor. If she moves forward toward me and to my left, I'll counter her with my own forward motion, stepping forward and sideways just one step into the space that she was about to occupy. I call it a "body block." Just that move on my part is enough to stop Tulip, whose body rocks back to her original sitting position. I respond by leaning backward myself, taking the pressure off Tulip but ready to move right or left again if Tulip initiates another break. Of course, the sooner you react, the better. Once you get good at it, you can simply lean forward an inch or two just as your dog starts the first shift of weight to move off of her stay. I get the best results by combining ethology and basic learning theory, so besides using relevant visual signals, I give the dogs treats *while* they are on the stay. I help them stay in place while I approach with the treat in my right hand and my left hand extended out like a traffic cop. When I get right up to my dog, I sweep the treat with an underhanded motion all the way to her mouth, then back away again, still holding out a helping "stay" signal with my left hand. Dogs learn that "all good things come to those who stay," and they develop a rock-solid stay that can be hard to break.

I also use body blocks to keep uninvited dogs from jumping into my lap, leaping onto my chest, or dancing on my head, as one overly friendly 90-pound Doberman tried to do. Because dogs don't use their paws to push other dogs away, I started watching dogs and wolves to see how they manage the space around themselves. Wolf ethologists are so familiar with body blocks that they've labeled them as distinct actions: "shoulder slams" and "hip slams" are seen all the time in wolf packs, where one individual uses her torso, either shoulder or hip, to take space away from another individual. Preestrous females, determined to keep their leader status to ensure their right to breed, are famous for slinging their hips around like hockey players on speed, slamming into other females to "keep them in their place." I'm not suggesting that you "slam" into your dog, heaven forbid. But it's much easier to work with dogs once you become conscious of the space around both you and your dog and who's about to move into it.

These body blocks are easy to learn, but they don't seem to come naturally. What is natural to all primates, including us, is to push others away with our hands (or forepaws). But to a dog, a raised paw can signify submission or a request to play or the beginning of a dominance-related mount, but it never seems to mean "go away." So I've stopped pushing dogs away with my paws. Instead, I keep my hands tucked into my belly and push dogs away with my shoulder or hip, using body language that they understand. Try it the next time some overly enthusiastic dog begins a charge for your lap when you're trying to relax in your chair. Long be-

fore she gets to you, tuck your hands into your belly and lean forward to
block her with your shoulder or elbow, sitting right back up after the dog
has moved backward. Most dogs won't give up right away: they'll try again
a few times. After all, they've probably been rewarded for crawling up into
someone's lap, even if it's just with attention, for a long time. It also helps
to turn your head away. (We'll talk about the importance of "look aways"
later in the chapter.) The key is for you to occupy the space before they
do, just as a Border Collie does when she darts around to the left to block
the sheep from going through the gate!

Space management isn't just about moving from side to side to
block space; it also involves how far you move forward or backward
to control another animal—or how much "pressure" you put on your
dog.

Feel the Pressure

*The three Barbados sheep that I have on my farm don't look like most
sheep. Designer-colored in black, brown, and white, they're as sleek as African
antelope and look stunning in my little orchard pasture of Irish-green
grass. Barbados don't act like other sheep, either. Fast and flighty, they
move like quicksilver at the slightest sign of trouble. They dart. They leap.
They run wild-eyed smack into the fence or into your head if you or your dog
put too much pressure on them. They are wild, reactive, and sometimes dangerous, and I adore them. Adrenaline junkies (and what dog trainer who
works with aggression isn't?) everywhere couldn't help but love them, because
they are so fast that you and your dog have to be equally quick or you're
doomed. One herding dog trial that used Barbados instead of the usual
wooled sheep lost five of them who hightailed it into the cornfields and were
not seen again—at least not until months later, when one was found in the
patio garden of an apartment complex. Another was found even later in a
county park, perplexing zookeepers and wildlife specialists alike at how an animal who looks like an African antelope could surface in suburban
Milwaukee.*

The Barbados escaped the trial field because they are so responsive to pressure, more so than white wooly sheep, and the handlers and dogs weren't used to it. Put too much pressure on a flock of Barbados, and you might never see them again. There's no animal that I know of that can better teach you this oh-so-important concept of pressure, although your dog has probably been trying all along.

Pressure is also about space, and it's about exactly how close you need to get to another animal to begin to influence its behavior. Good herding dogs learn exactly how much pressure to put on the sheep to get them to move. Besides blocking to the right and the left, dogs have to find the razor-fine edge of the sheep's flight distance, because if they go over it too far, they'll force the sheep to turn and fight or send them over your new fence. The job is always challenging, because the "pressure point" changes, depending on the day, the sheep, and the weather. A good, steady dog with an innate sense of pressure is worth his weight in gold, because he can move sheep and cattle without causing a fight or a stampede, smoothly moving the herd where you want them. The brilliant ones make it look so easy, you wouldn't know what all the fuss was about, until you watch a dog with no finesse, who moves in too fast and panics the flock. It's just as important with your dog as it is with sheep. Great dog trainers know all about pressure, while bad trainers misuse it and create trouble that could've been avoided.

You, too, know about pressure when you interact with your own species. Most human primates know how much pressure they can put on someone's personal space to avoid distressing the other person. We all know what it feels like on the receiving end: if someone gets too close to us, we usually find ourselves backing up. The other person doesn't have to touch us for us to feel his or her presence and want to move away. The difference between a comfortable social distance and an uncomfortable one can be very small, measured in inches (or less). It's the same between you and your dog, just as it's the same between a herding dog and a flock of sheep. Of course, just as the pressure point varies from flock to flock, and from person to person, depending on personality and cultural background, it also varies from dog to dog.

Great dog handlers know exactly how far forward to lean to put pressure on each dog with which they're working. Let's go back to the "stay" example. If Tulip is on a stay and starts to get up and move forward and to my left, I'll shift to the left myself to block her path, but I'm also going to shift my body forward to block her forward motion. But the instant that she pauses, I should stop leaning forward and "take off the pressure" by leaning back again. Just as she needs to get blocked when she moves off her stay, I need to reward her for going back to it, not continue to put pressure on her. This interaction between you and your dog, this dance of shifting your weight forward and backward, takes some time to learn, just as any sport or dance step does. In my office it seems as though people easily learn to put pressure on, but at first they go too far and don't take it off fast enough. You can practice with people and dogs, but be sure that you know the dog well before you consciously start to put pressure on him. Every dog is a unique combination of genetics and learning, but just as with humans, most fit into generic categories. Some goofy, socially oblivious dogs will launch themselves at you no matter how careful you are to step forward into them at just the right moment. Sensitive, submissive dogs will back up when all you do is tilt forward, even when you're several feet away. And you don't want to try this on testy, status-seeking dogs with an aggressive streak, because they may take offense and come back at you.

The direction in which a dog's body is shifted, whether forward or backward, is critical information to an Applied Animal Behaviorist. A dog may be snarling when I meet him in the lobby, but if his body is shifted even the slightest bit backward, I know that he's on defense rather than ready to attack. No matter how much he's growling and flashing his teeth, there's little danger if I don't put pressure on him. I'm much more concerned about the quiet, stiff-legged dog who stands still, shifting just a tad forward while he stares directly into my eyes. Dogs who alternate charging forward and retreating are ambivalent, torn between wanting to attack and wanting to flee. You can learn a tremendous amount about a dog by learning to read which way his body is leaning. Once you have a "template" in your brain, you'll find that you see it everywhere—in the little Sheltie who drops her shoulder and leans the slightest bit backward when you forget yourself and reach over her head with your paw. You'll see it at the dog park when two dogs greet, one dog leaning forward and the other shifting back. It becomes like a neon sign, and you'll wonder how you could've missed it before.

Our dogs, of course, are just as busy reading us as we are reading them. If you learn to shift your body backward slightly when you greet a new dog, you usually can ensure that the dog doesn't perceive your posture as threatening. When you're slightly sideways with your weight on your back foot, you've taken away what ethologists call an "intention movement" to proceed forward, and dogs can read it like a billboard. It doesn't have to be much; it's barely perceptible if one isn't aware of it. Of course, you'll want to do the opposite when you're working with some lunkhead who's all tongue and paws and thrashes around ignoring everything you say. Then you want to purposely move forward, both taking space and using your torso to signal your intention to take control, before you ask for that "sit."

Read My Lips

Sandy was a Cocker Spaniel, golden and curly-haired like some child beauty queen, as soft and infantile as a doll. But he stood like a cavalry officer in my office, ramrod-stiff, leaning forward as if to charge into battle. His eyes looked like flint as he stared hard at his owner in my office. The owner was there because Sandy had bitten her, not once but many times. The bites weren't nips, either; they were prolonged and deep. "Multiple strike" attacks, they're called, when the dog bites over and over again and causes serious damage. In the latest, and worst, incident, Sandy had worked his way up her forearm, biting hard and repeatedly until he finally latched onto her ear and wouldn't let go. She lived alone, and it had taken her a long time to get him off. Her arm had been badly injured, but her heart was broken. She loved Sandy like life itself, and I have no doubt that he loved her, too. Most of the time.

He was staring at her, I suspect, to induce her to get up and get him a toy out of the toy basket. He had walked over to it early in the session, looked at her, and then looked back at a prize toy. She started to get up to fetch it for him. The toy basket was low, open, and easily accessible. There was nothing to stop Sandy from picking up the toy himself, except Sandy's apparent preference for his owner to do it for him. I suggested that the owner let him get it himself. She explained that she always got Sandy's toys when he asked. I turned to look at Sandy, who remained standing beside the basket, tail wagging slowly, now staring hard at his owner. His owner shook her head from side to side and tentatively said, "No, Sandy, get it yourself." As she did, ever so slightly, the corners of his mouth moved forward about an eighth of an inch. (Does that sound like a tiny movement? Get out a ruler and move your finger across an eighth of an inch. You might be surprised at what an obvious movement it is.)

That little movement was the equivalent of a neon blinking sign. Bless his evil little heart for giving me warning. I managed to throw a beanbag in front of Sandy in time to stop him as he lunged toward her. By the time the beanbag landed in front of him, his eyes were hard, and his mouth was fully puckered forward, teeth showing, ready to bite. Because I saw the commissure (the corners of his mouth) go forward, I was able to predict his next move and stop him before he latched onto her again. In the months to come, Sandy learned a lot about patience, and his owner learned a lot about being a benevolent leader. She also learned to watch the corners of Sandy's mouth like a hawk.

I hope you don't have as compelling a reason as Sandy's owner to learn to read your dog's signals, but the corners of your dog's mouth can tell you a lot about what's going on inside his furry head. That's not just true of dogs, either. We humans pull our commissure back in a smile, and in a very general sense, we share with dogs an underlying emotion when we do that. Retracting the commissure in dogs signifies submission or fear. Sometimes it has a similar significance in humans: some researchers believe that human smiles evolved from the submissive grimaces seen in many primate species. We're all familiar with happy smiles, but think of all the smiles you've seen that were related, to some degree, to nervousness. Perhaps you, like me, have smiled when you wished you wouldn't, anxiously awaiting test results or submissively seeking favors from someone in authority. Primates also have a similar expression, somewhat akin to a nervous or submissive "smile," termed the "open mouth bared tooth display," which is associated with relaxed, friendly social contact. Not surprisingly it's seen more frequently in species with relatively relaxed social relationships rather than strict dominance hierarchies. I would argue that at one level a smile could signal both: social submissiveness rarely relates to unfriendly aggression, and thus a smile can signal to a stranger that you mean him or her no harm.

Primates, too (including humans, chimpanzees, and rhesus macaques), can signal confident threats to others with the commissure forward, but we can also push the corners of our mouths forward in an expression of delighted surprise. (Think of your face when you're "talking" to a baby or your dog: your eyebrows rise, your eyes widen, and your mouth rounds, corners moving forward as they do when you say "Ohhhhhh.") But usually that's a sign of offense in a dog and is called an "agonistic pucker." Any dog who barks at me with puckered lips gets my full attention. This is not a dog on defense; it's a dog ready and willing to act on his threat—not fearfully but with confidence.

One of the ways that I evaluate temperament in dogs is to give them a toy stuffed with food and then watch the corners of their mouth when I start to take it away. (I do this now with a fake arm, thanks to the brilliant idea of a dog trainer, shelter consultant, and seminar speaker named Sue Sternberg. After ten years of protecting myself with my reflexes and my ability to read a dog, I was thrilled to retire my hand and employ a stand-in. It's still potentially dangerous, though, because an occasional dog will work her way up the fake arm toward my hand or face, so, just as they say in the ads, "The people in this scene are professionals. Do not try this at home.")

When I look at a dog's mouth, I'm not just looking to see if he stiffens his jaw or shows me his teeth; I'm looking to see if the corners go forward or backward. Forward correlates with status-seeking dogs who are not the dogs you want in a family with three kids under five. Commissures pulled back in a defensive grin, even if the dog is growling and snarling at me, means the dog is on defense and is afraid either of losing her food or of what is about to happen. Either dog can bite, but it's important to know as much as you can about a dog's internal state before you give a prognosis and treatment plan. If you have a dog who threatens you in this way, you'd be wise to contact an experienced and humane dog trainer or behaviorist who can help you with a customized treatment plan.

To Fight or Not to Fight?

A common situation of visual miscommunication between people and dogs is when owners let their leashed dogs meet each other for the first time. The humans are often anxious about how the dogs will get along, and if you watch them instead of the dogs, you'll often notice that the humans will hold their breath and round their eyes and mouths in an "on alert" expression. Since these behaviors are expressions of offensive aggression in canine culture, I suspect that the humans are unwittingly signaling tension. If you exaggerate this by tightening the leash, as many owners do, you can actually cause the dogs to attack each other. Think of it: the dogs are in a tense social encounter, surrounded by support from their own pack, with the humans forming a tense, staring, breathless circle around them. I don't know how many times I've seen dogs shift their eyes toward their owners' frozen faces and then launch growling at the other dog. You can avoid a lot of dogfights by relaxing the muscles in your face, smiling with your eyes, breathing slowly, and turning away from the dogs rather than leaning forward and adding more tension.

Looking Away

Both humans and dogs turn their head away from those of our own kind for many reasons, a lot of which are shared between species. Primates such as humans, chimps, and gorillas often turn their faces away to avoid social conflicts. Primatologist Frans de Waal emphasizes the importance in humans and chimps of avoiding eye contact during tense social encounters and soliciting it during reconciliation. Shirley Strum describes olive baboons' turning their faces away to stay out of a conflict with another individual. An important principle in primate communication seems to be, "If we can't see each other, then we can't start something." That seems to be true for dogs as well.

My Border Collies are all trained assistants when I work with dog-dog aggression cases. I can bring them out without a leash and, because of their training, count on them to stop, sit, lie down, stay, move forward or backward on command while I concentrate on the dog at hand. But I never taught them to turn their head away when a dog barks and lunges at them. They do, though, and I'm grateful for it, because it is such an effective way of dispersing tension. Recently an 80-pound dog came to the farm for a session to decrease her rude behavior toward other dogs. Abby barks and lunges at every dog she sees, and we were working on teaching her a more polite response. Luke sat, as asked, quietly by the house, and when Abby launched herself toward him (safely contained by a strong leash a good distance away), he slowly turned his head to the side, as if deflecting all her nervous energy. Turid Rugas, a Norwegian dog trainer, calls turning the head a "calming signal," and I agree that it does have a calming effect on the dog who sees it (although I don't think that dogs are necessarily doing it consciously to relax the other dog).

Humans can do it consciously, doing what wolf researchers call "look aways" by turning our heads to the side when we greet a new dog or we sense that tension is mounting. You can also cock your head, which is something never done by a tense dog on offensive alert. Many mammals cock their head to gather more information about the world around them, and they almost always do it when they're curious and relatively relaxed. If you cock your head, you are signaling to a dog that you're relaxed, which can go a long way toward relaxing the dog as well.

Turning your head away doesn't just deflect tension. As with a smile, it can have many meanings. My huge Great Pyrenees, Tulip, looks away every night when submissive Pip grovels over to her for attention. Pip lies down on her side, thumps her tail, keeps her head low and her lips in a submissive grin as she flops her way over for attention from alpha bitch Tulip. Matriarch that she is, Tulip rarely deigns to give Pip the attention that she seeks. Tulip raises her huge square head a bit, nose in the air, and turns her head away from Pip. Submissive dogs seek interactions, but high-status dogs get to decide whether to grant an audience or not. Sometimes Tulip deigns to turn back and sniff Pip's face (while Pip seems to melt in ecstasy). Most of the time she continues to ignore Pip until Pip gives up and goes away.

What, then, is your dog to think if every time she comes over to you, you instantly drop what you were doing and respond with petting and attention? Who has control of the agenda in the living room? It's easy to train your dog to demand attention from you. That's what you unconsciously do if you respond every time your dog requests (or demands) something from you. You might ask yourself what she'll learn from that. Perhaps she'll learn that she is always more important than anything else that you might be doing. Alternatively what some dogs *don't* learn can create the biggest problem. I see dogs in the office all the time who, like a two-year-old child, simply have no frustration tolerance. They've always gotten what they wanted, but like any child, they must eventually cope with frustration but have no experience in how to manage it. Frustration is a common reason that dogs—or most any other mammal, for that matter—get aggressive. If you want your dog to be a polite house dog who is part of your family, then you need to raise her as you would any youngster and teach her how to tolerate not always getting what she wants the instant that she wants it.

If your dog pesters you for petting when you need to be doing something else, break off visual contact with him. You can use your torso to push him away with a body block (remember not to use your hands) or turn your head away (chin raised) in a benevolent but royal dismissal. It's amazing how fast dogs will go away if you break off visual contact with them. It's equally notable how hard it is for us humans to do that when we're trying to get our dogs to do something. All of our instincts seem to have us look at our dog, just as primates do when they are trying to communicate directly with another individual in the troop. But the look that works best, that we use ourselves when we're not thinking about it, is that slightly snobby, hard-to-get look when we turn our head away in dismissal. It works with dogs as well as with humans. Honest. Dogs can take you for granted just as anyone else in your social group can, and most of us hate being taken for granted. You might be stuck with it from some of the people you know, but you don't have to put up with it from your dog.

3

TALKING TO EACH OTHER

How Dogs and Humans Use Sound Differently and How to Change the Way You Use It to Better Communicate with Your Dog

It was springtime, and my Great Pyrenees, Tulip, was entranced. Every ounce of her huge frame was quivering over the dead squirrel, drinking in the smells rising from one of nature's recycling projects. Intoxicated by the pool of scents, Tulip must have heard me calling her, because she turned her head ever so briefly in my direction and then returned to what was important in life—attaching some of this marvelous odor to her own long, white coat. Tulip treasures a good roll in a dead animal, much as I cherish a long soak in a lavender bubble bath. So many times I have watched her sprawled in languorous joy on her back, an expansive grin on her face, grinding the essence of dead squirrel or cow pie, dead fish or fox poop into her fur.

"Tulip," I yelled again, and stepped closer to her. This time not an ear twitch. Not the slightest acknowledgment of my existence. My call was louder this time, because I was getting mad, irritated at standing in the pouring rain, getting wet because my huge, soggy Great Pyrenees was blowing me off. In about half an hour, I was expecting company for an elaborate dinner party. I didn't want the meal to be accompanied by a large, wet dog who smelled like old death. But Tulip didn't actually roll in the squishy mess under her, because I came to my senses and stopped being a dog owner and started being an animal trainer. "No," I said, this time quietly but with a pitch as low as the ground. Tulip stopped her sniffing and turned her huge, square head to look straight at me. "Tulip, come!" The "come"

came out like a cheery greeting to a neighbor you'd ask over for coffee. With a brief look at the treasure below her, Tulip turned like a dancer and ran to me. We dashed together to the house, and I let my poor, long-suffering floors get muddy yet one more time, while we tore to the refrigerator for Tulip's favorite treats.

Tulip had done exactly what I had asked from the beginning. "Tulip!" I had said at first, meaning "come" but simply saying her name and expecting her to read my mind about what it was that I wanted her to do. She acknowledged my presence politely, expressed some doggy version of "Wow, look! I found a dead squirrel, and it has maggots in it!" and returned to what she'd been doing when I interrupted her. Saying her name a second time gave her no more information than it had the first. But when I clearly communicated what I wanted, she did exactly what I asked. Tulip has learned that "No" means "Don't do what you're doing" and that "Tulip, come" means "Please stop what you're doing and come here right now." She did, too, as soon as I got my act together and told her what I wanted. Since I'm an Applied Animal Behaviorist, a professional dog trainer, and my Ph.D. research was on acoustic communication between trainers and their working animals, you'd think I'd have this down by now. But there's a catch: I'm a human.

Excuse Me. Were You Speaking to Me?

If there's anything that defines humans as a species, it's speech. Scientists have long asked what differentiates humans from apes like chimpanzees and bonobos. We started with a long list in the 1800s, which included tool use, altruism, social-political systems, and language, to name a few. The more we've learned about our closest relatives, the shorter the list has become. Look at what John Mitani wrote in *Great Ape Societies* in 1996:

> Ongoing research in captivity and in the field has progressively reduced a previously long list of traits that could be employed to differentiate the African apes from humans, and with this research, it has

become increasingly clear that humankind's uniqueness may depend on a single characteristic, namely our ability to use speech and language.

And boy do we use speech. Living, breathing verbal machine guns, we incessantly talk to our dogs. It's so compelling to talk to our dogs that I, and every other professional trainer whom I know, talk to deaf dogs even when we know they can't hear us. Trying not to talk is so distracting that it just gets in our way, so we do it anyway. This use of language is so essential to our nature that people with hearing disabilities have created a visual sign language, complete with its own grammar and syntax. Children growing up with no adult guidance create their own primitive languages. All humans, no matter what their culture or physical ability, seem driven by the desire to use language to communicate. Indeed, speech is so important to us that we often forget about the power of body language.

Not even chimpanzees or bonobos have a verbal language that approaches our complicated use of sound. Many species of animals, from whales to ravens to honeybees, have sophisticated systems of communication, but no species uses sound with the complexity of humans. We know from decades of research that apes can be taught to use visual symbols to communicate relatively complex information, and an African gray parrot named Alex learned to say and respond to dozens of words, including ones that signify abstract concepts like *larger, different,* or *color.*

Although communication research will no doubt uncover more evidence of linguistic abilities and intelligence in nonhuman animals, our sophisticated use of sound is unique. That makes it all the more surprising that we have so much trouble using language to communicate with our dogs. Look at me in the previous story, mindlessly saying "Tulip!" to get her to stop sniffing a squirrel carcass and come into the house. "Tulip" what? If someone calls your name when you're engaged in some engrossing activity, you'd probably say "What?" or "Yes?" or "Just a minute." You wouldn't necessarily know what the caller expected of you. Yet we put our dogs in that position all the time, saying their name and then expecting them to read our minds.

Dogs don't come speaking English, and they don't come reading your mind. If your dog doesn't listen to your commands, it well might be because he is confused. Of course, dogs can learn the meaning of many words, and like us, they have great hearing abilities and are primed to get information about the world around them from sound. Happy, well-trained dogs understand a wealth of information from the sounds that their humans make. Dogs even learn the meaning of words that we don't want them to—running under the table when you say "bath" or dashing over to the cupboard and barking when you ask your two-legged friend if she'd like to go to "dinner." But if you analyze our behavior carefully, sometimes I think it's a miracle that our dogs understand us at all.

The Best of Our Language Makes Us the Worst of Trainers

Devoted to their new puppy, John and Linda couldn't have been more fun in dog training class. They enthusiastically came to every class, laughed at my jokes (bless them), did their homework, and brimmed with love for their new Golden Retriever. "Ginger, come!" John said, calling her to come during a recall exercise. Ginger had just discovered that there were liver treats on an adjacent table and didn't even twitch an ear. "Over here, Ginger," John repeated, finishing with "Come on. Good girl. Come here. Over here." John's vigorous signaling resulted in loss of breath and rising frustration but not in convincing Ginger to leave the liver treats on the table. But she did learn to ignore a whole lot of interesting noises from her hapless owner. What's most notable about those noises is that they were so variable. If you assume ignorance of the English language, "Come here" sounds nothing like "Ginger, come!" but humans seem bound and determined to use as many words as possible for the same command.

It makes sense when you think about it. One of the most impressive aspects of our language is its flexibility. Look at all the ways we can say the same thing: "Come here," "Over here," "Come on over," "Come on down," "Come," "Hey, Ginger!" and on and on. This rich banquet of words is a blessing to us but a curse to our dogs. Learning a foreign language is difficult enough without having the word you're learning change from minute to minute. How would you do if the foreign word you were trying to learn changed form randomly? You'd probably do what a lot of our dogs do, which is just stop listening.

Almost every dog training book ever written advises dog owners to pick simple commands and use them consistently, and almost every dog owner in the world violates that rule repeatedly. How could the smartest species in the world be so idiotic when it comes to such a simple rule? I think there are at least two reasons. First, we humans use synonyms all the time, and learning to use the same word consistently as a command goes against our nature. There are great benefits to swapping words: it allows a layer of nuance and finesse that enriches us. But what a challenge it must be for our poor dogs to live in the equivalent of a foreign culture and have their hosts use different words for the same thing. It's a wonder our dogs don't all take off for the hills.

A second reason we may be so inept at picking one verbal command and sticking to it is that almost all species of animals, from single-cell amoebas to complicated mammals, illustrate a behavior termed "habituation." Habituation occurs when an organism (or even a single cell) begins to ignore something that occurs over and over with no relevant consequence. It's considered a simple form of learning that virtually all animals exhibit. It explains why you don't hear the train after you've lived by the tracks for a few months. It's why beleaguered spouses can successfully ignore nagging. And it might be why your dog doesn't even look up if you've called "come" too many times and then helplessly walked away when she didn't respond. She's learned that the sound "come" is like the sound of the wind in the trees, and she needs to keep her attention on more relevant noises, like a car coming up the driveway or the jingle of the keys.

Animals can even act unconsciously to prevent habituation. This might explain why some species of birds vary the notes within their songs. And it might be another reason why human primates so easily switch from one word to another. Perhaps we unconsciously drop one sound (especially if it didn't work) and try moving to another one, either to avoid habituation or in hopes that another sound will work better. That's a fine theory, but eventually we run out of new things to say, and our dogs just end up ignoring us anyway. In spite of our imprecise use of words to our dogs, there are many things you can do to help your dog understand you, and most of them aren't difficult or time-consuming.

Start to pay careful attention to the words you use around your dog. You might even write down what you think your signal words are. Be specific about exactly what words you use. Do you say "Lie down" or "Down," or both? After all, the words *complete* and *pleat* share the same sound, but they mean different things to us. How is your dog supposed to know if "Lie down" has the same meaning as "Down"? Would you, if it were two unfamiliar phrases in Swahili?

Think about *how* you say each of the words you use to talk to your dog. (You can say the same word differently and have it mean different things, as we all know when we hear our name whispered sweetly or yelled in irritation.) Try writing a symbolic equivalent of what each word sounds like when you say it. Does "Down" rise up in the air as you finish the word (like a question) or descend (like a statement of fact)?

Start listening to yourself and asking your family and friends to pay attention to what you actually *do* say to your dog. After about a day of this, you'll be ready to crawl into a hole. (No wonder so many dogs love their crates!) Most of us talk to our dogs like a thesaurus, substituting this word and that for the same command. Before you get too disgusted with yourself, just keep remembering that you're a human, and this is what humans do. If, on the other hand, you notice that you are clear and consistent, then more power to you. Give yourself a good chew on a fresh bone.

If you really get into this, arrange to videotape or tape-record yourself. Try to get some recordings when you're not conscious of being recorded. What's important is to be clear about exactly what it is that you say to your dog, asking how consistent you are within yourself and how consistent the entire family is as a whole.

Once your brain starts to pay close attention to what you say, with little effort you'll start to become more consistent. A standard and proven method of behavior modification is to ask people who are dieting, stopping smoking, and the like to keep a record of when and what they ate or smoked. Without even trying, people begin to eat or smoke less, simply because they are focusing their awareness on that behavior rather than doing something without thinking about it. So just pay attention and you'll automatically become more consistent.

What Do All Those Noises Mean, Anyway?

If you've thought about what words you use to communicate with your dog, the next step is to write down exactly what these words mean. In other words, what do you want your dog to do after you say something? This sounds so simple, and yet even professional trainers surprise themselves when they sit down and write out a dictionary of their commands. A lot of us aren't even clear in our own minds what we expect our dogs to do when we ask, and not surprisingly, neither are our dogs.

For example, many of us say "Down" to ask our dog to lie down and ten minutes later say "Down" to get her to stop jumping up on Aunt Polly. So which is it? What do you want your dog to do when you say "Lie down"? Lie down on her belly? Stop jumping up and stand there with all her paws on the ground? Leap off the couch? Of course, *you* know that the same word can have different meanings in different contexts, but we're supposed to be making things easy for our dogs, not doing IQ tests on them all day. Your dog's life will improve immensely if you learn to use a different command for each behavior that you want her to do.

Here's another example of how speech confuses our dogs: It's very popular now for trainers to teach dog owners to ask their dogs to sit and then praise them by saying "Good sit." But look at those words from a dog's perspective. If "Sit" means "Put your butt down on the ground," and you want your dog to do that every time you say it, what could your dog make of hearing "sit" after he's already done so? I know your dog is smart, but expecting him to read your mind about when "sit" means "*Do* something" versus when it means "*Don't do* anything; I'm referring to something that you've already done" is a bit much, even for the smartest of dogs. Rearranging the order of the words is a *grammatical* change, and asking a dog to understand the rules of human grammar is asking for the moon.

I drove my Border Collies crazy for a few weeks trying to teach them to wait at the door as a group and then go outside one at a time. Each dog could go out the door after I said his or her name, followed by the word *OK*. As soon as I said "OK," not surprisingly, all the dogs would get up and move forward, no matter whose name preceded it. I knew it would be hard for them, since they had all learned as individuals that "OK" meant "Go ahead and do what you want." But I thought that if I were clear and patient, they would learn to move only if they heard "OK" after their own name. After a couple of weeks, I was frustrated and my dogs were confused. Pip was so distressed that she started to stress-whine. Pip gets the connection between a sound and an action faster than any dog I've ever had, but she never could figure out that "OK" only related to her *if* her name preceded it. She'd sit waiting at the door, I'd say "Luke, OK," and she'd start to move forward and backward, clearly unsure of how to proceed, searching my face for clues until she began to look stressed when I moved toward the door. She practically wrapped her paws over her ears. It seems so obvious now that it hurts to remember it. If "OK" meant that "it's all right to get up now," it makes sense that Pip would respond when she heard it. So if your dog Chief can pick the word *sit* out of the middle of a sentence, what is he to make of "Good sit" after he already sat? With Pip I got caught up in using words as if I were talking to a human, and I think other owners replicate that mistake often.[1]

Here's another example of our remarkable ability to use the intricacies of language to confuse our dogs: a lot of people say "No bark" to their dogs to ask them to stop barking. "No bark" certainly sounds simple, because it is just two short words. But look at it from your dog's perspective.

---

1. By the way, I now release each dog at the door by saying his or her name in a lilting voice. It took only a day or two for them to learn it. Sigh.

First of all, have you taught your dog what *bark* means? After all, it's just a noise you're making, and the noise itself has no meaning until you've taught your dog what it is. The only intrinsic meaning it might have for your dog is that you're joining in the chorus, and since barking is contagious, you're more likely to encourage your dog than quiet him.

Second, look at the order of the words: if you first say "No" and then "bark," wouldn't your dog start to bark again if she knew what *bark* meant? We've come back around to the problem of "Good sit" again. "No bark!" is just another example of our expecting dogs to understand that a preceding word (*no*) changes the meaning of the next word (*bark*). I know some dogs will indeed get quiet after their owners yell "No bark," but "No" would have worked just as well.

Even if you are clear and consistent with your signals, be sure your dog defines them the same way that you do. For example, I suspect that most dogs and owners define the simple word *sit* differently. If you're like most pet dog owners, you taught your dog to sit by calling her to come, telling her to sit, and then reinforcing her after she did. To us "sit" is a posture. We define "sit" as a position in which the dog's hindquarters are flexed, her rear is on the ground, and her forelegs are straight, with front paws flat on the ground. "Sit." Simple. And it looks as if your dog defines it the same way, too, because most of the time when you tell your dog to sit, I'll bet she does just that. But what does she do if she's lying down and you say "Sit"? Unless you've specifically taught her to sit *up*, she probably will stay lying down. What if she's already sitting? Many dogs actually lie down if you repeat "Sit" while they're sitting. What if you ask your dog to sit when she's 15 feet away from you? If she's like most dogs, she'll happily trot to you and sit facing you, just as she was when you first taught her to sit. My guess is that most dogs think that *sit* means go to your owner's legs, stand in front of him or her, and go part of the way down toward the ground.

Of course, you can teach your dog to sit without coming to you or to sit *up* rather than sit *down.* But the point is that you have to teach it. Unless you go beyond where most dog owners go, your dog probably defines *sit* differently than you do. You might ask yourself what other words your dog has his own definition for. I'm reminded of my favorite cartoon, with a goofy, grinning dog saying: "Hi! My name is NO NO Bad Dog. What's yours?"

Imagine what it's like to be the dog at the other end of the leash—constantly trying to understand a lovable but confusing animal: your owner. I developed a new perspective of what it would be like to be a dog when I spent two years working for Professor Charles Snowdon in the Psychology Department of the University of Wisconsin at Madison trying to translate the signals of a tiny South American animal called the cotton-top tamarin. These highly social, squirrel-sized primates live in heavy vegetation and have developed an impressive repertoire of vocalizations. Just like your dog, scientists can only guess at what the noises of another species really mean, using what happened before and after the sounds they make as clues to their meaning. But even for a member of the world's most intelligent species, translating these sounds turned out to be an amazingly difficult job. For example, family groups of tamarins give "long calls" when they hear the sounds of neighboring groups. Are these sounds messages to the other troops, to their own family, or to both? What do they mean? How would you find out?

It's not easy translating the noises of another species, and take my word for it, your dog goes through a lot trying to figure out yours. Does "Lie down, lie down, LIE DOWN" mean the same thing as "Lie down"? Does "Come" mean the same as "Come here"? Just thinking about the way you use words to your dog will automatically help you tighten up your vocabulary.

Never Repeat a Command. Never Repeat a Command. Never Repeat . . .

Every dog owner who has read a training book has tried, usually unsuccessfully, to follow the advice about not repeating commands. In my experience one of the most universal tendencies of all humans is to repeat ourselves when talking to dogs. We're so driven to repetition that we do it even after the dog has done what we asked. "Sit, sit, *sit,*" says Bob, the third "sit" coming after Max has already sat down. Dog trainers leave the training center shaking their heads over trying to get the owners to give a command just once.

An example of my own most grievous repetition is when I first started working herding dogs on sheep. Talk about getting nervous: imagine going out in a big field and letting your dog loose around prey animals who can run at 20 miles an hour. Your job is to keep your dog from chasing the sheep over the fence, into the fence, or for that matter into the ground. In some situations the sheep will start to chase your dog. Whatever happens, a novice dog with a novice handler is a guaranteed adrenaline rush, and as soon as things started to heat up, like most novice herding dog handlers, I used "Lie down" far too often, as a kind of crutch to help stop things while I could figure out what the heck to do. (Herding can be described as chess with living pieces and only microseconds to decide on and execute your next move.) "Lie down!" I'd yell, immediately following with "Lie DOWN! LIE DOWN!" In no time at all, I had trained Drift, my first Border Collie, to lie down to, and only to, "Lie down, lie DOWN, LIE DOWN!" For all I know, he was waiting for the full signal before he responded, since there was no way for him to know what the basic unit of the signal really was.

Analyzing recordings from non-English-speaking animal handlers, as I did for my Ph.D. research, taught me how very difficult it is to determine the basic unit of a signal. If a Basque sheepherder, speaking in the unintelligible consonants of his language, said three short notes, then paused briefly and said the same one again, it was hard to know exactly what the "signal" was. Was it three short notes or four? If the notes all sounded like "grph," I couldn't necessarily tell if "grph grph grph" meant the same thing as "grph," just said three times. I struggled and pulled my hair and grunted and groaned trying to figure out exactly what the handlers' commands really were—and I'm supposed to be a member of the smart species.

The tendency of dog owners to repeat signals is overwhelming; go to any dog training class in the country, and you'll hear dog owners saying "Come" or "Sit" over and over again, while the instructors smile through clenched teeth, having just said, "Be sure to say 'Sit' just once." "Please,

please, please," (we say repetitively) "try this time to avoid saying it three or four times!"

Why are we humans so compelled to repeat ourselves, stringing words together like popcorn on a Christmas tree? Members of any species that includes linguistic wizards like Dickinson and Shakespeare ought to be able to stop themselves from mindless chatter. But we often don't, and I suggest it's not just because we're idiots, although we may look like them around our dogs sometimes. Surely a behavioral tendency that is so strong and so universal must reflect something beyond mere hardheadedness. Here's another place where looking at ourselves as primates might come in handy. Watch a video of chimpanzees sometime. Our closest animal relatives love to repeat notes. "Ooo," they say. "Ooo, ooo, ooo" comes next. It's not just chimps: most primates produce vocalizations in which similar notes are repeated over and over. Agitated squirrel monkeys fill the air with a variety of twitters, chatters, and cackles. Wedge-capped capuchin monkeys deliver *heh*s and *huh*s in rapid cadences. The cotton-top tamarins that I studied with Charles Snowdon squeak "eee" when they see a tasty treat like a mealworm, but the one note easily turns into a barrage of "eee, eee, eee, eee, eee" as they get more excited.

If at First You Don't Succeed, Just Get Louder!

We don't stop at repeating ourselves around our dogs. We tend to say each note louder and louder. We don't just say "Sit, sit, sit," we say, "Sit, sit, SIT!" And this isn't just when we talk to our dogs. Linguistic researchers have found that when talking to someone who didn't understand what we said, we tend to repeat exactly what we said the first time, only louder.

An undergraduate student at the University of Wisconsin at Madison and I found that humans do exactly the same thing around our dogs. For her senior honors thesis, Susan Murray asked owners in puppy training classes to tell their dogs to sit. Just as in human communication, if the dog didn't sit after the first time asked, the owner repeated the signal, but in two-thirds of the cases, the owner said it louder than before.

We behave as if volume itself could somehow create the energy we need to stimulate our dogs to respond. This tendency to get louder seems to be an integral part of our primate heritage. Not many animals can compete with an aroused primate when it comes to pure, ear-splitting noise production (parrots do come to mind, however). The tiny cotton-top tamarins with which I worked could shake the walls with their mobbing calls if they thought one of their troop was in danger. The noise was so deafening, it was actually difficult to think if you were in the same room. Our closest relatives, chimps and bonobos, are famous for their rising crescendos of calls when they get emotionally agitated. But noise to chimps isn't just about excitement. Within a chimpanzee troop, where males are always conscious of who's dominant and who's not, the ability to make a racket can move you up the social scale faster than buying a BMW. Jane Goodall describes the meteoric rise in status of Mike, a chimp who learned to augment his loud hooting during dominance displays with the crash of metal kerosene cans. The ensuing racket so impressed the other males that all but the dominant male immediately changed allegiances and approached him submissively. Mike eventually did become the dominant male, and his ability to achieve rock band sound levels appeared to play an important role in his quest for power.

We, too, use amplitude, naturally getting louder and louder if we don't get the response that we want. It's as though we try to make something happen just with the energy that we put into our voices. (Think of how hard you worked to train your child not to stand by the phone and scream "*Mom*" louder and louder rather than going to get you.) But dogs don't respond as primates do, and although a loud noise can certainly startle them and get their attention, it doesn't necessarily get their respect.

Barking dogs are often frightened dogs, and the louder they get, the more panicked they are. Keep in mind that barking is relatively rare in wolves, especially from adults.[2] Barking is rarely heard from experienced, confident adult wolves; it is mostly produced by juvenile wolves, usually in

2. Howling, of course, is commonly heard from adult wolves and acts to communicate the location of the pack. It also plays a role in group cohesiveness: I think of it like singing in church or tribal chanting before the hunt.

response to a situation that immature wolves perceive as alarming. As a matter of fact, the universal tendency of adult domestic dogs to bark is one of the many behavioral markers that suggests that adult dogs are actually a juvenilized version of adult wolves. Barking appears to be directed toward two different receivers. One is, of course, the intruder ("I see you. Can't sneak up on me. Better watch out!"), but barking is also directed toward the rest of the pack ("Help! Trouble at the west border!"). The pack usually comes running, responding to their pack member's danger signal.

The dogs who make my blood run cold are the ones I can barely hear, who stand stiff and still, staring straight at me while producing a low, quiet growl. If barking correlates with a juvenile and submissive condition, then it's doubtful that dogs read our loud vocal displays as dominant or impressive. Rather, they might see them as a sign of fear or as a sign that we don't have a lot of control. Many people to whom dogs are drawn are laconic and soft-spoken. I think their lack of "barking" is perceived as a sign of leadership, and dogs are drawn to their sense of self-confidence.

"Be Quiet!" He Screamed

Is there anyone in the world who hasn't, just once, yelled at his dog to *"Shut up"*? The irony of this ineffectual response usually escapes us during the heat of the moment. But think about it. Since the natural behavior of dogs is to join in the barking, they well might assume that we're barking, too, when we call out "Quiet!" or "Shut up!" Ask owners of multiple dogs and they'll tell you that their dogs' response to barking is not to get quiet; it's to bark themselves. At my house one booming bark from Tulip can raise Luke out of a sound sleep. He'll rise scrambling to his feet on the wood floor, barking and running pell-mell for the front door before he's even awake. He looks downright foolish, and I tell him so. "Luke, you don't even know what you're barking at." He looks at me as though I've missed the point. And perhaps I have. Barking is a group activity, and I'm not sure that it's relevant to him whether he knows what he's barking at. What matters is that Tulip is barking, and therefore, Luke is, too.

If a dog hasn't been thoughtfully taught what the word *quiet* means, he'll probably just keep barking. And even if he has been taught its meaning, if you yell it loudly, you've probably changed enough of the word's acoustics so that your dog can't recognize it. It's so very human for us, getting frustrated, to yell "Quiet" louder and louder, sounding for all the world like just another barking pack member, but it's not very effective.[3]

The difficulty of teaching people to stop turning the speaker up and to learn other ways of getting their dog to be quiet has training instructors shaking their heads and heaving a collective sigh of frustration. The key is to give agitated primates (which understandably describes many dog owners who desperately want their dog to pipe down) something to do that helps the dog stop barking and avoids the helpless frustration that leads to the owners' yelling in the first place. If you have a barker, don't try to stop his noise by being louder. Instead, get up and go over to him with a tasty treat between your fingers. This first step sounds easier than it is. Getting humans to move toward dogs at the appropriate time is a challenge for all training instructors. So know that you must focus carefully on this action, because although it seems trivial, people tend not to do it, even after they nod at my instructions and say they will.

Be prepared with easily accessible yummy treats. (Don't be cheap. Go for chicken or beef or anything your dog really loves, but keep the pieces very small.) As soon as your dog starts barking, say "Enough" and then walk all the way over to him, moving the treat to within an inch of his nose and making clicking or smooching noises to get his attention. If the treat smells luscious, and it's right beside his nose, he'll turn away from what he was barking at and sniff the treat. But don't give it to him yet. Palm it in your hand while saying "Good boy" a few times and use the treat to lure him away from what he's barking at. Then give him the treat. What

---

3. I have seen some dogs who appear to be as irritated by the barking of other dogs as we sometimes are. I've observed dogs who lunged and administered a disciplinary nip to the muzzle of a pack member who was an incessant barker. Once the offending dog stops barking, the disciplinarian goes back to calmly standing beside him. Of course, I can't possibly be certain of their true intent, but note that these "hall monitor" types never bark at the other dog; rather, their reaction is silent, unlike that of us noisy humans.

happened was that your dog was barking, you said his signal to stop, and you mechanically created a situation in which he did stop. After he stopped, he got reinforced for it with a treat. First, the treat acted as a lure to stop him from barking, and then the treat became a reinforcement for being quiet. Be sure to do this when he's not too excited to focus: don't start these sessions when he's crazed with excitement because there's a big family and two dogs at the front door. Set this up in the early stages so that you have control over the situation to avoid making it too hard for your dog (and you) to do it right. Have a friend knock just once or twice and then stop, while you lure your dog away from the door with the treat.

You may have to go all the way to him and put the treat within half an inch of his nose to get his attention off what he's barking at, but that's OK. What matters is that over and over, you set up situations in which he barks, you say "Enough" *as* you remove the reason that he's barking, and then you lure him away with treats. After he gets away from the door and he's been quiet for a few seconds (don't wait too long at first), he gets the treat. As time goes on, wait for longer and longer silences after your "Enough." This isn't as easy to train as something like "Sit," because it's much harder for your dog. Barking is tightly linked to emotions and physiological arousal (just as laughing, screaming, and yelling are in young humans), and it can be truly difficult for a dog to stop himself from barking, so be patient. It may take a few months of brief training sessions five to ten times a week, and you must start when your dog isn't so excited that he *can't* listen, but it's worth it. What a joy when your dog hears "Enough," turns away from the door or window, and comes to you, looking for her treat. Once it becomes learned, you can treat her intermittently rather than all the time.

Make Your Voice a Picture of What You Want Your Dog to Do

When I was at racetracks on the Texas border doing research for my Ph.D., I wanted to see if the sounds that we make to get our animals to speed up and slow down are the same, no matter what language we speak. I had already gathered lots of recordings of English-speaking dog and horse handlers. This trip was my first attempt to record professional animal handlers who spoke a language other than English. Regrettably my search for racetracks on the Texas border uncovered that there was no pari-mutuel betting in Texas. No betting meant little money and no plush, white-painted stables and brick-lined walkways like the ones I'd seen on TV. The track and stables I drove into were rundown and dirty and surprisingly empty. Little did I know that racing had been suspended there because of two murders in the last month. Seems the track I had chosen was a wasps' nest of two kinds of drug trading—illegal drugs for humans and illegal drugs for racehorses to enhance their performance.

I naively strolled into the stables, dripping with expensive tape recorders, microphones, and cameras, peeking into dark stable stalls looking for the trainers whom I had contacted earlier. Mostly I remember surprised silhouettes leaping up, grabbing objects, and diving for deep cover away from the door. Throughout the day I got good at identifying syringes, pills, and vials of "medicine" flying through the air on their way to the shadows behind a hay bale. Every sport, whether deep-pocketed or low-budget, has its share of trainers who bend the rules. The rules were bent over backward at this track, and strangers with tape recorders and cameras got no small amount of attention.

I was looking for a cross-linguistic sample of animal handlers and wanted to see how Spanish-speaking jockeys sped up and slowed down their horses. Later I would compare them with horse and dog handlers who spoke English, Basque, Chinese, Peruvian Quechua, and twelve other languages. But right then I needed Spanish speakers who had never learned English, and all the jockeys who were hanging around the old, run-down racetrack either spoke just English or spoke both languages.

"Wait for José," I was told; he'll be here any day, and he knows lots of trainers and jockeys who speak no English; he'll take you to them. They were right. José knew everyone, and everyone knew José, and although José was as perplexed as the rest of the stable about what I was there for, he agreed to take me around to trainers and jockeys who spoke only Spanish, so that I could record them working with their horses. As we drove off into the Hill Country of southern Texas, we stopped at a convenience store at the edge of town. José returned

(it was eight in the morning) with a six-pack. Popping a Bud, he lit a joint the size of a cigar and said, "OK, Treesha, we take you to lots of guys who talk to animals, OK? Want a hit?" I declined and felt for my Swiss army knife.

José kept his word. I must have gotten five good recordings of non-English-speaking trainers and jockeys. It quickly became clear why José knew everyone and was happy to drive me around. Each time we arrived at a new place, I studiously ignored the fat, oblong plastic bags surreptitiously passed from José to the trainers. I fussed with my equipment while José completed his main order of business and then explained why I was there. God only knows what José said to them; my halting Spanish couldn't begin to follow their conversations. They all clearly thought I was crazy, but still, they accommodated me as you would some endearing, harmless alien.

And in a way I was an alien, attending to the sounds that others make to animals as if I were studying another species. I felt like Jane Goodall, benevolently curious about the interesting noises from the primates around me, except the primates just happened to be human. What I learned about those interesting noises has had a profound effect on how I communicate with dogs. Professional animal trainers, who should know as well as anyone how to use sound to communicate to their animals, distinguish themselves from dog owners in one consistent way. They are able to separate their own emotional states from the sounds that they make, making sounds that elicit the response that they want rather than sounds that represent how they are feeling inside.

It's not as easy as it might seem. Human emotions profoundly affect the way we speak, not just in terms of the words that we use but also in terms of *how* we say a particular word. It's called the "prosodic" aspect of speech. I'm sure you've heard the phrase "It's not what you say, it's how you say it." *How* we say a word sometimes conveys as much information as the word itself, if not more. Just listen to the different ways that you can say your dog's name. "Maggie," you can say with velvet warmth while she nuzzles your face when you're cuddling together. *"Maggie!"* you belt out loud and high in fear when she starts to run toward the road. How we say our dog's name, or any word or phrase, is often driven by how we're feeling inside: just think of the times that fear or impatience have crept into your speech, even if you didn't want them to.

We talked earlier about how agitated primates repeat themselves as their excitement levels rise. Chimps call faster and faster in proportion to the amount of food that they discover. Cotton-top tamarins escalate into deafening spirals of repeated chirps when they get excited about food.[4] This tendency to produce what are called "graded" vocalizations is so common within the animal world that decades ago scientists used it to suggest that the noises animals make must *only* reflect their internal state. We now know that that's not true, for several well-studied species use sound symbolically to refer to something external to themselves (like different types of predators). But the tendency to link our internal emotions with the sounds that we produce is strong and takes no end of energy to overcome.

The sounds that we animals make when we're excited do a lot more than indicate our level of emotional arousal. They can also have a profound effect on whoever hears them, and that includes a nonhuman animal. I remember when a dear friend of mine, Todd, was inappropriately mounted onto an untrained, excitable horse. Todd desperately repeated "Whoa! Whoa! Whoa!" as his horse accelerated into a panicked gallop. The faster the horse went, the faster "Whoa" came out of Todd's mouth. But the faster he repeated "Whoa," the faster the horse ran. They were both locked in an escalating spiral that is easy to get into and hard to get out of. Agitated humans make sounds that reflect how they are feeling inside. Instead of helping the animal do what is wanted (or stop doing something), those sounds often agitate the animal that hears them.

I don't say this lightly: I spent five years of graduate research on this very topic. The patterns of sound that I found handlers using were overwhelmingly consistent. An analysis of 104 animal handlers and sixteen different languages found a universal use of short, rapidly repeated notes to speed animals up and single, continuous notes to slow or stop them. The kinds of sounds varied tremendously, from hand claps to whistles to

4. Charles Snowdon has found that as the tamarins become more excited, the structure of the "chirp" note changes as well as the rate of production. See the References for more on the correlation between acoustic structure and the internal emotions of the animal producing the sound.

smooches to words in their own language. But the pattern of sound was always the same: in all languages handlers stimulated animals to go faster with short, repeated claps, smooches, clicks, words, or whistles. English-, Spanish-, and Chinese-speaking jockeys, rodeo riders, draft horse handlers, and dressage riders all made repeated clicking and smooching noises to encourage their horses to go faster. Basque and Peruvian Quechua sheepdog handlers used short, repeated whistles and words to encourage their dogs to get moving. English-speaking sled dog racers belted out short, repeated sounds—words like "Go! Go! Go!" and "Hike! Hike! Hike!" and "Hyah! Hyah!"—to encourage more speed from their dogs.

In contrast, when handlers wanted to slow or stop an animal, they used one single, continuous note. No handler in the entire sample ever used clicks, claps, slaps, smooches, or repeated short words to inhibit their working animal, whether it was a horse, dog, water buffalo, or draft camel. Common English "slow down" signals to dogs and horses are "stay," "whoa," and "easy." North African handlers whom I interviewed told me that camels are trained to lie down to what sounds like "huush" or "kuush." Peruvian Quechua horseback riders used both one long "schuu" (also used by speakers of Basque, a completely different language, to stop donkeys) and a word that sounds like "ishhhhta" to stop their horses. Chinese jockeys slowed their horses with a sound something like "euuuuuu," said in an extended, descending voice. The whistles of sheepdog handlers were one single note, either a single, long, extended one to slow a dog or one sharp, up-and-down note to stop a fast-moving dog. A pattern with two versions of a "slow down" signal was replicated throughout the study, with one long, continuous note used to slow or soothe an animal and one sharp note to immediately stop a fast-moving one. If you think about it, it makes sense that "inhibiting" signals would fall into two different categories, since slowing or calming down is a distinctly different response than gathering up the energy to put on the brakes if you're in a dead run.

Perhaps the handlers used similar sounds because they were just doing what humans do, and the animals learned how to respond appropriately. But most professional animal trainers believe that certain kinds of sound work better than others when you want to excite or speed up an animal.

The racehorse handlers whom I interviewed believed strongly in the stimulating effect of short, repeated "sch sch sch" noises. They reported to me that jockeys aren't allowed to use "sch sch" to get their horse into a starting gate, because it will overstimulate the horses already gated. Herding dog handlers used exactly the same kind of noises to stimulate a hesitant dog to face up to a threatening ram. Barrel racers (a rodeo event involving speed and precision) used a continuum of sounds to influence their horses: two to four clicks to induce a walk, repeated smooches to move into a canter or gallop, and a series of "sch sch sch" to go as fast as possible. I found seventeen references in my field notes to handlers' refusing to repeat that "sch" noise in the belief that their horse would be overstimulated and therefore too difficult to handle during our taping.

Primates aren't the only animals that vary the use of short, repeated notes and long, continuous ones. Horses and sheep and dogs, to name just a few species, all use short, repeated notes to call their young. Young puppies produce short, repeated high whines to signal distress to the moms and solicit care from them. Male rats courting females are more successful in eliciting solicitous postures from females the higher their rate of note repetition. Lusty roosters do well to call quickly and call often: the faster they repeated the notes, the more hens approached them. Research on birds like herring gulls and house sparrows has found that short, repeated calls result in the recruitment of other flock members. The fact that herring gulls give these calls in the presence of food *only if there is enough to share* suggests that the call functions to elicit approach.

I did a separate study for my Ph.D. in which I tested the hypothesis that different types of sounds had different effects on the puppies that heard them. The results were crystal-clear. Based on the number of forepaw steps, we found that the pups' activity levels increased after four short whistles but not after one long, continuous one. Most relevant to dog lovers, four short whistles (comparable to syllables) were more effective than one continuous whistle at training our five-month-old puppies to "come." That makes sense, given that "coming" usually meant increasing activity.

The consistent use of sound by animal handlers from such varied backgrounds is reminiscent of other universal aspects of speech. Researchers have found that people have a similar way of speaking to both dogs and babies, and people around the world talk to babies in similar ways.[5] "Motherese," as it's called, is speech that is higher than usual and that goes up and down in pitch more than if the speaker were talking to an adult. Not only are babies more attuned to "motherese," but no matter what their native language, parents speak this universal "language" to their babies. Some aspects of motherese are useful when talking to dogs (described in the "Pitch Modulation" subsection below) and suggest a universal, evolutionary connection between all of us mammals. Sometimes, however, this form of speech does us little good. Baby talk has a slim chance of working on an aroused dog who's about to chase a squirrel, so the more flexible you are with your use of speech, the better your dog will listen. In the pages that follow, I'll give specific examples of how to use sound as effectively as possible to get your dog to do what you want her to do.

NUMBER OF NOTES

The general rule is to use short, repeated notes to encourage activity and one single note to discourage it. Let's say you want your dog to come when you call. Perhaps because so many of us see this as an exercise in "obedience" (translation: a test of our authority), many humans belt out the word *come* like a marine drill sergeant. If I tape-recorded the sound and analyzed it, it would look exactly like the sounds made around the world to *stop* animals. You could substitute any combination of letters, and you would still have a single sharp, short note that replicates the "*Whoa!*" and "*Ho*" that I heard from sixteen different language groups to keep an animal from moving. I'm always amused when an owner belts out "*Come*" in one loud, low command. Some of the dogs do indeed come, although some do with heads down and tails tucked, because you can eventually override biology with enough training. But why work so hard? Use a sound that inherently encourages your dog rather than discourages him and training will be more effective and, as important, more fun.

5. See the References for articles about "motherese" and "doggerel."

If your dog's name is short, you could call her to come by saying her name twice and clapping your hands, or you could try the "recall" signal of Scottish shepherds: "That'll do!" While teaching a recall signal, try encouraging little puppies to come by repeating "pup, pup, pup, pup" and clapping your hands as you run away from them. Smart dog owners clap their hands; make short, repeated whistles; slap their legs; and at all costs avoid harsh single notes that stop dogs in their tracks. Is your dog coming but not fast enough? Sing out "Good dog" as he lumbers toward you and start clapping as you run away from your dog.

You might ask why I'm suggesting that you repeat yourself sometimes while avoiding repetition at other times. The difference is in the function of your signal. If you're trying to increase your dog's level of activity, use short, repeated notes. But if you're communicating an action that inherently inhibits activity in your dog, like "Sit" or "Down," try to say it only once, just as the handlers I interviewed did. Think of the word that you use as a verb (do something!) and the *way* that you say it as an adverb.

But what if your dog is plunging through the brush after a deer? Not long ago, Tulip had been wide-eyed and air-scenting for days, and when I let her out of the house, she almost knocked me over. She began to charge up the hill after a deer who'd been bedded down in the flower garden. If I had cheerfully called "Tulip, Tulip! Come!" and clapped my hands with her usual recall signal, she would've kept on trucking. After all, I said that repeated notes encourage activity; I didn't say where that activity would be directed. The last thing Tulip needed at that point was sounds designed to stimulate her; she was so excited when she came back that she hyperventilated for ten minutes. I wanted to inhibit her, not stimulate her, so I did what the Basque sheepdog handlers and the Peruvian Quechua horse trainers did when they needed a quick stop on a running animal. I belted out one short "*No!*" Only when she had stopped did I direct her energy back toward me with hand claps and repeated words.

Think about the way you use your voice at the vet clinic when you and your dog are hanging out in the lobby. It's one thing to cool your heels when you wait for your own doctor, but hanging out in the lobby of the vet's office isn't all that relaxing for an owner or a dog. Is that 165-

pound Saint Bernard over there friendly, or was that a growl you heard? Will Chief break away and try to chase the cat that just came in? Here's your chance to use one long, continuous note to calm your dog, just as handlers all around the world would do. This is when you want to say, "Goooooooood boy, Captain, gooooooooooood boy. What a goooooooooood boy you are." What won't help is what I see a lot— slightly anxious owners repeating short, choppy versions of "Good boy, good boy, good boy" while their retriever strains wild-eyed at the end of the leash. The words are often accompanied by equally choppy petting actions, which arouse the dog even more. Here's where you need to learn to separate your own emotional state from the one you want in your dog. If you want to soothe or slow your dog, replicate the "Eeeeeeeeeeasy" of the dressage trainer that I recorded when slowing an anxious horse. Mimic the "Whooooooooooooaaaaaaa, son" of a racehorse jockey calming his horse before the race. Remember the "Steeeeeaaaaady" of a sled dog driver as his dog enters a tricky turn. This is exactly the way that parents all over the world speak when trying to soothe their babies, but it's harder to do when you're feeling agitated yourself. It can take a conscious effort to make sounds that reflect what you want your dog to do rather than how you're feeling inside. There's a bonus, though: speaking in long, steady tones can help calm you down, too. And don't forget to breathe. Long, deep breaths slow everything down, from your own speech patterns to your dog's response.

PITCH

We all know intuitively that pitch is important when we're speaking. Marine drill sergeants don't belt out orders in high, squeaky voices. Low, gruff tones may get soldiers to attention, but they're not going to calm a frightened young child. There's every reason to believe that pitch is just as important to your dog. Dogs and humans share an interpretation of high and low sounds (as do many other mammals). A low pitch signifies authority or confidence in both wolves and primates. Simply saying a signal in a lower voice than before can mean the difference between your dog's ignoring you or obeying. Cool Hand Luke couldn't be a better example.

More than anything in life, he loves to herd sheep. When we're done with the sheep chores, I call his name twice, "Luke, Luke," to ask him to come away from the sheep and follow me as I leave the barn. His response is so predictable, I could bet the farm on it: If I say his name in the usual way, with a relatively high pitch, he completely ignores me. Not a head turn. Not an ear twitch. It's as if it hadn't happened. If I say exactly the same two words, not louder but lower, he pivots on his hindquarters and runs to my side. It's the difference between asking and telling.

When I was competing in herding dog trials, I practiced for months to learn to say "Lie down" in a low pitch, after realizing how my voice tended to rise in pitch when I got nervous. The faster my dog went, the more anxious I became, and the louder and higher my voice got. And of course, the louder and higher my voice got, the faster my dog went. In general, women's voices tend to be higher than men's, so just like my female clients, I needed to practice using a quiet, low voice to inhibit my dog. In particular, it seems as though women's voices rise higher when we try to get louder, while men are better at keeping their voice low and speaking with power. I know that I'm not the only woman whose voice tends to rise just when I most need it to carry authority. Some men, on the other hand, need to practice using a higher voice to praise or encourage their dogs. Almost every training class has at least one guy's guy who shouts out "Good dog" in a voice that stops all the dogs and usually half the humans.

The rule is actually quite simple, and it's also almost universal among mammals: high sounds are associated with excitement, immaturity, or fear, while lower sounds are associated with authority, threat, or aggression.[6] As I work with owners in classes and clients in consultations, a consistent mistake that I see people make is the inability to change the pitch of their voices as needed, especially the inability to lower their voices when they ask their dogs to inhibit themselves. So practice saying "*No!*" or "Stay" in a low voice rather than a loud one and letting your voice rise when you call "Come" or when you praise your dog. If Fido ignores your

---

6. See the References for Eugene Morton's classic scientific paper on the universal tendency of aggressive calls to be low-pitched and broadband (like a growl), while fearful or appeasing calls tend to be high-pitched and narrow (like a whine).

sweet signals to come, switch to a low, growly "*No*" and then call "Come" again, just as sweetly as before.

PITCH MODULATION

Besides being either relatively high or relatively low, sounds can go up and down. This is called pitch modulation, and it, too, can have a huge effect on your dog. The handlers whom I recorded modeled a simple set of rules that I have incorporated into my repertoire ever since. They universally used a flat, unwavering pitch to soothe or slow animals and the opposite to stimulate them. And so those short, repeated words to excite animals were often rising in pitch. But the single notes used to stop fast-moving animals usually varied considerably in pitch, going up and down like a roller coaster within just one syllable. "Whoa!" for example, starts by rising in pitch and then falling. And it makes sense if you think about it: stopping fast requires a major muscular effort and a lot of attention. Sounds that change a lot in pitch are inherently going to get an animal's attention better than a continuous, flat sound.

SUMMARY

The bottom line is simple: Use short, repeated notes like claps, smooches, and short, repeated words to stimulate activity in your dog. Use them when you want your dog to come to you or to speed up. Use one long, continuous flat sound to soothe or slow your dog, as you might when you're trying to calm her at the vet's. Use a burst of one short, highly modulated note to effect an immediate stop of a fast-moving dog, saying "*No!*" or "Hey!" or "Down" when you need Chester to pay attention and stop chasing that squirrel in the backyard. For a "picture of sound," look at the sonograms in the photo insert to help you visualize what the sounds look like. It's easier to use sound correctly when you can see a picture of it in your mind.

Is all this really enough to stop Chester in his never-ending quest to finally catch a squirrel? No. Not even Pavarotti is going to be able to call most dogs off when they are dashing away from you, unless you've done a lot of training beforehand. You're going to have to teach Chester that there's a reason to break off the chase. But your voice is a powerful tool. And as with all tools, it works better when you learn to use it right.

Texas, January 1985

José and I drove back late in the afternoon. I was exhausted and relieved and happy to have gotten so many good recordings of Spanish-speaking horse handlers. Budwiesers and joints aside, José had been relentlessly helpful. All day long he had patiently sought out handlers, translated between us, and helped to lug around equipment and handle fractious horses. The sun was beginning to set when José suggested we stop and drive to a little lake where we could park and watch the sunset. I explained how I needed to get back to catalog and organize the recordings. The universal conversation between a young, healthy male mammal and an unreceptive female mammal ensued. José was doing his best to lure me to the lake, but he could see he was getting nowhere. Finally in desperation he said, to the woman who had been obsessed with getting high-quality recordings of sounds all day long, "Treesha, please come to the lake with me. I will make you such beautiful noises."

Here's hoping that the noises you make to your dog are beautiful, too, because they are easy to identify, easy to understand, and fun to respond to.

4

PLANET SMELL

You Have More in Common with Your Dog Than You Might Think

Ayla is a tiny cat, a perfect cat, who sleeps soft and silky on my chest every night. Until I brought her inside three years ago, she lived in the barn, keeping the mice out of the grain, sleeping curled up on top of my wooly sheep on cold winter nights. One spring the shearer was amazed to find felt instead of wool on one of the ewe's backs. Sheep like old Martha don't usually turn their own wool into felt, but the warmth and moisture from Ayla's snoozing body had matted Martha's wool into a circle of felt. Pretty endearing, coming home on a snowy winter evening to see your cat curled up on top of your favorite ewe, both bedecked with snowflakes like dime-store Christmas trees.

But now Ayla had been missing for three days. I returned home from a business trip on the third day of her absence and combed the farm, calling and looking everywhere. Late that night, searching by the barn, I heard one soft meow—or was it? So quiet, never repeated; it could have been Ayla, or just a bird in the woods settling into a cozy roost. I returned to the house for the flashlight and spent another hour peering into the messy piles of farm debris that grow like algae in southern Wisconsin barns. Nothing.

Early the next morning I searched again. This time I was sure the quiet call I heard was Ayla. Again, she meowed just once, but I heard it clearly this time, and I knew that she was in the barn; and I knew that if I didn't find her, she'd die; and I knew that I'd already looked and looked; and I knew that my chances of finding her in that old barn were lousy.

I looked a few more minutes and then sat down and cried. I had already looked for hours. I knew that injured cats usually hole up in a safe place and stay there. They rarely meow, even when their owners call, abiding by some primal desire to hide when hurt. My chances of finding her in the chaos of my old barn were nil. This is not just a simple space, this barn. This is the top story of a huge old dairy barn with endless passageways through the floorboards, four hundred bales of hay, and head-high piles of fence posts and wire and moldy siding. That cold, still morning I was sure that I'd never be able to find Ayla and that my sweet, tiny cat was dying somewhere within a few feet of me.

But Ayla and I weren't alone in the barn. My Border Collie Pip was in the barn with me, sniffing as always around the pigeon poop and fox tracks. Pip has not read the books on Border Collies. She wags her tail to sheep, like Babe without the secret code, and couldn't move a stubborn ewe if her life depended on it. Worthless on sheep, Pip is worth her weight in gold as an Applied Animal Behaviorist's dog, having rehabilitated more than a hundred dogs from their fear-induced aggression toward other dogs. Pip loves food, tennis balls, and other dogs, in that order. Next, she loves using her nose, reading the world around her like a newspaper written in scent.

While I was crying, I remember saying, "Oh, Pippy, where's Ayla? I can't find Ayla." I was pouring my heart out to her, as so many of us dog owners do, with no expectation that she'd join the search. A few minutes later I heard a noise and looked up to see Pip standing on top of a mound of hay bales, stacked 8 feet high and filling up half the barn. She had her nose jammed between two bales and was digging and whining. She'd never done that before, and she's never done it since. It had to be Ayla.

I must have slung fifty bales of hay before I found her, directly beneath where Pip had been digging: a 7-pound lump of starved, dehydrated cat, with a leg and shoulder so swollen I didn't even recognize them at first for what they were. She looked dead. The vet said she would've been in a few hours. She had a bad bite to the shoulder that had abscessed, and the infection raged while she hid in the hay bales, slowly dying.

Ayla is fine now. She's retired to the house, where she can curl up on warm, sheeplike laps. She visits the barn on occasion but now prefers her naps to be inside, close to the heating duct. Last month I presented her with a mouse caught but not killed in a trap. She turned and walked away. Apparently she is taking her retirement seriously.

Pip saved Ayla's life, and she did it with her nose. I have a nose, too. It works just fine. The rich, musky smell of wild plums hit me like a soft pillow last night as I walked through the valley. I go to sleep to lavender and bring eucalyptus on business trips to mask the odors of bad motel rooms. I can smell cat urine on a carpet as well as anyone in the world—a required skill for an Applied Animal Behaviorist. But it never occurred to me to use my nose to try to find Ayla. Of course, my nose doesn't work as well as Pip's, but did I even consider trying to use it? No. I looked. I listened. Pip smelled. I'm a human. She's a dog.

The Nose Knows

We all know how good dogs are with their noses. We see bomb-sniffing dogs in airports and hear about Bloodhounds who trail lost children through the woods. We watch our dogs sniff under other dogs' tails and wonder what in the world they're learning about one another. What we *don't* know is how very good our own noses are. Our abilities may pale compared to that of a Beagle, who I affectionately call "the nose with paws," but scent is profoundly important to us humans. We just don't seem to be aware of it most of the time.

As described in *A Natural History of the Senses*, by Diane Ackerman, research on humans' ability to smell is nothing less than astounding. People can tell whether a particular piece of clothing was worn by a man or woman just by sniffing it, even when they say they can't. Mothers can correctly identify the smell of their own infants, even when they say they're just guessing. Babies can tell by smell when their own mothers enter the room. Mothers can pick out T-shirts worn by their own children among those worn by others. Women can even identify the maturity of a person just by his or her scent—distinguishing accurately among an infant, a child, an adolescent, or an adult. Just like dogs, we can tell if a scent comes from a male or female. Helen Keller, left blind and deaf by scarlet fever as an infant, claimed that she could tell what people had been doing just by their smell—that odors of wood or the kitchen clung to them long after they moved into a different area.

The sense of smell mediates more of our behavior than we ever imagined. Women who live in close proximity to one another begin to menstruate in synchrony, all because of smells of which they're not even aware.[1] Men who are in intimate relationships with women have faster-growing facial hair than men who aren't, and girls who grow up around men enter puberty sooner than girls who do not. The sense of smell is even an important component of sexual pleasure: fully half of the people who have lost their sense of smell as adults report a decrease in sexual interest. Research on reproductive pheromones (which often can't be consciously detected at all, even if you try) has led to the use of a pheromone called alpha-androstenol in perfume. Not only does it attract members of the opposite sex (both in our species and in pigs—do be careful on a hog farm), but men rate photographs of women as more attractive if it's in the air, and women are more likely to initiate interactions if in its presence.

Although scent has a profound effect on our behavior, much of our response to smell is not within the realm of conscious thought. We humans may be the animal masters of self-awareness and consciousness, but our dogs have it all over us when it comes to the awareness of smells. It's even difficult to talk about smell: try describing a scent to someone who's never smelled it. Ackerman, in *A Natural History of the Senses,* calls smell the "mute sense, the one without words." We don't even acknowledge the lack of smell: we have labels for people who can't hear or can't see, but we have no commonly known term for someone who can't smell. Living without a sense of smell is no small matter. It's dangerous, for one thing; imagine not being able to smell smoke or gas or rotten food. And yet

---

1. If you let a woman smell something that has absorbed the scent from the underarm of another woman every day, she will begin to cycle at the same time as the woman whom she's smelled after about three months.

we never talk about people with a smell disability, as if it wasn't worth our attention.

Even many scientists, especially those who study mammals, pay little attention to the sense of smell. *The Human Brain,* published by the BBC in conjunction with its popular television series, has a section on memory, language, vision, movement, fear, and consciousness but nothing on the sense of smell. *The Biology of Mind,* by M. Deric Bownds, a brilliant book about mind and consciousness, has only one paragraph on olfaction, and that's in the section on memory. I spent hours looking in the indexes of my library of books on primate and human behavior. Very few of them had any reference at all to scent or smell or olfaction. The biggest exception is in the insect literature, where there is a tremendous amount of research on airborne signals, called pheromones, that drive a lot of an insect's behavior. Perhaps it is easier for us to associate a primitive sense like smell with animals that we see as far removed from us.

Visual as primates are, we have a long list of impressive responses to different scents. Cotton-top tamarin females respond to the scents of ovulating unfamiliar females by soliciting sex with their partners. The scent of her mother is enough to inhibit a mature, mated female cotton-top tamarin from ovulating, even if she's alone with her new boyfriend. In a recent study squirrel monkeys were found to have surprising olfactory abilities and were able to discriminate some scents better than rats or dogs. Many primates mark their territories by scent-marking: squirrel monkeys even urinate on their own feet, spreading it over their body in a kind of bath-in-reverse in order to leave a sticky scent trail behind them wherever they go. Several primates have specialized scent structures in their chests, throats, and wrists (where we humans put perfume on ourselves). The primates with which I worked, cotton-top tamarins and pygmy marmosets, scent-marked the branches in their cages, using smells to communicate to their own family and other troops housed down the hall that they could hear but not see. The bottom line is that all primates use the sense of smell a lot, but we humans don't think about it much.

Over the years I've occasionally succumbed to curiosity and got down on my hands and knees and sniffed where my pack of dogs were sucking air like vacuum cleaners. A few times I wasn't able to smell a thing, but most often I'm impressed with some rich, thick scent that smells markedly different than the ground a few inches away. My dogs appear to enjoy my behavior more than I do, increasing their sniffing and tail wagging, and licking one another and me as if something notable had happened. Perhaps it had. Perhaps it's no small thing when we humans become more consciously aware of smells than we usually are. Just writing this chapter has had an influence on how I perceive the world. (I was about to write "see the world" and was struck by yet another example of how visual we are. I consulted my internal thesaurus, not wanting to limit the concept to vision, and came up with "view." Whoops, visual again. See—oh, good grief—it is a big deal when we try to expand our sensory awareness.)

After just an hour of research for this chapter, I began sniffing my way around the house like some crazed rabbit, nose twitching, eyes squinted shut, little short snuffle sounds following me around like a drumbeat. I learned a lot. First of all, my house is even dirtier than I thought. A lot of things smelled dusty or moldy, although the air in the house smells fresh and fine. But beyond that depressing discovery, there was an entire world just waiting for me to notice. Almost every object I sniffed had its own distinct smell. I never expected each book I sniffed to smell different from all the others, but it did. There were some trends. Older paperbacks smelled moldy; new hardcovers smelled woody. A sweatshirt, only worn once, and then over a T-shirt on a cool day, smelled strongest under the armpits. My sheets still smelled like detergent. An old, dry dog bone smelled dusty; the remote control for the TV smelled sharp, chemical.

Try sniffing around your own house and yard. Keep in mind a few things that come naturally to dogs. First of all, you'll bring in more scent if you sniff in little short bursts rather than one long inhale. There's a reason that your dog sniffs in staccato notes. Sniff something with one long inhale, maybe for a second or so, and then sniff the same object with four to six quick sniffs within the same time frame. Often you'll smell much more with short, quick sniffs. (Don't sniff too hard; short, soft sniffs are all that's needed.) Second, don't hesitate to get your nose right on the object. As well as dogs can perceive smells, they don't hesitate to sink their noses deep into whatever it is that they're interested in. Don't be shy.

Do be careful if you have serious allergies. I'd hate for your experiment to turn into an asthma attack. And be aware of what's called "olfactory adaptation." We all know about it: it's the reason that you can sample only so many perfumes at one time. Your olfactory system has to reset itself once it's been satiated, and it simply can't discern different smells effectively once it's been swamped with a number of them already. So sniff a few objects and then give your system some time to recover before moving on.

The biggest surprise to me was when I smelled the fur on the top of my dogs' necks. I expected that they would smell a bit different, each one of them, but I was so shocked by how very different they smelled that my head jerked up like an animal in a Gary Larson cartoon. Pip, having recently rolled and subsequently bathed, still smelled like shampoo. Luke smelled almost astringent, while Lassie had a softer, fruitier smell. Tulip, the sheep-guarding Great Pyrenees, gets bathed more on the schedule of a guard dog and less on that of a house dog. As a result, her smell is very strong, distinctive, and sort of bittersweet. It's not unpleasant to me, but it'll never sell as a perfume. The least amount of smell was on Ayla, the cat that Pip sniffed out beneath the hay. I could barely smell her at all.

The Alien Planet of Smell

As a friend and I were getting ready to go on a bike ride, I was busy shutting windows, locking doors, and checking for food left out on the counters. Pip may stand big-eyed at the window when I drive away, but she's not distressed about my leaving. Mostly she's watching to be sure that I'm really gone, so she can shop for edibles. On the way out, I discovered a loaf of good, chewy bread on the counter, so I went to put it inside a cupboard. "Oh, I'm sorry," said my friend. "I didn't put it away because I didn't think the dogs could smell it. It's wrapped in plastic." My friend wasn't used to living with noses that put intelligence agencies to shame.

Titanium wrapping wouldn't deter the nose of Pip when she's on the hunt for food. If I'm ever buried in an avalanche, please let Pip be close by, above the snow and able to use her nose. She'd find me, I know, unless someone had dropped a Twinkie 20 yards away, in which case I'd suffocate while listening to Pip dig relentlessly through the snow for it.

Dogs have about 220 million scent receptors, while humans can boast only about 5 million. That's why some have argued that dogs can smell forty-four times better than humans. But scent reception isn't just about the number of neurons you have in your nose. As Stephen Budiansky points out in *The Truth About Dogs,* it also depends on what's being sniffed at the time. Dogs can detect some odors that humans can't notice until the scent is fifty times more concentrated. Other odors can be perceived by dogs at concentrations that need to be hundreds of times more intense for humans to perceive. Every species has particular odor combinations that it is better at perceiving, and the same is true with dogs.

Dogs are designed as scent machines, with mobile nostrils (try to move yours to the right or left without moving your head); a special bony structure, the vomero-nasal organ, which hangs on to large scent molecules like Velcro; and an olfactory bulb in their brain that is proportionately four times larger than ours. Dogs can detect human scent on a glass slide that has been touched just lightly, then left for two weeks outdoors or four weeks indoors. It's trivial for them to use smell to distinguish which stick you picked up and threw yesterday from all the other sticks lying in the yard. They can distinguish T-shirts worn by identical twins who ate different foods. Dogs are used all over the world to find buried land mines. There's simply no better method available, since mines are now mostly made of plastic, and metal detectors are useless. Glen Johnson, in his great book *Tracking Dog: Theory and Methods,* describes his German Shepherd, who detected 150 gas leaks along a 94-mile-long buried pipeline, deep under wet clay. Johnson and his dog were the utilities' last-ditch effort to find the leaks; they'd tried every technology available and come up with nothing else that worked.

Cornell Medical Center is investigating the use of dogs as cancer detectors, after a number of clients with cancer came in only because their

dogs reacted as if they could detect something wrong. Stanley Coren, in
How to Speak Dog, talks about a Shetland Sheepdog named Tricia who
kept worrying a mole on her owner's back. After Tricia tried to bite it off,
the owner finally mentioned the mole to her physician, who identified it
as a potentially fatal melanoma. Rin Tin Tin never looked so good.

Even though we know how good dogs are with their noses, we know
amazingly little about what they're really smelling. For example, we're not
sure what the focus of tracking dogs is when they follow someone's footsteps. We do know that all humans shed minuscule particles of dead skin,
called "rafts," that follow us like smoke from a moving cigarette. We de-
posit odors on the ground with each stride that we take, and dogs don't
need much of it to find us. About one–four billionth of a gram of sweat
is left on the ground by the average man's foot with each step. That, believe it or not, is more than enough for a dog.

But those are just some of the ingredients of the stew of smells that we
all leave behind us. We crush vegetation, disturb the soil, and broad-
cast particles of hair, molecules from our aftershave, our deodorant, our
clothes, and our shoes. The problem for dogs usually isn't finding the
scent; it's sorting out the multitude of scents that are there already. Even
the weather affects how much your dog can smell: wet versus dry, cold
verses warm, windy verses calm—all of these factors change the conditions every time your dog puts her nose down and attempts to follow a
trail.

To learn more about how your dog perceives the world, try enrolling
your dog in a tracking class. In the class that I took, we novices bonded
quickly, grinning over our clumsy efforts to manage the tracking line and
guffawing over our initial obliviousness to the world of scent trailing.
When we compared notes on our first attempts to set a track for our dogs
by ourselves, we each had a similar, humbling story. After leashing our
dog to a handy tree or pole, we had carefully walked forward to create a
track, placing each foot with care and thoughtfulness. In the early stages
of training a tracking dog, it's critical to give her one simple, clear track
to follow, with no confusing cross tracks, so each footstep was carefully
placed. In every other footprint, we added a nugget of food, to reward our

dogs for carefully following the scent of our steps. But at least once, when we novices got to the end of our carefully laid scent trail, each of us had sighed with pride in our accomplishment and then cheerfully walked back to our dog by the shortest route. By doing so, we walked directly over the scent track that we had just finishing laying, making mincemeat of the smells that we had so carefully deposited on the way out. It's a wonderful example of how rare it is for humans to think consciously about scent.

My favorite part of class was watching how a breeze affected the dogs. A wind blowing from the left would push the scent over to the right of the trail. The dogs would waver back and forth, moving in a sinusoidal S curve, trying to follow the molecules of scent as they moved through the air, losing them as they dispersed, and then turning back to the source, always searching out the highest concentration of whatever molecules it was that they were keyed on to. Scent is like a fog, a physical entity with its own physical integrity. Just like fog, scent settles in hollows, wafts though the air, and moves and flows in space, invisible to us but clear as a bright light to our dogs.

Scientists in Norway and Sweden were interested in whether dogs can tell the direction of travel of what they are tracking. Since we humans usually start them out at the beginning of a trail, they naturally go in that direction anyway. The researchers asked the question: If you start a dog out in the middle of a trail and give him no information about which way to go, will he choose to track in the direction of travel of whoever made the trail? Indeed he will, but only under some interesting conditions. If the trail consisted of discontinuous pools of odor, as footsteps are, the dog followed in the direction that the person walked. But if the track was left by something that always contacted the ground, like a bicycle tire or a sack dragged on the ground, the dog went both ways equally often. Possibly a continuous gradient didn't allow the dog enough difference between relative strengths to tell him the direction of travel. A similar effect was found in one of the T-shirt studies done on dogs. The T-shirts of identical twins couldn't be distinguished by the dogs unless the shirts were some distance apart. If they were side by side, they probably blended together, masking the differences and complicating the choice.

It's difficult to know how to interpret a dog's response to scent trails, given how little we know about the information that dogs are gathering. Clearly we need many more studies on the scent-related abilities of dogs. Right now, there are many aspects of a dog's life that we can only speculate about, given our primitive olfactory abilities and the dearth of research. For instance, it is common for house cats to attack their best feline friend after one cat has visited a vet clinic and picked up new scents, and I wonder if this could happen in dogs. Do recently bathed dogs smell bad to other dogs? Can bad doggy breath cause social isolation in dogs, just as in our species? Or since dogs love smells that disgust us, does "bad breath" smell good to dogs?

I've often wondered what role scent had in the behavior of aggressive dogs. The most common type of dog-dog aggression that I see is dogs who growl-bark and lunge as they pass by other dogs on a leash. But surprisingly often owners come with dogs who for all the world look as if they're just dying to play with that cute little Poodle across the street. Typically the preliminaries go well, dogs both take on friendly greeting postures, and then two or three seconds into the greeting, the dog in question explodes and attacks the other dog. Often we've been able to eliminate common causes, like inadvertent owner cues (tension on the leash, holding the breath, rounding the mouth) or a reactive response from the other dog. I'm left wondering if smell is an important factor in at least some of these cases. Could the attacked dogs smell like another dog with which the aggressor once had trouble? Or perhaps the victim dogs' hormonal state elicits an aggressive reaction. Maybe they just smell bad.

I took in a fearful little Australian Shepherd who was so damaged that she lived with me for part of a summer. She was terrified of my then husband, Patrick, who stood up to his full 6-foot 5-inch stature when she first entered the living room. She reacted in terror, bark-lunging at him with pupils the size of pancakes, and never got over her fear of him. I could merely hold his keys up to her nose and she'd begin to growl as soon as she smelled them. Surely the memory of a smell that was linked with a bad experience could relate to dog-dog encounters, too. I had a client whose dog seemed to attack visitors rarely and randomly, greeting most people at the door like long-lost friends but occasionally turning into a monster. She'd bitten several times, and her responsible family was desperately trying to protect their friends and yet not abandon their dog. We all worked hard trying to rehabilitate her, but we needed to find a pattern. What was it about some visitors that set her off? Or was it not the visitors themselves but something else? We couldn't find a pattern in whom she attacked and whom she loved: it wasn't about any of the usual factors, not sex or height or facial hair or hats. We finally figured it out. It was pizza. It seems a pizza delivery boy had kicked her when she was about six months old, a highly impressionable age for a dog, and if you entered the house having eaten pizza, you were in trouble. We conditioned her to associate visitors smelling like pizza with wonderful things (like getting to eat the pizza), and she's been fine ever since.

Can You Tell Me Where the Rest Room Is?
I Can't Smell It Anywhere

When we humans are out in public and need a rest room, we all behave consistently. First, we use our eyes, looking for the sign that says REST ROOM or WOMEN or MEN. Failing that, we use sound: "Excuse me. Where's your rest room?" But dogs don't look for a rest room, nor do they talk about it with whines, barks, or howls. They put their noses down and search it out by scent. That's why you have to eliminate any odor of urine or feces in the house if your dog has a housebreaking problem. Dogs who urinate or defecate in the house have a hard time resisting the chemical "sign" on your carpet that says "Go here!" Just because it's written in odor doesn't make it less compelling. Even dogs who were actually "house-trained" have pottied in the house because the dogs defined "house" differently than their owners. We define "house" as bordered by walls, but most dogs seem to define "house" as where you spend your time and therefore where the pack's scent is the strongest. Many of my clients' dogs only went in the back guest room, a place with none of the familiar odors of the family. In most of those cases, simply eliminating the odor of urine and then marking the area with a different scent can get the dog going in the right rest room again. Once the area is odor-free and clean, sit down on the carpet with your dog and a paperback and spend a little time each day there. In just a few days, that place will smell like a living room instead of a toilet to your pup.

It also helps tremendously to give your dog a treat every time that she goes outside—right after she goes, not after she trots back to the house. I'm always a bit surprised at how resistant so many owners are to doing this. Once our dogs are no longer puppies, we seem to have some sense of entitlement that grown-up dogs *should* go outside, because "they should know better." But if they're going to the bathroom in the house, you can either get upset about it and put on a threat display as any agitated primate would—scaring the heck out of your dog in the process— or you can get over it and give him a treat for going outside. Trust me, the latter works a lot better.

All Smells All the Time?

Just as we often aren't able to share in the remarkable world of smells in which our dogs live, we are equally unaware of its limitations. It seems simplistic to point out that all dogs don't use their noses equally well, but sometimes we tend to lump them all together as "wonder dogs" and leave it at that. But their skills and abilities do vary, and both genetics and experience play important roles. Individuals of some breeds are more likely than others to be good with their noses. In John Paul Scott and John L. Fuller's *Dog Behavior: The Genetic Basis,* the researchers described putting untrained Beagles, Fox Terriers, and Scotties in a 1-acre field in which they'd released a mouse. It took the Beagles about a minute to find the mouse and the Terriers fifteen minutes; the Scotties never found it at all. But genetics isn't everything. Experience is as important in nose work as it is in any of our endeavors. Sometimes there's a multitude of rich smells, and it takes a lot of experience for a dog to sort through the miasma of competing scents. Sometimes the scent that he's following is so weak that it's barely perceptible, even to a dog.

The same thing happens to us all the time, just usually with sound or vision. It happened to me in the sheep-ranching country of Wyoming, where a "ranch road" is any area of the desert that has had tire tracks on it in the last two years. Both interstate highways and Wyoming ranch roads can be found by using your eyes, but interstates are a bit easier to follow, unless you grew up as a sheepherder. I drove 26 miles down one of these "roads" one late afternoon, and by the time I reached the end (actually my truck and trailer fell apart about a mile from the ranch house, so I can't really say that I reached the end), my eyes were exhausted from trying to discriminate between bare patches caused by tire tracks and bare patches caused by anything else. Dogs have the same olfactory challenges sometimes, and it's only the committed and experienced ones that stay with it through thick and thin. By the way, this single-minded nature, a prized quality in tracking and trailing dogs, can make for a challenging pet. When Beagles and Bloodhounds put their noses down to the ground, I suspect that the rest of the world fades into oblivion. Think "adolescent with headphones on" and you'll know what I mean.

Remember when you were little and you imagined that adults had infinite power? Surely someone who could drive the car, open the juice container, and reach the sink could make it stop raining. I think that's the same expectation that we have with respect to our dogs and their ability to smell. Because they are so good at using their noses, we assume that they can smell anything, anytime. But dogs use other senses, too, and the brains of both humans and dogs tend to amplify one sense at a time. Many an owner has been snapped at by her dog when she returned home with a new hairdo or a new coat. Surprised by the vision of an unfamiliar silhouette barging into the house, these dogs were using their eyes instead of their noses. Their noses may be remarkable, but they're not always switched on.

Even if they want to, dogs can't smell anything unless volatile airborne particles float into their noses. Dogs may be able to smell a grain of cocaine in a warehouse full of coffee beans, but they can't smell anything at all unless they can come in physical contact with some of its airborne molecules. If your scent particles are being blown by the wind away from your dog, she can't smell you any better than your neighbor can.

Differences in Smell Preferences

A fox used to raise her babies every year in a den behind the barn but didn't return this spring. Her absence is probably due to an untimely death from mange. Last year a mange epidemic swept the foxes, coyotes, and wolves of Wisconsin. Most likely she was among the three foxes who over the summer slowly lost both weight and hair, until they finally died, starving and bedraggled, in my barn. The mange mites, of course, also came to the farm, ready to jump ship at the first possible opportunity for a live host. Tulip got it first, after trotting proudly out of the top of the barn with a limp fox carcass hanging from her jaws. Then Luke got it, badly. Some of his skin became completely bare of fur, starting at halfway up his tail and descending down his rump. He began to look like that cartoon of a guy bending over, pants too low. It's hard to look noble with an almost naked tail and a butt crack showing.

I engaged in a cyclone of research on mange mites and a multitude of assorted treatments until I finally declared it beaten. It's no fun for anyone when dogs get sarcoptic mange, but imagine what it's like when your dogs are part of your profession. My dogs all work hard for our living; they are invaluable in dog-dog aggression cases, and they get the bulk of the attention at speeches and book signings. Yet they and the farm were on quarantine for months.

Even so, I have mixed feelings about my absent fox's disappearance. Certainly I became conditioned last summer to worry that every time I saw a fox it would bring mange back again. But before the epidemic, which comes and goes like most cycles of nature, I would glory in her presence. Every spring I watched her raise her kits between the road and a steep slope of woods, just 50 yards from my barn. I loved her babies, who played on magical evenings on the front lawn, leapfrogging around the pink and white peony bushes. I

*loved hearing her cough-bark, watching her trot purposefully across the county
highway with food for her young early in the morning.*

*But even before the mange struck, the fox had brought something with her
that dampened my pleasure: a smell so strong and awful, it could gag you. If
she'd kept it to herself, it would have been one thing. But she didn't. She
painstakingly scent-marked my farm every night, leaving neat little piles of
fox poop on my front porch. The piles weren't the problem. My dogs were, because they threw themselves with passion onto her scat and ground it into their
ruffs as if it were invaluable. If you haven't smelled a dog who's rolled in fox
feces, then your life is slightly better than mine, because it's a horrible smell,
skunky and repulsive, and it clings to dog fur like a burr.*

I would never pretend that I understand what is going on in the brain
of my dogs when they're rolling in fox poop. And of course, it's not just
fox feces that gets my dogs' attention. To all dogs, the stinkier the smell,
the more attractive the object, including dead fish; fresh, sloppy cow pies
(the more liquid, the better); and partially dried squirrel bodies. Maggots
are a plus, a value-added commodity in canine economics. It's impossible
not to imagine that dogs enjoy themselves when they're rolling in slime.
Their eyes begin to glaze, their mouths droop in a relaxed grin as they
duck their shoulders and grind their backs into some foul, rotting mess.
After satisfying themselves that they are properly anointed, they trot
home with the high-headed, confident stride we might adopt when life is
good and the day is ours.

A myriad of theories try to explain why dogs roll in smelly things, but
they're all just guesses. One of the best known is that dogs are putting
their own scent on the "resource" to mark it as their own. I'm not sure
about this given that dogs scent-mark resources all the time by urinating
and defecating on or around them. (Tulip, who grew up eating outside,
still occasionally squats in place as she eats her last bite of dinner on the
porch.) Perhaps dogs roll on things that they might later want to put in
their mouths, and so they roll on the object, rather than urinate on it. I've
seen so many dogs lick up urine that I'm skeptical (but open-minded)
about this possibility. Others have suggested that, as predators, dogs are

trying to camouflage their scent to prey animals by smelling like something else. I suspect this just makes them smell like a dog or wolf who rolled in something stinky. Besides, if I were a vulnerable prey animal and I smelled an 80-pound dead squirrel moving toward me, I'd probably start getting a little jumpy. But mostly I'm not so fond of the "camouflage of scent" theory because of the behavior of prey animals themselves. Working Border Collies on sheep gives you a good idea of how animals, at least hoofed ones, pay attention to the world around them. Sheep, deer, and horses are highly visual, always looking for signs of predators. That's one of the reasons that they have eyes on the side of their head: it allows them to "keep an eye out" even when their head is down to graze. Scent is no doubt important in predator detection in some species, but the sight of an approaching wolf surely would have a substantial effect on a deer herd, even if the wolf did smell like a dead rabbit.

My favorite theory is what I call the guy-with-the-gold-chain hypothesis. It starts with how dogs and other canines make a living. Dogs and wolves aren't just hunters, they're scavengers, and scavengers can't be too picky about getting their meat refrigerator-fresh. They eat what's available, and what's more, they want to live in a territory where there is lots of food available. Perhaps, it's been suggested, dogs roll in dead things or stinky poop as a way of advertising to other dogs, "Hey, look at me, I live in a high-rent district with an abundance of good things." This seems to me to be the most plausible theory.

But perhaps there's something else. Maybe, just maybe, they also do it for the same reason we put on perfume. They like the smell. And just as we might put perfume on ourselves to attract others, we also put it on to please ourselves. Maybe it makes dogs smell good, both to themselves and to others. Stanley Coren proposed the same theory in his book *How to Speak Dog*. I love the section in which Coren declares rolling in obnoxious smells (obnoxious at least to us) to be the equivalent of the "same misbegotten sense of aesthetics that causes human beings to wear overloud and colorful Hawaiian shirts." It will help from now on, when I'm bathing yet another slimy, greenish dog, to imagine her in a fuchsia and orange flowered shirt, complete with baggy shorts and bad socks.

But enough about dogs. What about us? We humans put alien smells onto our bodies, too. We just like different ones. What must dogs think of a species that grinds up jelly from deer bellies (musk), a squishy liquid from sperm whales (ambergris), secretions from anal glands (civet), and the genitalia of plants (flowers are reproductive parts, pure and simple) to smear all over our bodies? We love this stuff as much as dogs love a good squirrel carcass. Perfume is a $5-billion-a-year industry. New scents are developed in secret research that is as carefully guarded as the development of biological warfare agents. That's why perfume and sweet-smelling products like bath oil are, appropriately enough, the ultimate generic gift of Christmas and birthdays. Almost everyone likes to smell good and to smell good things. We're very aware of that aspect of the world of smell. We notice if the air smells sweet and fresh, or heavy and foul. Bad breath can poison a conversation and be a social nightmare for its producer. Some people can yearn for the scent of a lover or child as if hungry for life-sustaining food. Almost everything that we buy is scented, whether we notice it or not. Manufacturers know, for example, that good-smelling furniture polish is rated more effective than the exact same polish without an added scent.

Our obsession with good smells isn't new. The athletes of ancient Crete rubbed themselves with scented oils before the early versions of the Olympic Games. Alexander the Great adored perfume and incense, as did all the men of ancient times. Syrians, Babylonians, Romans, and Egyptians all doted on the scent of flowers and sandalwood and saffron. Indeed, the first gift to the Christ child was incense. So although we ignore the sense of smell in much of our life, we share with dogs a lust for anointing ourselves with scents that make us and others feel good.

What we don't share is what constitutes a "good" smell as opposed to a "bad" one. We're not the only ones who are appalled by the olfactory interests of the animal at the other end of the leash. Ever put on perfume or aftershave, your very favorite, and let your dog sniff it? I just dabbed on my wrist some Chanel No. 5, a true classic of jasmine and other floral sweetnesses, and asked my dogs to sniff it. Luke and Lassie sniffed, turned their heads (and stomachs?), and backed up. Tulip and Pip insisted on ignoring my wrist and sniffed to see if there was food in my fist. Finally satisfied that there was no treat there, they sniffed my wrist and wrinkled their noses. If they could, I suspect that they'd have had me outside under the hose, scrubbing off that disgusting smear of perfume while muttering some doggy version of "Don't blame me for this bath. I didn't grind this disgusting stuff all over your body."

It makes sense that we'd be attracted to different types of smells. Omnivores like our early humanoid primate ancestors were always seeking out plump, juicy fruits, and that legacy drives our attraction to fruity and flowery smells. Dogs are hunters and scavengers, attracted to, rather than repelled by, the scent of ripe carcasses. In the big scheme of things, one attraction makes no more sense than the other. When you think about it, soaking in plant genitalia or whale goo really isn't inherently any more sensible than rolling in cow pies. That perspective helps me a bit when I'm not quick enough to stop one of my dogs from her blissful wallow in some wretched, stinking mess. But given the power of smell to attract—or in this case, to repel—it frankly doesn't help enough. The next time Tulip comes home smiling and stinking to high heaven of fox feces, I think I'm going to soak her in a bucket of Chanel No. 5. That'll teach her.

5

FUN AND PLAY

Why Dogs and Humans Play Like Kids
All Our Lives and How to Ensure That
Play with Your Dogs Is as Safe as It Is Fun

*Tulip was the one Great Pyrenees puppy that I knew I shouldn't get.
Restrained by a gate from playing with her littermates, she was the only white
fluff ball that threw a fit. Her sisters sat quietly, resigned to watching everyone else have a good romp. Tulip leaped and barked and did everything but
grab the gate in her paws and shake it like a convict in a bad prison movie.
I was watching the litter in order to pick the right puppy for me and the farm.
Bo Peep, my first Great Pyrenees, had died suddenly of cancer, and her death
had left a gap in my farm like a missing puzzle piece. My sheep were de-
fenseless without a big, white guard dog who barked deep and low like a can-
non. I missed her soft, square muzzle resting on my stomach when I lay in the
high pasture, my back pressed to the earth, the sheep chewing their cud in the
sun around us.*

*And so I had come here to find my next sheep-guarding dog and was
stampeded by big-pawed Great Pyrenees puppies. But which one would be the
right one? Bo Peep had been the perfect dog for me and the farm. Sweet as
country butter to people, noble and quiet with the sheep, Bo Peep had been
a poster child for overcoming a disability. She had only one back leg, and
the one she had was weak and unstable. Born with her kneecaps off to the
side, she had kept me and veterinarians busy for years with surgeries and
long hours of rehabilitation. One leg was repaired but never functioned nor-*

84

mally; the other we finally had to amputate. She could walk upright on three legs for a few steps, but mostly she cheerfully dragged her hindquarters along with her sturdy front legs. Moving more like a fluffy seal than a dog, Bo Peep nonetheless repaid us all for our rehabilitation efforts. For nine years she was a working guard dog for the sheep and the ducks, her disability not preventing her from carrying out her duties. Most of the time livestock-guarding dogs protect their charges indirectly by barking and scent-marking, so it wasn't as though she were out fighting bears all night. Here in southern Wisconsin, the predators on lambs are coyotes and stray dogs, and they tend to avoid farms with dogs as big as sheep on them. But on rare occasions guard dogs have to be more protective. Bo Peep earned a place in the guard dogs' Hall of Fame by picking up a 60-pound stray dog who was trotting out of the yard with Uncle Burt the Stud Duck in his mouth. Bo Peep, moving surprisingly fast, flopped her way across the yard in seconds, picked up the dog by the scruff until he dropped Uncle Burt, and then nosed the duck back to the safety of the barn. But now she was gone, and in her absence my animals needed protection, and I needed a bear-headed, seal-eyed dog to fill up the hole in my heart.

It's hard to replace a dog that's one in a million. I wanted a dog like Bo Peep that was docile but not fearful, so I could trust her with children, and that would be quiet and mellow with the sheep. Sheep-guarding dogs most often fail because they are too playful—they end up playing some of their charges to death. Ten-pound baby lambs and hundred-pound dogs both love to frolic, but they're not the best of playground partners. The dogs have more fun. So when I gently turned Tulip over on her back and held her still with the palm of my hand on her chest, I was looking for a dog who would squirm a little, lick my hand, and then settle with sweet acceptance.

"Sweet acceptance" is not in Tulip's vocabulary. I might have named her "Eloise," after the menace of a little girl who poured water down the mail chute at the Plaza Hotel in New York City, made famous in a series of wonderful books. While Tulip writhed like a fish under my hands, squirming in protest, she looked straight into my eyes. But it wasn't with that hard-eyed, make-your-blood-run-cold look I've seen on the faces of some puppies. Her eyes gleamed like a sparkler on July 4, shining with joy and gleeful playfulness. She and I looked deep into each other's eyes, and in that brief moment I was dumbstruck with love. Like some foolish adolescent, I let Tulip steal my heart in less than a second.

Oh, to my credit, I told the breeders that she wasn't the right puppy for me. I wisely chose a quiet, passive puppy. But that puppy died before I could take her home, and the breeders decided they wanted to keep my second choice. So I took home my third choice, rejecting Tulip as too spirited to be a good sheep-guarding dog.

Great Pyrenees puppies look a lot alike, but the one that I brought home looked suspiciously unlike the pup that I thought I'd bought. By the time I got home, I was sure. The package of fur and paws and shiny eyes that smiled beside me was none other than my playful, incorrigible friend. After a few phone calls to the breeder and confirmation of the inadvertent switch, I settled into my inevitable fate. I named her Tulip, after the white flowers I had planted when Bo Peep died.

Tulip is in the house as I write this, guarding the spring lambs from the couch. Now seven years old, Tulip is a mature female and long past the age at which most mammals would be playful. But her eyes still sparkle, and she still leaps and spins like a puppy while romping with me and the Border Collies up the hill. A few years ago I found her lying at the crest of the hill, far from the flock. She didn't get up when I called, which isn't like her. When I got closer, I found a week-old lamb nestled between her thick white legs. I was overcome with gratitude that my guard dog was protecting what I thought must be a sick lamb. Too bad that thought was a fantasy, as I realized when the perfectly healthy lamb tried to get up and return to his mom. Tulip watched the lamb dash a few yards away and then, eyes shining, chased him like a soccer ball, gently stopping the lamb with her huge square jaws, punching him down to the grass, and lying beside him. Tulip wasn't protecting the lamb; she was playing with him as my other dogs play with tennis balls. So even though she's a grown-up, Tulip goes off duty as a guard dog each spring until the young lambs are older. She plays with me and with dog toys that are more appropriate than baby lambs. She just came over and pushed her warm, *square muzzle into my lap. She still has my heart, but that's OK. She'll guard it well.*

The Eternal Youth of People and Dogs

Dogs and people aren't normal mammals. Most mammals play a lot when they're young and then gradually become more and more sedate. It's not just because older animals are too busy staying alive and finding food for themselves. My grown-up sheep, who are provided with food, water, and protection, don't play like lambs. My neighbor's red-and-white calves drag race in wide circles around their sleek but passive mothers. Surely the adults could allow themselves a momentary frolic in the afternoon sun; their only danger comes from coyotes who might attempt a midnight raid on a newborn calf. But grown-up cows rarely play. They eat; they chew their cud; they lie down on occasion to rest their legs. As with most species of animals, the grown-ups just don't play very much.

There are a few other animals, besides dogs and humans, who also show high levels of play as adults. If you need a good laugh, get a video of river otters careening down mud banks or watch a group of kea parrots entertaining themselves by deconstructing a car in New Zealand. I once watched in wonder as ravens, one by one, kicked snow from their perches on top of light poles onto a pedestrian walking below them. Each raven was standing on a different light pole, spaced about 30 feet apart, and as the man walked below each pole, that pole's raven kicked snow on top of him. When the man looked around, startled at the snow falling on his head, all the ravens burst into a cacophony of cawing. I don't begin to presume that I know what those ravens were really doing, but "playing a game" is the best explanation that I can come up with. But animals like ravens and otters and humans and dogs aren't typical at all. Most adult animals just don't play very much.

But dogs? My middle-aged Border Collies live for the cue that I'm about to pick up a ball. Seven-year-old Tulip plays along, preferring her own ball, which she alternately tosses and chases with the abandon of a puppy. Tulip's level of exuberance may be extreme, but most adult dogs still love to play games, well into their mature years. And I follow right along, just as happy to play a game as the dogs are. At the age of fifty-three, I am hardly a juvenile, but I still love to play. And so do my friends, and so does the whole global community of humans and dogs, for that matter. Our species is obsessed with play: we are either participating ourselves or watching others play for us. We turn every new invention into a toy. Look at computers—machines designed for high-level data processing, the most boring and serious of all tasks—which have been turned into a multibillion-dollar industry of computer games. "Whoever dies with the most toys wins" is funny only because it underscores a basic truth about our species: we're fixated on play long after we've grown up.

Of course, we play less as we age than we did as youngsters. Almost all juvenile mammals play, so much so that play defines youth more than any other activity. Young lambs leap up into the air from a standstill, twisting sideways at the top of their jump. Watching a group of them alternately rise and fall in the air is like watching popcorn pop. Pronghorn antelope yearlings spar with their horns in mock fights. Cats of all forms, from kittens to tiger cubs, box around anything they can get their paws on, from leaves to butterflies to crumpled paper. Young laboratory rats chase and pounce on one another and engage in a behavior that for all the world looks like tickling. Two- to three-year-old chimps do little but eat and play. Sometimes they play solitarily by swinging in trees and spinning in circles, but more often they play together, chasing, leaping onto one another, play fighting, and wrestling.

As most animals age, the frequency of their play decreases until it ceases altogether. But Peter Pan species, like humans and dogs, retain their playful natures into adulthood. I don't want to oversimplify this: adult animals like wolves and chimpanzees still play, but not at the high levels seen in dogs and humans. This tendency to continue exuberant play into adulthood is one of the factors that leads most scientists to consider dogs and humans as "paedomorphic," or juvenilized versions of their more "grown-up" relatives. Paedomorphism is the retention of juvenile characteristics at sexual maturity, characteristics that usually fade away as an animal matures. In these animals the normal developmental process is delayed for so long that in some ways they never grow up. Almost every animal, no matter how simple, has different characteristics early in its development than it has later on when mature. Sometimes these characteristics are physical—for instance, some insects have vastly different physical forms as juveniles than they do as adults. We all are familiar with caterpillars changing into butterflies. "Juvenilized" insects have evolved so that they never morph into their ancestral adult form; they become adults while looking like juveniles. But sometimes these characteristics are behavioral. Often there is a link between anatomy, physiology, and behavior, and animals that not only look like the young of their juvenile ancestors sometimes act like them, too, even when they're grown-up. Paedomorphism is a fascinating evolutionary phenomenon to which I'm afraid I can't do justice here in this brief discussion. What matters in our inquiry about humans and dogs is how changes in the process of development can create adult animals who, like most juvenile mammals, remain remarkably playful even as they age.

Changes in developmental processes have much to teach us about how and why dogs can be so different from wolves and yet still be of the same species. A Russian scientist named Dmitry Belyaev was interested in how the process of domestication resulted in animals who are less aggressive than their ancestors. Borrowing a group of foxes from Russian fur farms, Belyaev selectively bred only the most docile of foxes. He had to choose carefully, because most of the foxes with which he was working didn't take kindly to handling. Out of each litter, he only bred the foxes that were least likely to try to flee or bite and that were the most likely to lick the outstretched hand of the experimenter and to approach voluntarily. In just ten generations, 18 percent of the foxes born were what he classified as the "domesticated elite"—eager to establish contact with strangers, whimpering, and licking the experimenters' faces like puppy dogs. By the twentieth generation, 35 percent of them were eager to be petted rather than trying to flee or bite as most adult foxes would.

What makes this study so interesting, and so important to science, is that when the researcher selected for just one trait, that of docility, changes occurred in a multitude of other aspects of the foxes' behavior, anatomy, and physiology. The floppy ears of young canid pups stayed with the foxes into adulthood. The adult "domesticated elite" continued to act like pups even as they aged, showing less fear of unfamiliar things at a later age than the normal population of foxes; and reacting submissively to strangers by raising their paws, whining, and doing full-body wags as young pups do. Amazingly they developed patches of white in their fur, like so many of our domesticated animals.[1]

The foxes also developed problems with over- and undershot jaws (just as our domestic dogs do), curly tails rather than the straight ones of adult wolves and foxes, curly or wavy fur, a drop in adrenal production, and higher levels of serotonin production. These last two physiological changes relate to an animal's overall level of stress, lower levels of corticosteroid production from the adrenals and higher serotonin levels being associated with individuals who are less stressed by unfamiliar things and more open to change. In their book on the evolution of dogs, *Dogs,* Raymond and Lorna Coppinger make a good argument that this all gets down to "flight distance"—or how likely an individual is to go on alert at the approach of something unfamiliar. Adult animals are more wary than their young. After all, part of the joy of watching children and puppies is their naive innocence about the dangers of the world around them. It's refreshing to temporarily cast off the grown-up burden of being "on alert." Perhaps that's one of the reasons that play is so healthy for us.

The common factor in all these traits of Belyaev's foxes is paedomorphism, or the retention of juvenile traits in the adult form, also replicated in our domesticated dog: overall, adult dogs act much more like juvenile wolves than adult ones. This selection for juvenile characteristics can, in the case of dogs, be attributed to two different explanations. The traditional argument suggests that domestic dogs evolved from wolves because of artificial selection, whereby humans selectively kept and bred the most

---

1. Wild or feral cattle, horses, and dogs all tend toward a lack of white, looking entirely brown or black from a distance. Their domesticated relatives like holstein cows and pinto horses and Springer Spaniels often have the same piebald coat that Belyaev inadvertently developed in his "domesticated" foxes.

docile of wolves. Another argument is that docility developed through a process of natural selection, whereby dogs with shorter flight distances began gathering around human settlements to scavenge on their garbage.[2] I like the natural selection perspective myself, although I would argue that both processes could have occurred simultaneously. What's relevant to us at our end of the leash is that dogs, for whatever reason, have a suite of characteristics associated with juvenile canids, even after they've grown up, including being remarkably playful.

And we humans, playful and childlike into our old age, play right along with our dogs until neither one of us can get up off the couch anymore. This tendency has led to the suggestion that humans are paedomorphic primates. It's not necessarily a new hypothesis—a man named John Fiske made the argument as early as 1884—but it continues to be a reasonable one. There's more than just our playful nature that suggests eternal youth has played a role in our evolution. One of the defining characteristics of humans is our creativity, our willingness to try new things and new ways of interacting with our environment—all traits normally associated with youth.

Overall, the young of our species, and the young of most mammals, are much quicker to welcome change than their elders. It's not just in humans that older individuals frown on the openness of youth to change. In a now-famous experiment, researchers introduced sweet potatoes to a troop of Japanese macaques. The juveniles, not the adults, initiated eating the new food, although some of the younger adults eventually followed suit. One enterprising two-year-old female named Imo learned to walk into the ocean to wash the sand off her potato. Later she invented a similar technique in which she scooped handfuls of wheat grains from the sand and dropped them onto the surface of the water. The sand sank and the grains floated, now clean and fresh and nicely salted and ready to be picked up and eaten without the unpleasant grit of sand mixed in. This behavior eventually spread throughout the troop, with the exception of the very young, who lacked the motor skills to pull it off, and

2. See the References for more information on the fascinating topic of the evolution of domestic dogs.

the older adults, who seemed to have no interest in the kids' newfangled ideas.

But even though humans are more open-minded and flexible when they're young, from a broad comparative perspective, adult humans are amazingly flexible compared to the adults of other species. One could argue that part of our astounding success as a species relates to our ability to interact in new ways with our environment. Our love of play goes hand in hand with that flexibility, and it's one of the defining characteristics of our bond with dogs. We both love finding new ways to play with each other, especially with those strange, round objects called balls.

Play Ball!

Two red fox juveniles, born in a den behind my barn, trotted into the front yard one evening and got my attention by playing leapfrog over and around a hedge. While the female dashed around to the right of the hedge, the male would flatten in a stalking posture on the other side and leap forward when his sister appeared. Occasionally the stalker couldn't or wouldn't wait, and he'd bounce straight up and over the hedge, landing on top of his playmate. This would temporarily change the game to one of wrestle play, but soon they'd be back to their version of "tag, I'm it." They played for long, full minutes like that, while I, barely breathing, stood motionless in the window. At some point I noticed a tennis ball, lying perhaps 15 feet outside the circle of their game. I distinctly remember wondering what they would do with it if they encountered it. Not much, if anything, I assumed. They had no experience with balls as play objects, and besides, they were busy with other games. But just as I found myself thinking, "Wouldn't it be delightful if one of them picked it up?" one of them did. He picked it up without hesitation and, turning his head down and sideways in preparation, flung it up in a high arc, 16 feet above the ground. When it landed, he pounced, picked it up, and flung it away again. Then he turned to his littermate, and just as abruptly as they had entered, they trotted purposefully out of the yard and down the road.

I was enchanted. But what struck me later, beyond the pure delight of frolicking foxes, was the broad-based appeal of balls. Our mutual love of those round objects that we call balls is truly amazing. I knew a Golden Retriever named Max who virtually lived and breathed with a yellow tennis ball in his mouth. There are dogs of all breeds who'd do almost anything to find yet one more ball. My friend Deb's yellow Labrador Retriever, Katie, is so ball-obsessive that she looks for them everywhere. She finds them everywhere, too, including in a wilderness preserve in the Rockies, even though Deb had purposely left their own tennis balls behind so that, just for once, she could go on a normal walk with her dog instead of throwing balls for hours on end. My Border Collie Luke, who is normally so mild-mannered that I compare him to Ashley in Gone with the Wind, used to mug his cousin Pip mercilessly if she happened to get to the ball first, thundering alongside her at a dead run and grabbing it out of her mouth on the fly. And as for us humans, you can turn on the television right now and find fifteen games from around the world that involve those strange round objects.

I must confess that I don't completely understand ball games, being something of a mutant here in Wisconsin, where the fate of footballs, golf balls, baseballs, basketballs, soccer balls, and tennis balls is headline news every day. During my required softball practice in elementary school, I used to stand in right field chanting under my breath, "Please don't hit the ball to me, please don't hit the ball to me." But of course, they did, knowing my tendency to run away from hard, fast-moving missiles targeted toward my head. I take comfort that I am not alone. Plenty of dogs out there haven't read the book that they're supposed to love balls and either ignore a passing ball or run away from it. My Border Collie Mist never even turned her head toward a moving ball; rather, she herded my retrieving Border Collies as if they were sheep, running wide circles around them, stopping when they stopped, stalking up with serious intensity toward them as they waited for me to throw the ball. But we athletically challenged individuals of each species are the exceptions, overwhelmed by the majority of humans and dogs who throw, kick, hit, chase, and retrieve anything that rolls.

As ubiquitous as ball play or "object play" is in people and dogs, it is not common behavior in most of the animal world. Even in the young, playing alone or with something other than a sibling is only seen in a few bird species (especially parrots and corvids like crows and ravens) and some mammals (most species of primates and carnivores, goats, red deer, bottle-nosed dolphins, and mustelids like otters) but never in insects, fish, or amphibians.[3] Reasonably enough, object play is found mostly in species that are generalists and whose method of obtaining food involves a lot of handling and manipulation. That's true in primates, who all play with objects to some extent. Chimps are the masters of object manipulation in the wild, using carefully modified sticks to hunt for termites and thoughtfully selected tools to crack nuts.[4] They also turn certain types of leaves into sponges and use them to soak water out of crevices. No wonder, then, that their young grow up playing with sticks and leaves and any other interesting object that they can find to pick up. In captivity orangutans are famous for their ability to manipulate objects, being especially adept at picking locks.

Play directed toward objects is virtually the same in all primates, human and nonhuman, during the first year of life. Up to the age of twelve months, most human and nonhuman primates interact with objects in the environment by investigating them: sniffing, touching, and especially mouthing anything that we can move toward our mouth. But only apes (chimpanzees, bonobos, gorillas, and orangutans) and one species of monkey (capuchins) have been seen to engage in play that includes throwing an object. Only apes, capuchins, and humans, I should say, because our own children are masters at flinging objects willy-nilly, usually onto the kitchen floor right before company comes. It's not until

3. Reports by scientist Gordon Burghardt of captive turtles playing with basketballs have initiated an interesting inquiry into the possibility of object play in reptiles.

4. Only chimpanzees from certain areas have developed this skill, which humans have found to be extremely difficult to perform successfully.

the age of eight or nine months that human children first begin purposefully dropping or throwing things—and then, as any parent knows, get ready to back up.

This tendency of humans and dogs to play with objects like balls is firmly based in our natural history as primates and canids. But as always, "nature" (our genetic blueprint) provides a foundation on which "nurture" (the environment) can build. How we grow up affects how we play, whether with objects or not. Dogs who are rescued from abusively sterile environments often don't play with any kind of toy. One of my saddest cases involved evaluating a group of dogs that had been tied all their lives on a short chain inside a dark barn. Meeting these particular dogs would have broken your heart. After an entire year of rehabilitation efforts at the Fox Valley Humane Association in northern Wisconsin (the dogs couldn't be placed in homes until the legal issues were resolved), the dogs were still so terrified of new people that some defecated in fear when I entered the room. Besides their pure terror of strangers, the most notable behavior of these dogs was their complete disinterest in toys. They wouldn't play with balls, wouldn't chew on rawhide, and after a cursory sniff, ignored any object put into their kennel.

This lack of interest in playing with toys is almost universal in dogs raised in impoverished environments and isn't the same as the disinterest of my Mist, who just wasn't a natural retriever. Unlike the permanently damaged dogs in the abuse case, Mist was happy to gnaw on a good chew toy and had some toys that she enjoyed. Dogs raised in the complete absence of any environmental stimuli, like many dogs in puppy mills, often develop into adults who won't play with any object, ever, not with balls, rawhide chew bones, or Frisbees. Perhaps there is a "critical period" for object play, just as there is for socialization, in which dogs are hardwired to learn how to play and what to play with.

This influence of environment on play is not unique to dogs. Although the basic forms of how kids play with objects is universal, the amount and complexity of their play seems to be influenced by the opportunities afforded them. Women in hunter-gatherer societies don't have a day-care center down the street, but they still have to perform a multitude of jobs that require two hands and a lot of concentration. By necessity some children spend most of their early years bound to their mothers, in a sling on mom's back or chest. Strapping their child to their body not only allows mothers to get work done but also keeps their babies safe from danger. Children who grow up attached to mom have limited opportunities to play with objects in the environment, and they show a predictable decrease in the frequency and complexity of their object-related play later in life. One lovely exception is the children of the !Kung culture, who are belted to their mothers all day but can and do play with mom's elaborate ornamental necklaces.

I know little about rehabilitating children from impoverished environments, but I do know that dogs who spent their early years trapped in an empty kennel or at the end of a chain can sometimes learn to play with objects. It can easily take up to one or two years, but if you use hollow toys (like Kongs or Goodie Ships) and stuff them with food, the dogs can learn first that objects are interesting because they might contain food and eventually that objects are inherently interesting in and of themselves. (This also works with some dogs who may have had a wonderful start in life but just don't exhibit an interest in balls. Owners who are determined to play ball with their disinterested dogs can hollow out tennis balls, stuff food inside, and sometimes create a dog as obsessed with balls as they are.)

Keep Away

We don't just share a love of ball play with dogs; we share a tendency to play the same games. Variations of "keep away" are as popular with dogs as with kids. Some of my clients are hurt when their dog won't bring the ball back to them. But why should dogs bring the ball back when they can play an even more exciting game called "catch me (and the ball) if you can!"? And, boy, do dogs love this game. Dogs seem to glory in being the one who "wins" an object and keeps it away from the others, especially if others want the ball themselves. They are masters at staying just far enough out of reach so that you can't catch them but close enough that they keep you engaged in the game. They're not doing this to torture you, although it might feel like it. They're just playing a game that they play with other dogs and that they'd like to play with you. Because we are who we are, we can't resist playing along. Helpless victims of our own obsession with balls, we just can't bear the idea that we threw the ball and *didn't get it back*! After all, if we weren't as ball-crazy as they are, we wouldn't have started the whole thing in the first place. Chimpanzees play keep away, too. Jane Goodall described young chimps' approaching others in a floppy kind of "play walk," holding a toy. If another chimp reached for it, the initiator dashed off, looking over his shoulder all the while. It's just no fun if no one else wants what you've got, not for chimps or for dogs.

Some dogs take it a step further. It's not enough for Luke to catch the ball and run with it; Luke then runs toward the other dogs as if trying to get their attention, ball held high as if raised in the air by an Olympic athlete running a victory lap with his country's flag. If there isn't some element of taunting in all that body language, then I'll retire from my work with dogs and take up working with fruit flies.

It's actually not too difficult to get a dog to bring a ball back to you once you learn how. It helps to start by understanding that dogs are just trying to teach you to play their game while you're trying to teach them yours. Who ends up training whom first depends on you. Keep in mind that dogs are naturals as animal trainers, while humans aren't, so you'd better be on your toes when you start to try out "fetch" with a new dog. But if you can follow just a few rules, you'll have a dog who's much more inclined to bring the ball back than not. Start with young dogs by throwing the ball only a short distance away. Most people who are just getting their dog started throw the ball too far for the dog to stay focused on it. Don't throw it very often at first either; just two or three times is enough. Ten-year-old Cool Hand Luke, now obsessed with balls, came to me at one year of age with no interest in them. After a few months he'd chase one and bring it part of the way back, but only for three or four times. Then he'd lose interest and shift his attention to something else. So I'd stop before he lost interest, after two or three throws. Gradually he stayed interested longer and longer, until now he stops only when he's out of breath or I'm worried that he's getting overheated.

After you throw the ball, wait until the dog has his mouth on it. Once he does, your job is to move *away* from the ball, clapping and smooching to attract him in your direction. If you walk *toward* him, you've just initiated a chase game, but in the wrong direction. After all, he has the ball, he has your attention, and you're moving toward him. What's any good dog to do? He's going to take off *away* from you because you've initiated the first steps of "tag, I'm it!" by running toward him. But if you can override your own natural tendency to get sucked into his version of keep away, you can outtrain him and pull him into chasing after you. Somebody has to chase somebody else: that's the rule that both species share. You get to decide who chases whom.

Turn so that you're not facing your dog, clap, smooch, and take some steps away from him so that he'll start chasing you. Now you get to be "it"! If you're lucky, he'll come all the way to you and drop the ball, but don't count on it. More likely he'll come forward a few steps and drop the ball 5 feet from you. Or he'll drop the ball the instant that you call and run trotting back to you with an empty mouth. Another common variation is to run partway back to you with the ball in his mouth and veer off in hopes of getting you to chase him. Your job is to "shape" his behavior so that you reward successive approximations of what you want. If the first time he comes forward three steps and drops the ball 10 feet from you, that's OK. Walk slowly up to it (perhaps turn sideways so he doesn't start to dash away) and throw it again. You can also throw a second ball as soon as he drops the first. But next time try to get him to come a little closer to you by running actively away from him as he approaches. Gradually expect him to come closer and closer, eventually coming all the way to you.

If he drops the ball before he heads back toward you, try being a bit quieter when you call or waiting to be sure that he has a good grip on it. If that doesn't help, go back to the ball and wave it around in front of his face to get his interest back on it, then toss it just a foot or two away. On the other hand, if he starts to bring it back but veers off as he approaches you, just beat him at his own game. Before he can peel away next time, you turn and run in another direction, playing hard to get better and faster than he does.

But what if your dog comes all the way to you with the ball in her mouth but won't let you take it away? Don't pry your dog's mouth open or get gruff and angry about it. Think of young children who greet you at the door with their new treasure but simply can't bear to give it up, even for just a moment. You wouldn't get mad at a three-year-old for not wanting to give you the toy; you'd patiently teach him that it's OK to hand it over. Just like children, most dogs need to learn that they won't lose in the long run by giving up the ball, and you're the one who can teach them. There's a variety of ways you can teach your dog that it's fun to give up the ball. First and foremost, be sure that whenever she does give it up, you throw it back instantly. That's instantly, as in an instant. Not two seconds later after you've clutched it to your bosom and said, "Good dog. What a good dog!" She doesn't want your praise or your petting, for heaven's sake, not then. (Think your kid would be appreciative of a neck rub in the middle of a ball game with his or her buddies?) She wants the ball. Give it to her, *quick!*

Just learning to give or throw the ball back the instant that the dog releases it solves about half the fetching problems that most people have with their dogs. Most of the other problems are solved when people learn to move away from their dog to encourage him to fetch rather than moving toward him. Above all else, remember that in both chimps and dogs, it's no fun to have the ball unless your play partner wants it, too. If your dog simply won't stop teasing you with the ball, turn away from him, fold your arms, look away, and pay no attention to him. I used to turn and abruptly walk in the house when Luke began to get coy. It works like a charm. I can't tell you how many clients' dogs I've seen, reported to be impossible to get to return the ball, who would literally push the ball into the back of my leg if I played hard to get. Just remember to throw it the microsecond that you get it. (Try to resist the urge to say, "Nah nah nah nah nah, I've got the baall!")

Play Can Be Dangerous

Humans and dogs share another way of playing, but unlike ball play, this one can get us and our dogs into trouble. Both of us love to engage in what primatologists call "rough-and-tumble play," or play fighting. It really needs little description beyond its title: we can all easily conjure up an image of dogs or kids wrestling around on the rug. But even though this behavior is shared by both species, it's more common in primate males than females. Male primates not only play fight more often than females; their play is rougher and more intense. As a matter of fact, the females of almost all primate species avoid play fighting with males. They don't do it as often as males, but when they do play fight, it's with other females. In both humans and other primates, play fights are usually between individuals of the same age, same sex, and similar physical ability.

Not so in dogs: males and females equally seem to love rolling around and sparring together. A noted researcher on play in animals, Marc Bekoff, found no sex differences in play fighting in timber wolves, coyotes, bush dogs, or crab-eating foxes. In less scientific observations, I've never noticed any obvious differences between sexes in the frequency or intensity of rough-and-tumble play in any of my litters, in any of my own adult dogs, or in my clients' dogs. I've never seen or heard anyone suggest that male dogs play fight more than females.[5]

We humans may do our playing with dogs rather than chimps, but the way that we play fight is more like the way our primate relatives play fight than the way dogs do. Like most primates, we have major differences in the way that males and females play. Even in our species, wrestle play is mostly a guy thing. If one person in a couple that comes to my office likes

---

5. But neither have I seen any good research on sex differences in play in domestic dogs. It's remarkable how little research has actually been done on the behavior of domestic dogs compared to their wild canid cousins.

to wrestle play with the dog, bet on the guy every time. I can think of two cases in thirteen years, out of about four thousand cases, in which the woman loved to wrestle play and the man didn't. But all dogs love it, and the people who play fight with their dogs seem to love it as some of us love sweet air and good food. So I don't take it lightly when I advise certain dog owners to stop playing rough-and-tumble games with their dog. I don't like my job when I watch some sweet, happy man's face fall as if I'd just taken away his favorite game in life. How could I be such a party pooper? Sister Trisha says, "Uh, uh, uh, boys, no having fun in the house." Sigh.

But I do suggest it in some cases, because I've seen so much heartbreak related to play fighting between people and dogs. I know there are hundreds of thousands, if not millions, of pairs of dogs and humans who play fight all their lives with no problems. But then there's that one dog who had always been wonderful with children who turns a rough-and-tumble play bout into a nightmare. In one tragic example, one owner of a Golden Retriever said in our interview, "At least he didn't bite him on the face; he had him by the back of the neck." In the middle of an exuberant wrestle game with a ten-year-old neighbor boy, the dog had, like lightning, gone from playful to serious. He was found growling, holding the child down on the ground, teeth sunk into the back of his neck, until the owner was able to pull him off. My blood ran cold when I heard the story. That was a bite that could have killed, and it's lucky that the boy was still alive. I can still see the dog owner's face, eyes huge and vulnerable, tears streaming down his cheeks, as we discussed euthanizing his best friend. (He did, although it broke his heart. He decided that he couldn't take the risk of it ever happening again.)

Most problems, thankfully, aren't so serious or dramatic. More commonly I see cases like the Collie/Labrador cross who play fights joyfully every evening with 230-pound Bob and won't stop nipping and biting at 110-pound Julie all day long. Julie's arms were covered in scratches and bruises when I met with her; she looked as if she'd been abused. Bob and the dog thought it was amusing. Julie and I didn't. I don't want to overstate this: play fighting doesn't always lead to trouble. But if you want the odds in your favor, or your dog is already in trouble with his mouth, then think carefully about how you play with him.

While you're thinking about it, recall that wild animals play fight only with well-matched partners who are of similar size and physical ability. That may be true with 230-pound Bob and his 85-pound Lab (Bob is bigger, but the dog is faster), but an 85-pound dog, all muscle and teeth, holds too many cards over anyone, no matter how quick and brave, who weighs 110 pounds. If Bob and Julie were to have a 35-pound child, the mix would get even more imbalanced. There's a reason to match size and age and physical ability during play fights, because even when the participants are well matched, sometimes somebody gets hurt. Even when wrestling with your best human buddy, one of you could twist a knee and end up needing surgery for torn ligaments.

Besides, mistakes in play fights are different when humans wrestle with dogs. We grab with our paws, while dogs grab with their mouths. The biggest difference between the structure of play fighting in human children and that of other animals is that humans don't include biting in play bouts, but dogs do.[6] Researchers on play behavior have found that generally humans are wrestling to obtain a superior position over their playmate, while dogs play fight to give each other inhibited bites. Some of us may have pretty strong hands, but those hands don't contain the equivalent of carpet knives, as do the mouths of dogs. We use our hands, they use their mouths, and their mouths are designed to rip open the tough skin of a deer or an elk. Think about opening up your leather purse with your teeth instead of a zipper. Your dog can do it in an instant. And in an instant one tiny mistake from your dog can open up your child's forearm or cheek. Mistakes like that aren't common, because dogs and people both "self-handicap" and are pretty good at moderating their power if they're playing with someone weaker and smaller than they are. A dog's ability to control the pressure of his jaws, even in an excited frenzy, is truly amazing. But still, mistakes can and do happen, and they can be so serious that it just doesn't seem worth the risk.

Another common problem with play fighting, which in my experience causes the most trouble, is that, just like kids at recess, dogs can lose their tempers in the middle of a game. Why shouldn't they? We're the species with

6. Biting is out of bounds even in serious "play" fights like boxing matches, as Mike Tyson discovered when he bit Evander Holyfield in the ring.

more intellectual control over our actions and emotions, and yet we get angry in all kinds of situations. On the playground boisterous play can turn into hurt feelings, tears, and sometimes aggression in an instant. Teachers need to be outside to monitor recess for a reason. Play is arousing—that's part of why we drama addicts love it—but emotional arousal can lead to a lack of inhibition, and not just in children. Look at what happens during and after popular sports events. Thousands of people riot in the streets after some ball games, breaking windows and burning cars—even when their team won. "I went to a fight and a hockey game broke out" is funny because there's so much truth in it. I spent the only professional hockey game I ever attended dodging soda cups and roundhouse punches, thrown with equal abandon by the fans around me. Dogs get aroused, too, but they can't yell at the umpire, and they don't throw very well. Since that just leaves their teeth, be grateful that they aren't involved in organized sports.

Sometimes trouble comes not from excitement or a temper tantrum but from what the dog considers to be appropriate discipline. Luke once corrected his two-year-old daughter, Lassie, in the middle of a wild game of rolling, lunging, and mock biting. I'm not sure what she did that elicited a correction from Luke, but he disciplined her with a growl-bark and an inhibited muzzle bite that was so fast my brain didn't process it until it was over. It didn't seem to be about emotional arousal, at least not Luke's, because it was over in less than a second, and Luke seemed cool and calm and matter-of-fact. Although dominance roles often reverse during play, I suspect that there are rules to doggy play, and youngsters can be corrected for breaking them. Many of the play fights in wild animals end because one individual gets too rough. At that age Lassie's play could spiral up into a frenzy, and my guess is that Luke was reminding her that she needed to learn to regulate her arousal level, no matter how exciting the play. Probably one of her mock bites had a bit too much real bite in it, and Luke was letting her know that she was out of bounds. In dogs, corrections involve swift, inhibited bites to the muzzle. (That's probably why so many bites to children are to their faces, although surely the fact that kid's faces are right at canine level also plays a role.) Well-socialized, benevolent dogs like Luke are careful with their jaws and don't discipline their youngsters hard enough to cause any damage. But the skin on a five-year-old child's face is not equivalent to the skin on a dog's face, and a bite hard enough to get a pup's attention is a bite hard enough to puncture your child's cheek.

Ideally play is joyful and childlike, a physically and psychologically healthy exercise for both people and dogs. Psychologists and spiritual counselors advise us all to put more childlike play into our lives. I think it's great advice: play is good for our spirits, our bodies, and our minds. It teaches us, both dogs and humans, to coordinate our efforts with others, to learn to inhibit ourselves even when excited, and to share the ball even when we want it for ourselves. So please don't interpret my words to mean I'm suggesting that you don't play with your dog. My dogs and I play every day. I throw balls for them, and I just bought the *big* box of crayons for me.

But just because something is childlike and joyful doesn't mean that it is trivial, because how you play with your dog has serious implications. The safest way to play with your dog is to play fetch together, to play mental games like "hide-and-seek" (a great way to keep your adolescent dog busy while you make dinner), to play discrimination games ("Go get your *big* chewy"), and to teach your dog silly, lighthearted tricks. Leave the play fighting for well-matched individuals of the same species, so your play sessions with your dog always end in joy and laughter rather than tears and heartbreak.

Last night Edgar, an adolescent wirehaired Dachshund, came over to visit. In twenty seconds his nose located the errant tennis ball under the couch. He began digging and whining, desperate to extract the fuzzy golden globe. We showed him bones, chew toys, rope toys, interactive rubber toys, and heaven knows what else. He wanted the ball. Later that night I turned on the local television news. As much time was devoted to the fate of golf balls, baseballs, and basketballs as to world peace, world hunger, and medical epidemics. No wonder we love dogs so much. No one else understands our obsession with balls so well.

6

PACKMATES

The Social Nature of Humans and Dogs

Calvin, the little, white fluff ball curled up on my client's lap, had gone home from the pet store with Mary when he was almost seven months old. He had spent the first six weeks of his life in a puppy mill. After being born with his littermates in a tiny wire cage, a cage he never left until he was delivered to the store, he spent his next five months in yet another cage, although this one was cleaned daily. Protected from germs by a glass between him and people, he rarely got to interact with anyone beyond the pet store staff, and he never met other dogs except the brother and sister who had accompanied him. Occasionally, but not regularly, a dog-loving employee would let him out to play after closing time. When my client Mary found him, he was curled up, alone, his littermates sold, two big brown eyes in a pool of fur.

Mary was doomed the moment that she saw him. Recently divorced, she was lonely and tired, and the sight of little Calvin, terminally cute and desperately in need of rescue, pushed all her buttons. Mary needed something to rescue, because she needed rescuing herself. She wanted something to cuddle and pet. Calvin needed escape from his sad, lonely existence. You might have thought it would be a match made in heaven, but in this case it turned into a living hell.

I always ask clients what the primary problem is that they've come to me to work on, but Calvin's owner was hard-pressed to pick just one. Now three years old, her cute little dog urinated and defecated in his crate, on the bed, and all over the house. Every day when Mary returned home from a hard day of work, she had to bathe Calvin and wash out the crate, both being smeared with urine and feces. But that was just one problem. Calvin was also terrified of strangers and wouldn't stop barking when she had visitors over. As he'd gotten older, his barking had become more threatening, and last month he had nipped the ankle of Mary's neighbor. It wasn't a serious bite, but last week he had done it again, and this time he had drawn blood.

His behavior was so disruptive that Mary hadn't had much company lately, and she was beginning to rely more and more on Calvin for social contact. But Mary was starting to miss her human friends, and worse, Calvin was becoming aggressive to her, too. She'd begun to pick him up before she opened the door to her few visitors, but the last time she had, he snapped at her. He slept on Mary's bed and had begun growling at her when she inadvertently rolled into him at night. He had even bitten her foot once while she was sound asleep.

Initially Calvin had been afraid of other dogs, so much so that Mary had had to drop out of obedience class. But lately Calvin's crouching in fear had changed to lunging and snarling, and now her walks in the neighborhood were becoming nightmares, so she had to keep him away from other dogs as well as from people. And yet, as tired and frustrated as she was, Mary still adored Calvin, and Calvin clearly adored Mary. A pack of two, they were inseparable. He greeted her with boundless joy when she came home from work, shadowed her around the house, and loved cuddling on the couch as much as she did. In my office Calvin watched her every move, and Mary couldn't keep her hands off of him.

When I tried to interact with Calvin, he made it clear he wanted nothing to do with me. Happy only in Mary's lap, he stiffened and stopped breathing when I spoke to him. He wouldn't take treats from me, even extragood ones that I threw on the floor so that he could stay far away from me. When Mary put him down on the carpet, Calvin panicked and began hyperventilating until she let him up on her lap again. Mary was desperate to get help. She loved Calvin so much, and yet she couldn't continue living like this. She *asked me what she could do to get him turned around. I asked her how long she had.*

First, I gave her the good news: there was a lot she could do to help make her and Calvin's life better, and she could get started right away. But there was also bad news: Calvin's early development could never be overcome completely. Like humans, dogs are a highly social species whose normal development requires social interactions during specific times of their puppyhood. Calvin could learn to be more comfortable around unfamiliar people, but he would never become the well-adjusted dog he would have been if he'd been raised in a normal environment. My prognosis on house-training Calvin was guarded, because dogs who learn at an early age to potty where they sleep are exceedingly difficult to house-train when they are adults. The problem with the best chance of a successful change was his behavior toward Mary, but that would require Mary to stop treating Calvin like an infant and more like the mature, grown-up guy that he was. Mary had the equivalent of a twenty-five-year-old son living in her house who got attention, food, and free massages just because he was cute. To change his expectations of entitlement, Mary didn't need to get harsh with him or stop loving him; she just needed to recognize that, in spite of his sweet little face, Calvin wasn't a needy infant who required her constant nurturing to survive.

Six months later Mary's work started to pay off. Calvin began to associate visitors with wonderful treats and no longer barked and nipped at them. He preferred that visitors not pet him, but he no longer saw them as invading aliens. Calvin continued to adore Mary, but he had started to learn some social manners and no longer had a temper tantrum when he got irritated. It would take a lot of effort to teach him to get along well with other dogs, but Calvin could walk in the neighborhood now without barking and snarling at other dogs who pass by. He'll never be fully house-trained, but he's much better now. During the day he's allowed out of the crate, and Mary doesn't have to wash a stinky dog every night when she comes home from work.[1] Now when she's gone, he relieves himself in a doggie litter box in a back room. It's not

---

1. Chapter 8 presents some of the suggestions that Mary followed to improve Calvin's behavior, especially toward her. A full explanation of all the things that Mary did would take up a book in itself (see the sources mentioned in the References).

ideal, but it's good enough for Mary and the little dog she loves—one of the millions of dogs who was permanently disabled as a puppy, by people who produced and marketed him as if he had been a case of soda pop.

Making Social Bonds

What's so terribly sad about this story is that Calvin's problems were mostly preventable. Like people, dogs have certain times in their mental development in which they learn about the world around them, one of which is called the "critical period" of socialization. Extensive research on dog behavior found that puppies who were isolated from human contact between five and twelve weeks were never able to react normally to people later in life. Now called a "sensitive period" because it doesn't appear to be quite as cut-and-dried as first thought, these early weeks have a profound effect on the behavior of an adult dog. During this time puppies— and their wolf cousins—are primed to take in information about who their social companions are. It's so important that the wolf puppies at Wolf Park, a research and education facility in Indiana, are taken away from their mothers at eight to ten days and raised exclusively by humans until they're returned later in life to the pack. Without those interactions during this important developmental period, the adult wolves would never accept humans into their pens. There's no time later in a canid's life equivalent to this sensitive period; you can't "make up" the time you lost later on. If you provided the same amount of contact for the same amount of time to an adult wolf, it would have less of an effect. The same goes for dogs. That's why it is so important to have an understanding of the effect of early development on an adult dog's behavior. Once a dog has grown up, you can't go back. As with Calvin, you can make substantial progress, but you can only work with what you've got.

A lack of socialization during the important months of early development leads to some dogs' being terrified of unfamiliar people, especially the dogs who also have a genetic tendency to be shy. As early as four or five weeks, while still at the breeder's, they need to meet people, lots of them, and learn that people of all shapes and sizes are part of what's normal in the world. Once they go to their new homes, puppies need time not just with their new families but with visitors, and as soon as it is safe, they should go out and about to meet the bank teller and the neighbors down the street. I can't tell you the precise age at which you should start taking your puppy out. All owners have to decide for themselves, because there are risks you need to be aware of. For instance, before your puppy is fully immunized at around fifteen to sixteen weeks, you want to minimize his exposure to pathogens like parvo virus. But the first and most important period of socialization is over around week twelve or thirteen, so you need to balance the medical risks with the behavioral risks of keeping your puppy isolated until the sensitive period of socialization is over. Regrettably these two risks create a conflict. Many owners solve this dilemma by ensuring that their pup meets lots of new people at home and goes to lots of safe new places (like the neighbor's fenced backyard) until the pup has had two sets of vaccinations. Usually that's around the age of nine to ten weeks. Avoid potentially troublesome places that may carry infectious diseases (like dog parks) until the pup is fully immunized, as long as he continues to learn that people and dogs outside of your family are members of his extended social group.

It Takes a Village, and It Takes Some Time

Don't stop at thirteen weeks. Research has shown that the boundaries of these periods are not black and white, and just like children, puppies don't develop at exactly the same rate. Additionally there are other important periods in the social development of a dog, which isn't surprising given the experience required to achieve social grace in a species with complicated relationships. Dogs seem to go through an important developmental period around early adolescence, usually from about six to eleven months, so be sure to continue your dog's social education for at least the first year of his life.

My Border Collie Pip is a good example of this. As the puppy of a behaviorist and trainer, she lived the life of a social butterfly. For the first seven months of her life, she met a smorgasbord of people and dogs at training classes and on visits to friends. But one day, at eight months of age, she hid behind my legs when an unfamiliar man approached her, as if she'd never seen one before in her life. Having noticed a cautiousness at this age in some of my clients' dogs, I acted right away before it led to trouble. For a few months I asked every man I could to throw a tennis ball to Pip before he got within 15 feet. (Recently, while explaining this process at a seminar, I said, "And for three months every man she met was preceded by balls." I wish I could be as funny on purpose as I can be by mistake.) Now she adores men and assumes that all guys she meets have come to play fetch with her.

I've met so many confident puppies who become fearful as adolescents that I eventually gave this tendency a name, "juvenile-onset shyness," so that I could speak about it. This behavior is not the natural, early "fear period" of increasingly mobile, young canids that they develop as a life-saving cautionary approach to the world around them. These are puppies who are relatively confident until they hit some important developmental stepping-stone and become cautious as teenagers.[2] Because in some dogs this cautiousness can lead to fear-related aggression, all dogs should be kept well socialized during (at least) their first year of life.

Your puppy also needs to socialize with other dogs as well as people. It's not enough that you have another dog at home or have the neighbor's dog play with your new puppy every day. Social animals like dogs and humans have a strong sense of "familiar" and "unfamiliar," and dogs need to learn that part of what's normal and familiar in life is to meet unfamiliar people and dogs. As a behaviorist, once I started to see how dogs sort the world into "familiar" versus "unfamiliar," I was able to understand a lot more about their behavior. Take poor little

2. I worked with troubled adolescents for a few years and found that young humans showed the same tendency to become shy or hypersensitive during equivalent ages.

Calvin, for example. He had no experience interacting with any dogs besides his littermates, until he was about a year old, when Mary acquired him. Then, from his quiet apartment, he was carried into a small room with twelve boisterous, barking dogs for obedience instruction. He was terrified, and as he got older, he used threat displays to keep the other dogs away.

When I was busy studying dog behavior as part of my Ph.D. work, long before I taught dog training classes, I didn't know the importance of the distinction between familiar and unfamiliar. I had gotten a new Border Collie puppy, named Mist, but was overwhelmed with the demands of graduate school and so didn't take her to puppy socialization classes and places where there were friendly, unfamiliar dogs of all shapes and sizes. She met scads of people and was as trustworthy with little children as any dog I've ever had. But I worked with dogs all day long in my research for twelve- to fourteen-hour days, and I assumed that the other five dogs at my farm were enough to socialize her. At that time I had Bo Peep, my first Great Pyrenees, and four other Border Collies. It was an impressive pack, and Mist lived with them, played with them, and slept with them in the house. But for that first year of her life, she met very few unfamiliar dogs. When she got older, Mist was aggressive to dogs she didn't know. Mist's behavior was not just due to her early environment: behavior in dogs and humans is always a complex interaction between genetics and environment, and Mist had been born with tendencies that made the problem even worse. As many owners can, I found ways to drastically improve her behavior, and as long as I could manage the introduction between her and another dog, Mist could be trusted around other dogs. But I wouldn't have had to work so hard if I'd known then what I know now. Like people, dogs need exposure to lots of new humans and dogs to learn to be comfortable around strangers. Basically dogs need to learn that strangers aren't strange. Otherwise, they might end up like some furry equivalent of a hermit hiding in the cabin, threatening visitors with a shotgun aimed out the window.

Social to the Bone

Humans also need social interaction during development to be our normal selves. Just like laboratory primates isolated from others, human babies that don't receive close, nurturing physical contact and social interaction from adults begin to hug themselves and rock back and forth as they age. If they manage to mature, most of them are never able to show empathy for others or form meaningful attachments later in life.

But when we are raised normally, we humans are the antihermits of the animal world, ever seeking companionship and social interaction. Some of us may prefer more private time than others, and we may get overtired by too many people or too many phone calls, but we rarely seek complete solitude for long. Indeed, the ultimate punishment in prison is solitary confinement. We use "time-outs" now as a consequence for misbehaving children, but the idea isn't new. Children in England were "sent to Coventry" for punishment, meaning they were banished from social interaction. "Shunning" is used the world over as a consequence for inappropriate behavior. In some cultures even entire families are shunned for the social sins of one of their relatives. The Cheyenne Native American culture banned whole families, in one case banishing a family for the social transgressions of one of its members, even though in battle they had risked their lives and killed many of the enemy. But in spite of their bravery, the tribal council refused to recognize or reward their acts. Because they were banished, they functionally didn't exist, and not acknowledging them was considered the gravest of all possible punishments, worse than death or physical torture.

Enforced solitude as an extreme punishment is an excellent example of how important social interaction is to our species. If it weren't, taking it away wouldn't be so powerful. This dependence on sociality isn't characteristic of all animals. Many animals live a life of solitude as adults, from grizzly bears to tigers. Many more species, like some fish and butterflies, spend a lot of time in groups, but just because they are in a group doesn't mean that they have a lot of social interactions. Butterflies, for example, congregate around a valued resource, like the minerals in a puddle in a gravel driveway, but they are drawn by needing similar things, not by an attraction to one another.

Primates, who are otherwise a remarkably varied group, are consistent in their high degree of sociality. Primate social relationships tend to be complex, involving relationships that differ in degrees of familiarity and intensity with a variety of individuals. Male chimpanzees have such strong social ties that no adult male can achieve or retain dominance without a coalition of other males to support him. Frans de Waal titled his book about these coalitions *Chimpanzee Politics* for good reason: status-seeking male chimps play a complicated game of currying favor with the power brokers while always assessing the potential of a takeover from another group. Some individuals do their best to play both sides of the aisle, staying in the good graces of those in power but always positioned to switch allegiances if it serves their own best interests. If a chimp were elected to the House of Representatives, he'd have trouble with the use of language and abstract concepts, but he'd understand the power struggles as well as anyone else.[3]

It's been hypothesized that the relatively large neocortex (forebrain) of most primates is a result of our need to manage complex social relationships. Without a lot of brainpower, you can't keep track of dozens of individuals in your social group (and if food is abundant, possibly hundreds of individuals), all of whom have intense, ever-changing relationships with one another. Our social interactions don't occur randomly. All human cultures, from hunter-gatherers to city slickers, share certain universals in the ways that we, as primates, interact with one another. This social destiny has a profound influence on the way that we relate to our dogs. Sometimes we can get ourselves (and our dogs) in a whole lot of trouble when our primatelike social behavior clashes with the natural behavior of dogs. Much of the rest of this chapter describes what some of those problems are and how to avoid them. Ironically even some of the shared aspects of the social behavior of humans and dogs can create trouble.

3. *Newsweek* reported that Newt Gingrich said he'd used *Chimpanzee Politics* as a model for assuming control of the House of Representatives.

Social Intimacy

We may be different from dogs in the visual signals that we use when we greet members of our social groups, as described in Chapter 1, but in some ways we're not so different at all. Both species share an awareness of personal space and the importance of matching physical intimacy with social intimacy. Remember the way the guy greeted his new wife on "Who Wants to Marry a Multimillionaire?"? He walked straight up to a woman he'd never met in his life, put his hands on either side of her head, and thrust his tongue down her throat. I can't even write about it without turning my head in disgust. Granted, any woman who puts herself in that position doesn't get my vote for good judgment, but I would've been the first to bail her out of the pound if she'd bitten him. His behavior was so inappropriate that it seemed aggressive. Dogs are not so very different: both species are always conscious of what level of closeness feels appropriate. How would you feel if, as an adult, you were expected to allow any stranger to grab your head and jam his face into yours? Of course, we humans vary in how touchy we are. Some people are happy to hug strangers, while others rarely hug even their own children. Dogs also vary in their reactions—from the stereotypical happy Labrador who assumes all humans are just as touchy-feely as he is to the dignified Akita who expresses affection by meditating at your feet. So please keep in mind both the differences and the similarities between primates and canines when you see a cute dog walking down the street. Maybe, just maybe, you look to the dog like that pushy person at the party who gets too close too fast and makes you want to run away. Imagine if you were on a leash and couldn't escape.

A Little off the Sides?

Grooming is another behavior that humans share with many of our primate relatives. In most species grooming involves one individual's carefully parting the hair of the groomee and removing dirt and parasites.

But cleanup is not the only function of grooming. It plays a major role in the social relationships of most primate species, acting to bond individuals together and soothe social tensions. That is probably why most primates spend an amazing amount of time grooming one another. Stump-tailed macaques spend 19 percent of their waking activities in grooming. Rhesus macaques, the grumps of the primate world, spend only 9 percent of their time grooming, but that's still actually quite a lot of time during a day mostly spent searching for food. The most time-consuming activity of female baboons is grooming the males. Chimpanzees and bonobos are dedicated groomers, spending as much as an hour at a time carefully parting the hair over the body of another in their group. The groomee often looks like we do when we're getting a good massage—blissfully relaxed.

This tendency to respond to touch by relaxing is not something that all animals do. Being "social" to many species means being physically close to other individuals and having some kind of social interaction with them, but that interaction doesn't inherently include being touched for much of the day. Yet in every stage of life, our closest animal relatives spend a large amount of their time touching another and relating touch to being pleasantly relaxed or playful. In the wild, chimpanzees and bonobos are indefatigably touch-oriented, spending much more time touching others than most species. Infant chimps and bonobos are in almost constant contact with their mothers. As they develop, they spend hours in physical play with their buddies, which includes a tremendous amount of physical contact. As they get older and play wanes, the amount of time that they spend grooming increases.

Frightened primates, even adult ones, cling like burrs to one another if they are scared enough. That's as true of our species as it is of other primates. It is heartbreakingly easy to find pictures of frightened humans, whether victims of some natural disaster or the tragedy of war, chest-to-chest, wrapped in the arms of another human being. These images are almost exact replicas of pictures of terrified or distraught chimpanzees clutching one another for comfort. Most animals don't leap onto one another and embrace when they're scared; they just run like heck. Frightened horses and sheep want to run away, not cuddle with one another. Frightened birds and cats usually don't want to be petted; they want to be left alone to hide, even by their mates. The bottom line is that our species, like other primates, is a touchy-feely one, and our emphasis on physical contact is very much a part of our genetic heritage. Whether it's with a member of the family or even with a stranger in a crisis, the need to make physical contact in both good times and bad is deeply ingrained in our psyche. Touch may be the most important sense that we have. As difficult as it must be, many people learn to cope well when they lose their sense of sight, of hearing, or of smell and go on to lead rich, fulfilling lives. But losing your sense of touch would immediately cut you off from a connection with the world in a way virtually unimaginable to most of us. Perhaps this explains why we sometimes simply can't keep our hands off our dogs.

Even in the best of times, when we're not stressed or needy, many of us enjoy petting our dogs as much as any other aspect of dog ownership. This is not a trivial need. Quiet stroking can significantly change your body's physiology, lowering your heart rate and blood pressure. It releases endogenous opiates, or internal chemicals that calm and soothe us and play a significant role in good health. Lucky for us, most of our dogs adore being touched. Most normal, well-socialized dogs cherish getting belly rubs and head massages and butt scratches. Many dogs like grooming so much that they're willing to work for it, pawing or barking whenever needed to remind their human not to stop.

But just as some humans don't want to cuddle all evening, some dogs don't enjoy a lot of physical contact, preferring to lie on the rug beside their owners rather than nestled up to them. Some dogs and owners are mismatched, with a cuddly owner and an aloof dog or vice versa. Sometimes these cases become serious, when a dog finally hits the wall after years of trying to communicate to his owners to please stop pawing at him, loses his temper, and does some damage. Other dogs love petting except when they're tired and get grumpy over petting that they'd enjoy in the morning but not at night.[4] It's sad when a dog who craves touch and contact lives with an owner who isn't very cuddly— reminiscent of a human couple who have such dissimilar physical needs that neither one ever really gets what he or she wants.

As physical as we primates are, even we have times when grooming or touch feels inappropriate or irksome. It's one thing to have a friend affectionately kiss you on the forehead when you're alone; it's another thing altogether if you're at a car dealership negotiating the price of a car. I think the same is true for dogs. Probably the most common, inappropriate use of petting is when owners pet their dogs on the head for doing a difficult recall. Here's Spike the German Shorthaired Pointer, playing with three other male dogs, and his owner calls him to come. Spike is pumped, he's been playing hard among a group of competitive, same-age, same-sex buddies, but he's a good boy who's been well trained, so he dashes over to his owner to see what she wants. "Oh, good boy!" she says, leaning her face toward his in that rude way we have, and pats him on the head. If Spike is like thousands of dogs that I've seen in this context, he does everything but say "Yuck" or some canid equivalent of "Ah, Mo-om, cut it out." Spike is in play mode, and there's a bit of a competition going on with the other dogs, and maybe, just maybe, he really doesn't want to be petted right then. "Oh, but he loves petting," his owner tells me. So do I, but not when I'm playing sports.

I'm using anthropomorphic examples here to bring home a point, although there's a danger of misinterpreting your dog's behavior by putting yourself in your dog's place. A dog owner who assumes that his dog defecated in the living room because she's "mad" at him for leaving her alone during the day is forgetting that dogs are fascinated by feces. Dogs spend long periods of time checking out poop, sniffing it, and sometimes eating it. The Navajo word for dog sounds something like "thlee shaw" and means "eater of horse poop." It makes no sense that your dog would offer you such a wonderful present if she were mad at you. Some people think that their dog is defecating on the rug to spite them, so they yell at the

4. Sometimes "touchiness" can indicate that a dog has a medical problem that needs attention, so be sure to eliminate a physical cause if your dog won't tolerate petting.

dog, perhaps rubbing her nose in it or, worse, physically hurting her. Dogs who are treated this way cower in terror (not guilt) when their owners return home but are much more likely to defecate on the rug out of nervousness or fear in the house, because who knows what that maniac will do next time he comes home.

So sometimes imagining ourselves inside a dog can cause problems, but other times it can be useful. In the case of petting, I think it's useful, because it can explain the fact that some dogs will come *less often* if the "reward" for coming is getting patted on the head. To many dogs, in this circumstance, it's a punishment, not a reward. You should see the faces of these dogs in our training classes as their owners stroke their heads: they turn away, lips pulled down like a human who just smelled rotten eggs. They didn't want petting, not right then; they were playing with their buddies, and they wanted to keep it up. What pleases these playful, athletic dogs is for their owner to provide more play, perhaps throw a ball when the dog comes, not to switch gears into a massage session. Sometimes just saying "OK" and letting them go back to play with their buddies is a great way to make them glad that they came. It seems to dazzle them. "I can go play some more? Wow, you are so cool!" Now Spike is going to be glad he came and be more likely to do it the next time his owner calls. With this kind of active dog, save the massages for later, when you're curled up watching TV together. Of course, if you have a dog who would do anything to hear you coo and give him a chest rub, it works just fine to pet and praise him when he's come away from a play session. But just like you, your dog probably wants different things at different times, and he may not want to cuddle on the ball field.

Another time to avoid petting is when your dog is highly aroused or agitated. Dogs and humans share a kind of a threshold of arousal, a level of emotional excitement that changes our response to touch. Under that threshold, touch is soothing, as it is when your dog is slightly anxious at the vet's or when you're nervous at the doctor's office. In those cases "grooming" feels calming and helpful.

Photo courtesy of Frans de Waal

Photo by Jim Hofstetter

Photo by Karen B. London

Chimpanzees and humans often express affection by putting an arm around each other. But to a dog, a front leg over another's shoulder is usually a display of social status.

We humans greet others by moving directly forward, hands extended, looking straight into one another's eyes.

Dogs, on the other hand, avoid direct eye contact and direct approaches when they're meeting a new dog, and use smell, rather than eye contact, to get to know one another.

Humans aren't the only species who express affection by kissing one another. Chimpanzees and bonobos are world-class kissers.

Lots of dogs like to lick the faces of people they know well, but even then, many of them avoid direct eye contact and approach from the side. Most dogs appreciate the same courtesy from us, especially from strangers.

You can tell how much we love hugging dogs just by looking at our faces. Because of our primate heritage, we seek what's called "ventral ventral" contact—pressing our chests together—as a way of expressing affection and feeling connected.

Look at the faces of the dogs on these two pages. Do they look as happy as the humans?

Photo by Cathy Acherman, courtesy of the Coulee Region Humane Society

These well-intentioned dog owners are doing what most of us humans do when we want our dog to come, which is to pull on the leash and turn toward the dog, looking directly at his face. Each of these actions is very effective—in getting a dog to stand still.

Erica is illustrating the right way to encourage a dog to come—she's moving in the direction that she'd like Tulip to go, smiling and clapping as if it's all a fun game.

Photo by Karen B. London

Tulip rolls on a dead mouse. Like many dogs, Tulip loves nothing better than a good roll in something smelly—the stinkier and squishier the better.

We like strong smells too, but notice how Lassie's daughter, Tess, turns her head away from the perfume that I've sprayed onto my wrist. She's just as disgusted by the smells I love as I am by "eau de dead mouse."

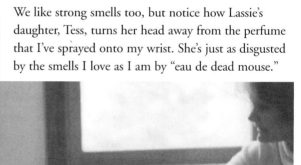

Photo courtesy of Frans de Waal

You can't miss who's dominant and who's submissive here. In most social species, high status individuals express their social rank by standing tall and looking as large as they can, while subordinates get low and small.

Given our size differences, even the kindliest of greetings from a human can appear like a dominance display to a dog.

Photo by Cathy Acherman, courtesy of the Coulee Region Humane Society

Tulip looms over Kodi during their first introduction, while Kodi tries to get as small and as low as he can, in order to appease Tulip.

Kodi doesn't respond to a more submissive dog like Pip by lying down. This time it's Pip who tries to get small.

When Kodi lies down after a play bow, Pip ducks her head, trying to stay smaller and lower than Kodi.

Photos by author

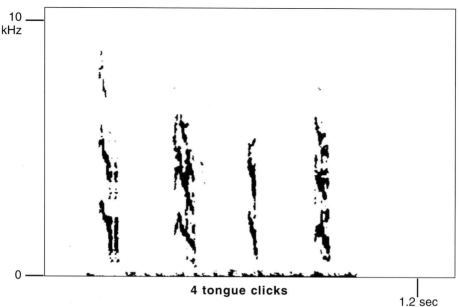

10 kHz

0

4 tongue clicks

1.2 sec

The images on these two pages are sonograms, or pictures of sound. Pitch, or frequency, is on the vertical axis in kilohertz, and time goes horizontally. Above is a picture of the sounds that a horse handler made to speed up her horse by clicking her tongue four times.

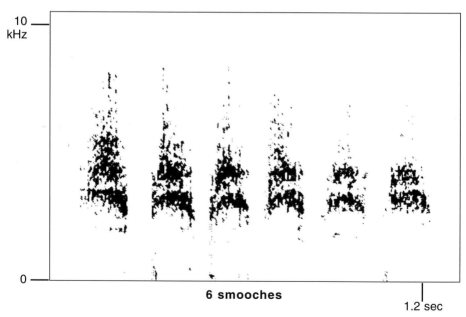

10 kHz

0

6 smooches

1.2 sec

These six notes are smooches used by the same horse handler to get her horse to move into a fast gallop. The faster the professional handlers wanted their animals to go, the faster they repeated short notes with a lot of power across a range of frequencies.

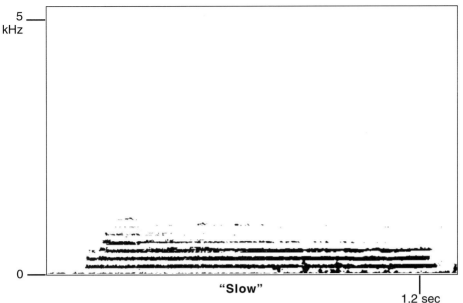

"Slow"

1.2 sec

This long, flat note is typical of sounds that professional handlers make when they want to soothe or slow an animal. You can do the same by saying "staaaay," or "gooooooood," in a flat, quiet tone.

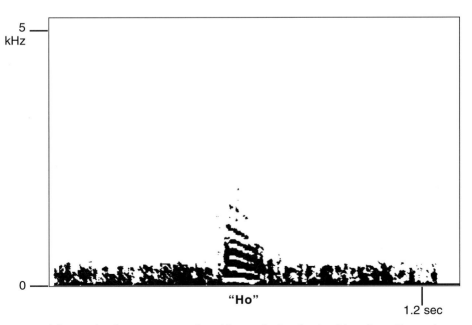

"Ho"

1.2 sec

This single, short note is produced by professional animal handlers all over the world who want to stop a fast-moving animal. If you want to stop your dog from grabbing your dinner off the coffee table, say "Hey!" or "No!" or "Ah!" quietly to get her attention and stop her. (Then be sure to tell her what you *do* want her to do!)

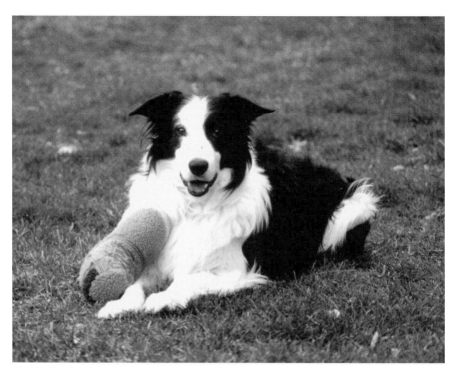

Cool Hand Luke

Lassie

Pip and her litter of puppies

Luke, Lassie, and Pip in front of the flower garden

Tulip with her sheep

Tulip on her favorite sheep-guarding platform—the couch

Luke herding the flock, moving them toward me by blocking their movement in any other direction

Lassie's first encounter with a huge flock of sheep. She's used to no more than 30 sheep at a time, and this flock contained well over 150. You can tell she's a bit intimidated, because although her hindquarters are pushing forward, her shoulders and front legs are not. The sheep can read these subtle changes in the way a dog's body is leaning, and your dog can read subtle changes just as easily in your body.

Ayla, the cat whose life Pip saved, cuddled up on a warm, wooly back on a cold winter day

Luke is always ready to play ball.

It's natural for us primates to want to calm an animal by putting a hand on it, and not always just for the receiver's sake. Merely seeing others in a state of upset is in itself upsetting for many of us. Jane Goodall made the case that in times of agitation the chimps she observed weren't only being altruistic when trying to calm others down: they were trying to calm things down for their own sake. She suggested that chimpanzees, like humans, find it upsetting to see others in emotional turmoil. That's why grooming, which appears to have a very important function of dispersing social tension, may be as much for the groomer as for the groomee. In chimpanzees fights are almost always followed by intense grooming bouts. Primatologist Frans de Waal even noted that the chimps he studied showed higher levels of grooming when confined in a small indoor facility, where tensions would be expected to run higher than outdoors. In such a small space, strained relationships could have serious consequences, given that individuals couldn't escape from one another, so the animals compensated by increasing the amount of time that they spent soothing and calming one another with grooming. It seems very natural to put a hand on someone to try to get him or her to calm down. Perhaps we, too, reach out to dogs not just to calm them but to keep their distress from distressing us.

But touch doesn't always calm the ones who receive it, not if they are pumped-up and agitated. I've seen several owners who were bitten by their dog after they tried petting the dog to calm him down when he was agitated and aroused. Often owners will tell me that they're sure their dog didn't mean to bite them, that the dog must have thought that it was another dog attacking him when he felt himself being touched. Sometimes I suspect that that's true, and sometimes I'm quite sure that it's not. Humans can turn on those we love when we are emotionally charged up and frustrated, pushing well-meaning friends away, and sometimes not very gently. That kind of "redirected" aggression is common in many species, from birds to rodents, and there's no reason that it should be surprising in dogs.

However, if your dog isn't too aroused, you can help to calm her with touch, but it's important to be aware of how you're touching her. Owners who are anxious often pet their dogs with short, rapid little pats to the head and neck. Do it on yourself and see how soothing it is. (Not very.) Just as it's important to keep your voice different in tone from your internal emotions when you're trying to influence your dog, you need to learn to massage your dog with long, slow strokes when you want to soothe her, even if you yourself are nervous. It's all that I can do in the lobby of the vet's office to stop myself from leaning over and gently stopping someone's hand from bouncing off his or her dog's head. Pat, pat. Pat, pat. The more rapid the patting, the more aroused the dog. And of course, the more anxious the dog, the more anxious the owner. By the time my name gets called, I'm nervous just from watching them.

As easy as it is to get sucked into this emotional spiral, however, it's also easy to change. Once you become aware of what you're doing, it's relatively easy to consciously slow yourself down. Nothing helps me relax more than to focus on my breathing for a moment and take full, deep breaths. Slow your own breathing down and it will help slow your dog down. It'll feel good to both you and your dog, and it might even relax other owners and their animals in the vet clinic lobby.

One last comment about petting: not all dogs enjoy being pounded on like drums. Some dogs do like hard, boisterous petting, just as some guys like hearty punches to the biceps, but some dogs prefer a more thoughtful touch. As social animals ourselves, we learn to modify our touch depending on who we're with. Not many grown men would greet their wives with a punch to the arm, but they might greet their buddies that way at the bar. The petting preferences of dogs do not seem to be sex-related, but dogs are as varied as people in how they like to be touched. Some of this variation is related to breed: tough field-bred retrievers plow through briars and ice water when they're looking for a bird, and so they are often fond of manly slaps to the rump. Sighthounds were bred to course across the desert sands and can be as touch-sensitive as the princess and her pea. Every individual is different, and if you pay attention to her reaction, every dog will let you know what feels good and what doesn't.

The moral of the story is to be mindful about how and when you touch your dog. Just because your dog "loves petting" doesn't mean that your touch is received like a precious gift every time you give it. Be thoughtful when you feel extra needy and start petting your dog more than usual. Some dogs will love it, but some will feel overwhelmed. Others will start exploiting you (see the next chapter) and get more and more demanding. And just because she's a dog and not a child doesn't mean that you can pound on her ribs and slap her on the head and she'll love it.

Aw, Look! A Puppy!

Humans are suckers for puppies. We melt like butter in July every time we see one. Go out with a puppy and you'll be surrounded by smiling humans who just *have* to pet her. They'll coo and simper as if you'd just had a baby yourself and become sweet and engaging when just a minute before they were busy and aloof. Of course, it's not just puppies that we coo over. We're suckers for any mammalian babies, from kittens to infant elephants.

There's a reason for that, and it derives from our nature as social animals who are totally dependent upon adults for our survival. Helpless at birth, we don't have a chance in the world without intensive, long-term parental care. That extended period of development with parental care is a characteristic of primates, and it sets us apart from many other animals. Look at foals and lambs and young antelope: they are all born able to run alongside their mothers within just a few hours of birth. But many intelligent and highly social animals—like primates, elephants, wolves, and domestic dogs—are born needy and helpless, requiring parental care not just immediately after birth but for a long time to come. In that sense we primates are more like dogs than most other animals.

Although puppies are born as helpless as a newborn child, dogs grow up a lot faster than we do.[5] By three weeks of age, puppies begin their first foolish steps (although admittedly they are usually backward). At a year of age, a dog may not be physically mature, but she is strong and fast and capable of some serious work. Year-old dogs excel at canine sports like ball play and Frisbee (although overdoing it can harm them), and a year-old herding dog is fast enough to outmaneuver the flightiest of sheep. But a child that's a year old is just on the verge of learning how to walk and hardly ready to start tennis lessons. Compared to lambs, dogs are slow developers, but compared to dogs, we humans mature at a snail's pace.

This slow development has a purpose. It takes a lot of learning and experience to manage in a society as complicated as a primate's. If you're a chimpanzee, bonobo, gorilla, or human, it takes decades. During this process of slow-motion development, children may be dependent, but they're not without power. Children are armed with a set of visual signals that can drop an adult to his knees. The sweet face of a big-eyed two-year-old has the power to melt even the toughest grown-up. Our young are not designed like a miniature version of adults. They have anatomical characteristics that elicit caretaking from adults as light attracts fluttering moths. In relation to the rest of their bodies, children have proportionately larger heads and eyes than adults, along with larger foreheads, larger "paws," and eyes farther apart. This set of babylike proportions calls forth a reaction that is hardwired. "Aw," we say, when we see a photo of an infant, responding with warm feelings of nurturance. The reaction is so universal that psychologists call it the "aw phenomenon." Show a slide of a cute little child on a screen, and an audible "Aw" emanates from the audience. This response isn't foolish, and it isn't trivial; it's biologically important. If adults don't respond to those signals, then they're not going to be very successful parents. If they're not successful parents, then they're not going to pass on many of their own genes. Thus, natural selection has created a species that goes all gooey when we see babies and babylike features. After all, if two-year-olds

5. They are also born deaf and blind and remain that way for their first few weeks of life.

didn't look as exquisitely darling as they do, how many of them would make it to three? Any youngster who demands as much of a parent as a young ape does, whether human or chimp, had better be armed with some pretty effective artillery, because he's going to need something to keep his long-suffering parents engaged throughout those many years of development.

Just about any mammal with a head and paws too big for its body tends to get the same nurturing response. Baby dogs, baby cats, and baby bears all elicit the same response in most humans, because they all have a universal set of childlike features that go right to our heart. It's as though we can't avoid responding to that particular type of visual signal without wanting to take care of something. It even works in rodents: Walt Disney's Mickey Mouse started out in the late 1920s looking more like an adult rat than the big-eyed, big-headed, big-handed "cute" little mouse that he is today. An expert in evolutionary biology, Stephen Jay Gould, wrote an article about our attraction to infantile features that included comparative measurements of Mickey, showing how the cartoon character became more popular as he became more childlike.

Other species are also under the thrall of infantile features. Perhaps the most famous example is Koko the gorilla, who adopted All Ball, a Manx kitten that she nurtured until he died in an accident. In spite of her gargantuan size, Koko gently carried the tiny kitten around and groomed him as if he were her own infant. She was apparently devastated when All Ball died: she became listless at first and then began to wail gorilla distress calls. It's not just primates that react to babylike features: some songbirds can be duped by fish who rise up above the water's edge and gape like baby birds. A gaping mouth is the feature that elicits parental behavior in birds, the avian equivalent of big heads and large eyes, and so the poor birds dip down and stuff food into the mouths of the fish instead of their own young.

We humans react to young dogs as we do to young children, because they, too, have disproportionately large heads, foreheads, feet, and "hands." Big eyes and goofy paws have led millions of dogs into carpeted living rooms and heated, padded doggie beds. These characteristics probably played a substantial role in the process of bringing dogs into our homes, when villagers just couldn't resist adopting some big-eyed little puppy. But our attraction to infantile features has a dark side, too. Too many people respond to those infantile features and get a dog when they don't want a dog at all. They see a puppy and want to take care of it, but puppyhood only lasts a few months. By five months a puppy starts to turn into a gangly adolescent, complete with an attitude and a tendency to ignore his elders. Humane societies and shelters can place as many puppies as they take in, but they struggle to find homes for the multitude of surrendered adolescents who swamp their kennels. When dogs lose their "cute factor," they lose one of the hooks that makes the work involved in raising them worthwhile. Regrettably for them, just like human adolescents, they still need a lot of time and energy at that age, but providing that time and energy isn't always as rewarding to the adults. It doesn't seem to matter whether the teens are two-legged or four-pawed, it takes a dedicated caretaker to put up with them in adolescence when they're being difficult but aren't so cute anymore.

The Tragedy of Puppy Mills

One of the most tragic consequences of our reaction to cuteness is the inadvertent support of puppy mills. Puppy mills are dog factories, assembly lines for puppies that house breeding males and females in conditions that would turn your stomach. Puppy mills are everywhere, although they flourish in the South and the Midwest. They are one of the best-kept secrets in American society, and they cause tremendous suffering to untold numbers of animals. The last one that I visited raised each litter in small, hanging wire cages. The urine and feces were supposed to fall through the wire, except, of course, most of the waste remained in the cage, so the puppies played in it for lack of anything else to do. (Good luck house-training those puppies.) The mother dogs were trapped with their litters for the entire seven weeks of their development, until the pups were sent to pet stores. Not letting a dog out of a tiny cage for seven weeks is abusive enough, but not letting a mother dog away from her puppies for even a few minutes is downright vicious. This particular puppy mill had more than three hundred adult dogs and one adult caretaker. There was no attempt to work with any individual dog and thus virtually no ability to judge the temperament of the dogs that were bred. The owner told me that "of course, all the dogs were gentle—even the caretaker's children could go into the pens."

But you can't necessarily predict how a dog in an empty pen will behave once he's part of a typical busy family. When I visited, I saw a variety of temperaments, from fearfully shy dogs to pushy, demanding ones. One set of dogs continually attacked another dog in the same cage every time we walked by. The dog was basically trapped inside a cage with a gang who beat him up daily for the hell of it. Many of the dogs had serious physical deformities, like over- and undershot jaws. Those problems can be serious and are genetically mediated, so no responsible breeder would have bred them. Dozens of the dogs at this particular puppy mill were covered in continuous tangles of matted fur, with hairs pulling on almost every inch of their skin. Most depressing to me is that this puppy mill (still going strong, by the way) is by no means the worst of its type. I stumbled across another one in which permanent cages were stacked three high, the higher dogs urinating and defecating onto the ones below. Each lower dog lived on a 1- or 2-foot-high mash of compressed urine and feces, her flesh covered in angry red sores. Their filthy water dishes were equally full of waste, with the colorful addition of green algae scum.[6]

Hidden from view, these concentration camps for dogs provide millions of puppies to pet stores and "agents,"[7] where unknowing dog lovers take one look at that cute little fluff ball in the corner and just have to take her home. Even people who know better can't resist rescuing the poor little pup: after all, there she is, all big-eyed and needy, and what will happen to her if someone doesn't take her home? Once a puppy doesn't look

6. For a variety of reasons, puppy mills are notoriously difficult to shut down. For now the best way dog lovers can help to put them out of business is to ensure that they never buy a pup that was raised in one. See the next section for advice on how to avoid them.

7. Agents are people who broker dogs for large commercial operations, often posing as family dog lovers who "just happen" to have some puppies in the backyard.

like a puppy anymore, she's lost much of her value.[8] Stores can't exactly stack the dogs on a back shelf until their fall sales come around. This isn't just a problem for the store; it's a potential crisis for the puppy. Even staying in the store for more than a week can compromise a puppy's development. Pet store "puppies" (read "adolescents") learn to potty where they sleep and often can't be house-trained no matter what. Others are so socially damaged that they are miserable at best and dangerous at worst. By buying that cute little puppy, you are supporting puppy mills, allowing them to continue raising unsound animals from miserable, enslaved parents.

Responsible Sources for Puppies

Don't buy a puppy if you don't want a dog. You may be buying a puppy, but in a measly three months, your puppy will turn into a gangly adolescent who needs shots and training and socialization and exercise and toys and grooming. The list goes on, and it goes on for many years. All this takes lots of time and money, and 98 percent of it is for a dog, not a puppy. Dogs can live from ten to twenty years, and that short three-month period of adorable puppyhood is going to be a pretty dim memory when you're cleaning up projectile diarrhea from the walls after your teenage dog got into the garbage. I am not trying to discourage you from getting a puppy if you've made a thoughtful decision to raise a dog. But it's important to do a reality check and remind yourself that buying a puppy is better described as buying a "dog-to-be."

Second, if you do get a puppy, get it from the right place. The three responsible places to get a puppy are from a responsible breeder, a humane society (animal shelter), or a rescue organization. By "responsible breeder" I don't just mean someone who shows her dogs in dog shows and has a lot of ads in magazines. I mean someone who is serious about raising dogs who are physically and mentally healthy and is equally serious

---

8. I've asked several pet stores what they do with dogs and cats that they can't sell. They responded that the animals always eventually find homes. As someone in business myself, I find that hard to believe.

about finding good permanent homes for the lives that they have created. By my definition responsible breeders take responsibility for their pups for the entire life of the pup, period. No questions asked. Two years ago I took a dog back that I had sold as a puppy nine years before to a dairy farm. The owners were moving off the farm, and as I insisted when I sold him, they brought him back to me when they didn't want him anymore. I was grateful that they brought him back, even though the last thing that I needed was another dog. But other responsibilities took second place to standing behind a dog that I had bred. Responsible breeders are appalled at the thought that their pups might end up clogging up animal shelters somewhere and move heaven and earth to keep track of their puppies for their entire lifetime. If you're considering buying a puppy from someone who won't take the puppy back at any time for whatever reason (or whom you'd be uncomfortable giving the puppy back to), then thank her and go elsewhere.

The other responsible places to get a dog are from humane societies or rescue groups: there are millions of dogs who just need a second chance, and a shelter or a rescue group is a wonderful place to find them. They won't have as many puppies as they do adolescents or adults, but the animals there need homes just as much as, if not more than, any puppy. So often I hear people say, "Oh, I couldn't even go into the shelter! I'd feel so bad!" But many shelters are fine, happy places that test dogs' temperaments and have banks of volunteers who exercise, play with, and train dogs, and they need your help to create happy endings. If you find yourself feeling all nurturing and parental, maybe you could even use that energy to help them out. Rescue groups for dogs need help, too, both in finding places to rehome dogs and in finding temporary foster homes for them. Rescue groups are usually associated with a particular breed, and the individuals in these groups expend amazing amounts of time, energy, and money to link needy dogs of a particular breed to good homes. Often they have a lot of information about the dogs that they've fostered, so you can adopt a dog who seems well suited to your home and family situation.

Whatever you do, don't let yourself get seduced by pet stores, "agents," or "no-kill shelters" that also just happen to raise ten litters a year. Watch out for long stories from people who placed newspaper ads: "Well, my sister owns the mother, but she's busy, so I thought I'd drive the pups over from Iowa to help her out." The real story is that "the sister" actually owns a puppy mill and has a bank of agents who peddle the puppies to the unsuspecting public.

It's hard to make a thoughtful decision when you're looking at the cutest little bundle of puppy you've ever seen in your life. Infantile features have such a strong effect on us that just looking at a pup can change the balance of hormones in your body. These hormones are not to be sneezed at; they are serious forces inside you that can have a profound influence on what you do. So when you're looking at puppies, just remember the birds who couldn't stop themselves from feeding fish instead of their own babies and ask yourself what's driving your decision to take home that big-eyed little puppy you're looking at—the "Aw" phenomenon or a thoughtful decision that you'd like a dog for the next fifteen years? I won't look at a litter of puppies until I've decided whether I like the parents, because once I sit down with a pack of sweet-breathed, velvet-bellied puppies, I'm had. Once when I went to look at a litter of Great Pyrenees puppies, the breeder asked me to stay outside while she put the bitch away, since the dam was "a little protective of her puppies." Female dogs that don't trust strangers around their puppies aren't carrying the genes that I want, so I thanked her and drove away. The breeder, who bred truly fine sheep-guarding dogs, couldn't believe that I wouldn't at least come in just to see the puppies, but I knew that once I did, I'd end up listening to my hormones and taking one home when I shouldn't.

In spite of all this advice, if you find yourself in a pet store (or anywhere else) that sells puppies and you are overwhelmed with the desire to take one home, ask the salesperson where the puppy came from and insist on driving out there to see the place yourself. The staff at every pet store that I know of will assure you that *it* would never get puppies from a puppy mill, but perhaps you've noticed that lots of nice salespeople in lots of nice stores will tell you lots of nice things that don't always turn out to be perfectly true. Insist on meeting the parents of the pup yourself and the people who raised it. Demand to see where the mother dogs are kept while they are raising their puppies. Talk in person to the veterinarian who oversees the dogs. If all is well, then fine, buy the pup. If not, complain to the pet store, call the humane society, contact your legislator, and at minimum let someone else who is not as educated as you buy the puppy. Try to rescue the poor mother and father and get them out of that hellhole. Just because they're not adorable puppies anymore doesn't mean that they don't need you.

Cute as a Button

The other problem of our attraction to infantile characteristics is the relatively recent trend toward breeding dogs for childlike faces. Besides having some body parts out of proportion, a flat face is another feature of young mammals. Puppies all start off with flat little faces, looking like tiny Mack trucks, all squared off and flattened in the front. As dogs mature, their muzzles extend into a form that allows them to catch and eat meat. Many of our current dog breeds (many of which are surprisingly new, only a hundred years old or so) have resulted from our efforts to create dogs with teddy bear–like features—big eyes, large foreheads, and flat, puppylike muzzles. But just because we find flat faces pleasing doesn't mean that they are good for dogs. The face of a cute dog with a smashed nose, like a Bulldog or a Pug, results from an abnormal shortening of the facial bones, called brachycephaly. Considered a severe disability in humans, it's caused by a mutation that interferes with the essential processes of life: breathing and keeping your brain at the right temperature. This may look endearing to some people, but the dogs' well-being is compromised. Dogs like Bulldogs simply can't breathe or pant normally, as owners who have listened to them snore at night or tried to go jogging with them can attest. By shortening their muzzles, we've created nasal passages that can't do their job and a jaw that can barely hold all of its teeth.

I don't mean to pick on a particular breed,[9] because our very human propensity to be attracted to youthful features isn't the only tendency that can get dogs in trouble. Humans are also attracted to things that are different: we tend to like animals that are flashier or bigger or smaller than the rest. For instance, look at the North American Plains Indians' favoring of pinto horses rather than ones of only one color. During the same era, the effect European dog breeders had on the size of dogs has been amazing. If left to breed independently of humans, dogs weigh about 25 to 35 pounds, but many of the breeds that have been developed recently weigh from little more than a pound to well over 200 pounds.

Perhaps our drive to create extreme shapes and sizes goes along with our own tendency to be endlessly childlike and curious, attracted to "newness" and drama as most youngsters are rather than drawn to stability as is characteristic of older animals. Being curious and attracted to things that are different may serve us well in many ways: quite possibly we humans are as successful as we are because of our ability to cope with new environments. Currently retaining our youthful curiosity into adulthood leads to advances in all areas of our lives—from discoveries of new food sources to difficult surgeries that save lives to understanding how best to raise healthy and happy children. But this interest in things new and different doesn't always improve the life of our dogs, not when we breed dogs so large that they only live nine or ten years or so small that they can't deliver their own young without major surgery or so physically disabled that they can't breathe comfortably. It's easy to castigate some breeders and breed clubs, as has become popular in certain circles, but blame doesn't lead to anything useful. Rather than putting dog lovers on the defensive, it is more helpful to our dogs to first start understanding *why* we do what we do and then make thoughtful decisions about what to do next.

It's not that people who breed extralarge or extrasmall or flat-faced dogs don't love them. This isn't about love, not at all. I spend my life with

---

9. It's not that I don't like the behavioral characteristics of many of the brachycephalic breeds: I've fallen in love with countless Pugs and Bulldogs, and I know that their owners love them dearly, too. But even though it's a bit painful, it's important to examine the effect that we have on domestic dogs as objectively as we can.

people who live with, breed, and compete with dogs of all breeds, and believe me, you should be so loved. But all behavioral virtues, in certain contexts, can spiral into trouble. Our interest in breeding for that fascinating new coat color or that cute little face is seductive and can lead to extremes of anatomy that simply aren't good for dogs. "Everything in moderation" is good advice for breeders, too. I'm reminded of the saying "Our vices are the excesses of our virtues." Dogs were shaped the way they were for a reason, and our tendency to manipulate their anatomy can be a virtue if moderated but can compromise their well-being if it becomes excessive. Ouch. I know this observation hurts. But when we're playing God, as we've been doing with domestic dogs for centuries, then we need to be sure that our power doesn't outstrip our wisdom. After all, shouldn't we be their "best friends," too?

7

THE TRUTH
ABOUT DOMINANCE

How Social Status Relates to the Behavior
of Both Humans and Dogs

Male Chesapeake Bay Retrievers tend to be big-chested, muscular dogs, the kind of dogs that love hard, pounding pets to the ribs. Bred to break the ice for duck hunters in the frigid weather of Chesapeake Bay, they are famous for being tough, independent, and just a little bit stubborn. Although I try to avoid stereotyping breeds, because it can blind you to the true nature of the dog with which you're working, Chester looked like a cartoon of a classic male Chessie when he trotted into my office. He had the huge square head that goes along with a lot of testosterone in dogs and humans. (Think of the jaw structure of a classically handsome man compared to that of a delicate-chinned, beautiful woman.) He looked muscled up like a weight lifter, as strong as a small bull.

I sat up a little straighter, breathed in, and asked what the problem was. "Dominance aggression," his owner, John, told me, diagnosed by his veterinarian. It seemed that Chester didn't take kindly to John's corrections. When John said "No" to Chester inside the house, Chester would run into the bedroom, leap up on the bed, wait for John to come after him, and then, staring directly at John, lift his leg and pee on the pillow.

After talking with John for several minutes, I started my usual evaluation, in which I interact with the dog to see what I can learn from him. One of the things I'm looking for is whether a dog will respond to handling with a cold, hard stare directly into my eyes. A cold stare is one of the visual displays that high-status dogs will give to another as a warning. "Back off, buddy, or I'll follow up on this threat" isn't a bad English translation. You don't need a Ph.D. to know that you could be in trouble if a dog as big as Chester goes still and looks you straight in the eye with his own eyes as hard as flint. But chilling as it is, that direct stare is a useful visual signal that helps explain why a dog is doing what he's doing, so I started working with Chester to see if I could elicit it.

Few dogs, whether male or female, status-seeking or submissive, seem to like people handling their paws. How different from us they are in this: we humans like to hold hands and get hand massages and manicures. Some male dogs especially object to their back paws' being handled, and there's a lot to learn about a dog by gently picking up a back paw. Some of them lick your hand; some of them freeze anxiously, the corners of their mouth pulled back in a fearful grimace. Others stiffen their bodies and glare at you with eyes like cold, hard steel. Most dogs never look at you like that: unless you're a professional trainer or have owned a particularly difficult dog, you've probably never seen it. I saw it in the eyes of a wolf-dog hybrid who took the time to shoot a look like a bullet at my eyes, right before he sank his teeth into my hand. (I had thrown a piece of meat 5 feet away from the bone on which he was chewing. I picked up the bone while he ate the treat on the floor and then handed him back the bone, all to teach him not to worry if someone picked up his "treasures." In less than half a second, he took the bone from my hand, spat it out while he shot a furious look into my eyes, and then bit my other hand, hard and deep.)

Usually the look is a true warning and gives you time to act on it, within a quarter of a second or so, before you get hurt. As long as I act, the dog has no need to follow up on his threat, and there's little danger. I don't foolishly push a dog until he has no choice but to react. While I quietly handle his back paw, I watch his face out of the corner of my eye. I will also test him by reaching toward him when he has a bone in his mouth to see if his expression changes or will gently hold on to a front paw after he tries to pull it away. In all these tests I'm learning a lot about the dog—how he reacts to something mildly aversive, what he does when I start to take away his treasure. One of the ways that a dog can react is to go still and "hard-eyed," a look that corre-

lates with pure offensive aggression—not defensive aggression motivated by fear, not submission, and not passive helplessness. I see it from dogs who aren't willing to concede an inch and who are signifying their willingness to back up the threat that they have just made. I see it in the few dogs that I think can be accurately described as "dominant aggressive," like the wolf-dog hybrid whose look I interpreted as "Don't you ever do that again" and who disciplined me with a single, hard bite to make his point.

As I moved my hand down Chester's back leg and held up his back paw, I was prepared for him to change instantly from the big friendly lug he'd been so far to a dominant aggressive dog.[1] Chester's eyes didn't change in the slightest but stayed soft and liquid. He continued wagging his entire body from the shoulders back. His mouth stayed open and relaxed, his tail low and loose while he licked my face. I asked him to lie down. He did, his tail wagging so hard it moved his entire body back and forth along with it. I gently rolled him over, and he slurped his huge, silly tongue all over my hands. I let him up, gave him a bone stuffed with cheese, and then reached to take it away. He looked up and licked my hand, and then went back to his bone. I reached all the way over and took it away. He stood there grinning and let me do it.

Chester may have been built like a professional wrestler, but he wasn't acting like a dominant dog in my office, and he didn't seem to be at home either. John reported that he could pet Chester anytime, he could groom him, pull burrs out of his tail, take away his toys and dinner bowl, and push him off the bed without a problem. Chester adored visitors; he let children play with his toys, hug him exuberantly, and sit on top of him on the floor. As a matter of fact, the only problem John had with Chester was when he said the word no.

None of this was making any sense. I went back to basics and asked John again about the history of the problem. John explained that he had been warned that Chesapeakes can be stubborn, willful dogs and that "you must get dominance over them right away." The first time that Chester squatted in the house, seven weeks old and newly arrived, John was sure to give him a good, masterful correction. "NO," he boomed, and ran to Chester, grabbed the scruff of his neck as he'd been taught by the breeder, and shook him hard. This hap-

---

1. This is a dangerous exercise with some dogs, and I discourage anyone but experienced trainers and animal behaviorists from trying it.

pened several times in the next few days, John escalating the power of the "No" and the intensity of the scruff shake each time. No coddling for this tough hunting dog, puppy though he might be. On the second day, Chester urinated, as submissive dogs who are frightened often do, after John yelled "No" and reached toward him. But when Chester's ears flattened and he rolled over and urinated, John realized that his correction had gone over the top, and he immediately stopped his charge toward Chester. This same scenario, with John yelling "No!" and running toward Chester, followed by Chester cowering and then urinating, was repeated several times over the next couple of days.

You can connect the dots from here. Chester learned that if he urinated when John said "No," John would stop his offensive charge. Later Chester learned to combine urinating with a delightful "tag, I'm it" game that he was successfully teaching John and turned it into a romp onto the bed and a leg lift on the pillow. His look at John from the bed probably wasn't a cold threat. I'll bet that Chester was simply watching John to see what he'd do next. My own suspicion is that Chester, like lots of adolescents, loved watching his elders go crazy with frustration and had found the perfect button to set John off. Chester wasn't exactly a helpless victim here: he'd taken what he'd learned and was using it to get a rise out of John, but that's a far cry from dominance aggression. Where was the aggression, after all? Chester had never even growled at John, much less tried to hurt him. The behavior was turned around by John's changing his correction word from "no" to "wrong". Chester learned that if he stopped what he was doing when he heard "Wrong," something good happened. Chester loved this new game, and last I heard, John hadn't had to change his sheets because of Chester in a long time.

Dominance?

Chester's behavior had little to do with dominance aggression. It was a response from a smart dog who had learned how to handle an inappropriately aggressive correction from his owner. It didn't lead to real trouble in that case, because his owner was wise enough to look for help before he acted on an incorrect diagnosis and some bad advice from his buddies.

But the misdiagnosis of dominance aggression and the all-too-common bad advice about "getting dominance over your dog" does lead to trouble, lots of it, and sometimes the results could break your heart.

I will never, ever forget watching a videotape of Scooter, a big-eyed, sixteen-week-old Golden Retriever puppy. One look at Scooter—golden soft, baby-headed, and big-pawed—and you'd want to take him home and cuddle. Too late—Scooter's dead. He was euthanized at four months of age for dominance aggression, the result of horrific advice that dog trainers had given his well-meaning owners. Scooter, like most retrievers, was obsessed with objects. He adored toys the day he came home and proudly trotted around the house with anything he could get into his mouth. The responsible owners took Scooter to puppy class and asked the trainers what to do when Scooter stole socks from the laundry, the remote control from the coffee table (always a favorite of dogs), or shoes from the closet. "You must do what wolves do!" the trainers said. "Go to him, grab the scruff of his neck, and get right into his face. Yell 'No' in a loud and growly voice. You must let him know right away that you are in charge, that you're dominant, and that he can't get away with stealing things."

The owners complied: I saw their attempts on the videotape. Scooter, in the first stages of this treatment, looked befuddled and scared. Holding on to a child's toy tight within his mouth, Scooter flinched when his owner (who looked just as miserable) grabbed the skin of his neck and shook him while repeating "No" over and over again. But Scooter didn't drop the toy. I don't think it occurred to him to do so. All Scooter knew was that his owner was attacking him. He clenched all his muscles, shut his eyes, tried to assume a posture of appeasement, and waited for her to go away. But of course, that didn't result in the toy's dropping from his frozen mouth, so his owner yelled louder, her face within inches now of Scooter's, and shook him again. As the tape continues, Scooter begins to growl as his owner shakes him with her face just inches from his, and eventually he starts to growl and lunge when she comes anywhere near an object that he treasures, even if it's not in his mouth.

The last scene is indeed scary, with Scooter bug-eyed and snarl-

lunging at his hapless owner as she reaches within a few feet of a toy lying at his feet, but I still feel sick thinking about his death. Scooter was not a little angel. His possessiveness of objects was extreme, and I never would have trusted him in a home with little children. But I talked to the vet tech who'd been called in late in the case, and she said that the pup had never growled in any other context, adored the little boys of the family, and was a shining star in obedience class. Certainly lots of dogs don't respond aggressively to harsh punishment and threats, but the advice given to the owners made Scooter's possessiveness much worse and eventually ended up killing him. What's so sad about this case is that dogs who are object-possessive, but docile in all other contexts, have an extremely high rate of successful treatment, and most three-month-old puppies can be taught to gently give you what was in their mouth. If dogs learn that they're going to get something extra wonderful when you reach toward them and their "treasure," they quickly learn to trade up. After a few months of training, using positive reinforcement instead of violence, almost all dogs will drop the object in their mouth when quietly asked, whether you have a treat in your hand or not. I once rewarded a five-month-old Border Collie puppy for handing me a rotting rabbit carcass by giving it back to her for a few minutes. The people watching were appalled, but she was dazzled and trusted me completely ever after.

I wish that stories like those of Scooter and Chester were rare, but they're not. Just as people were taught to "Spare the rod and spoil the child," people have been advised for years to "get dominance over their dogs," and so often getting dominance meant getting aggressive. Even the Monks of New Skete, whose book *How to Be Your Dog's Best Friend* inspired me and at least a million other people, advised owners to act like wolves and do "alpha rollovers"—to throw dogs down onto their backs to ensure that their dogs would accept them as leaders. The book's main author, Job Michael Evans, later said that he deeply regretted this advice.

Well-socialized, healthy dogs don't pin other dogs to the ground. Submissive individuals initiate that posture themselves. The posture is a display signal from one animal to another, a signal of appeasement, not the result of a wrestling maneuver. Forcing dogs into "submission" and screaming in their face is a great way to elicit defensive aggression. It makes sense that a dog would bite, or at least threaten to, in this context. Within their social framework, you're acting like a lunatic. Not only that, but a mature wolf would never attack a puppy that already had something in his mouth. He might growl at a puppy to warn him off an object that lay between them, but once the puppy had it in his mouth, the adult wolf would let him keep it. Mature wolves are amazingly tolerant of puppies, allowing them to steal their toys, chew on their tails, and harass them mercilessly. Besides, wolves do a lot of things that we have no reason to emulate, from eating the placenta of their newborns to killing visitors from other packs, so recommending that we humans should do something simply because wolves do it isn't exactly a compelling argument. Besides, dogs aren't behavioral replicates of wolves. That makes four reasons not to use alpha rollovers on your dog: dogs aren't wolf replicates in the first place; wolves don't use alpha rollovers themselves to discipline other wolves; the action elicits defensiveness and sometimes aggression; and it teaches your dog to mistrust you.

The advice about using threats to get dominance over your dog is amazingly pervasive. Dog owners and trainers everywhere have picked it up, as have veterinarians, police K-9 trainers, and your neighbor down the street. I think it's useful to wonder about why people who would never hit their child are so quick, even against all their instincts, to follow the advice of "experts" and get physical with their dog to gain "dominance" over her. I suspect that it's based, albeit loosely and inaccurately, on an essential truth that every human inherently understands: social status is important to both people and dogs, and we all know it.

Any human, even one with the poorest of social skills, can walk into a room full of strangers and quickly pick out the person with the most status. Others will cluster around her so that she's the center of attention. People will be more likely to bring her food and drinks, to open doors for her, and to try to get her attention. You can also look to see who touches whom: the higher someone's social status, the less likely the rest of us are to touch her without her permission. Think about how you would react to meeting royalty and how likely you'd be to run up and give him or her a hug. Remember when the queen of England visited the States and some woman from New Jersey slapped her arms around the Queen in an all-American hug? The British were appalled. But if the queen had wanted to, she could have initiated the hug, and no one would've mentioned it.[2]

People can gain high status in a variety of ways, but no matter how they manage to obtain it, and whether it feels fair or not, individuals with a lot of social status can do things that others can't. Erik Zimen, one of the world's foremost researchers of wolves, a profoundly status-conscious species, put it this way in the book *Wolves of the World*: "The dominance relationship between two animals is expressed by the degree of social freedom each animal allows itself during an encounter." Certainly there are still social constraints on those in power in our own and other species, but there are fewer constraints on those in power than on others. I recently saw Minnesota Governor Jesse Ventura bragging on television that he broke the speed limit whenever he wanted to, driving at 145 miles an hour at one point, with no expectation of ever getting a traffic ticket. He felt secure that his social status as governor gives him freedoms that the rest of us don't have. Whether speeding (and bragging about it) is objectionable to you or not, we all understand that the governor has more social status than the rest of us. Usually it seems appropriate. (I'm reminded of Animal Behavior Society conferences at which the well-established scientists can dress casually and make jokes that the graduate students would never consider making.)

The importance of social status is just as obvious in interactions between dogs, who remind us daily how important it is to them. Like chimpanzees, who use every greeting ceremony to clarify rank, dogs employ similar postures to communicate social status each time that they meet. Watch the tails of two dogs while they are greeting each other, and you'll get an excellent idea of how each dog sees himself or herself compared to the other. Look to see who raises the base of the tail and whose tail gets

---

2. Well, perhaps they would have, given the queen's reputation as being a bit aloof, but the talk wouldn't have been about her violating a social norm.

lowered (the base of their tails is the relevant part, not the tip). In some pairs the differences are extreme, with one dog's tail held high like a flag and the other dog's tail submissively tucked under her belly. In other cases tail posture differences might be more subtle, but overall body postures contain clues, too: one dog might be leaning forward more than the other, perhaps standing straighter and higher, ears forward rather than back—that's the dog with more social status. If both dogs look like mirror images of each other, with their tails high and their bodies erect and stiff, then you are well advised to distract them and get them thinking about something besides each other. Both dogs are communicating that they would like the higher social rank, thank you very much, and it's rarely pretty when two social climbers get in each other's faces.

Dogs also illustrate their attention to hierarchy by urinating in specific orders, with higher-status dogs "overmarking" the urine of others. You can see it every night at my house. Before we climb the stairs to bed, I take the dogs out for one last pee. When we first started this routine, low-on-the-totem-pole Pip was the first to squat, while Lassie and Tulip waited for her to finish so that they could urinate over Pip's, Lassie next, followed by Tulip. That's the order that you see among wolves, in which high-status individuals overmark the urine marks of lower-status individuals. If you have a group of dogs, especially dogs of the same sex, watch and see whether there is an order to who goes when and whether one dog overmarks the others' urine predictably. Lately there's been a change in my dogs' routine, because last winter I got tired of waiting out in the cold at ten o'clock at night while four dogs sniffed around for the latest news about chipmunks. I started giving them treats as soon as they finished to speed them up (it works wonders). Now they tend to pay a bit less attention to who goes first and more attention to getting their treat, but I've yet to see Pip urinate over the puddle that Lassie left, and you can still bet money that Luke will wait for Lassie to go so he can urinate over it.

Social status is also obvious in play, and although a lot of social differences are ignored in play (as they are in our species also), they're not irrelevant. Tulip will grab the ball away from Pip, but Pip will defer to Tulip, even if Pip could get the ball first. I've never had a dog who loved ball play as much as Pip, but Queen Tulip has more social freedom than Pip, and that means she gets the ball if she wants it. Sometimes she doesn't want it, because just like other queens, Tulip gets to say what's important and when.

Humans and dogs are predisposed to having hierarchical social systems because both species need ways of resolving the conflicts that inevitably arise in group living. These potential conflicts can include who goes out the door first, who gets the best sleeping place, or who gets to mate with whom. As we humans know well, one of the ways to resolve these conflicts is by fighting. But fighting is not the best solution when conflicts can come up repeatedly during the day: it takes a lot of energy and is dangerous. Individuals can avoid having to fight every time that a conflict arises with a system of social rankings in which each individual has a predetermined rank in the group. This must be a reasonably good solution to the inevitable conflicts of group living, because it's ubiquitous in the world of social animals. An individual's rank can change and in egalitarian societies is highly fluid, but each individual's position is as real, at any point in time, as his physical presence.

Putting It in Perspective

I have to admit that I would rather avoid this whole subject of social status, because it's become so contentious and emotionally loaded in the world of dog training that I risk the equivalent of an electronic collar correction by broaching it. Rather than looking at the overall concept of social status, the focus in dog training has been on "dominance," and to the detriment of our dogs, dominance has often been equated with aggression. They are very different things, but confusing dominance with aggression is so common that in some circles all talk about dominance is politically incorrect. Some Ph.D. behaviorists, veterinary behaviorists, and trainers are opposed to even using the word *dominance* at all. At one professional meeting, the word became so loaded that Wayne Hunthausen, a veterinary behaviorist, and I began to jokingly call it "the concept formerly referred to as dominance," complete with its own Prince-like icon. I sympathize with those who object to using the word, I really do. The word has been so misused that it's tempting to drop it from our vocabulary altogether.

But we can't avoid the fact that humans and dogs are derived from animals that live within a carefully organized social system. Our relationship with our dogs will profit most by our trying to understand how social systems are organized in both species and then going on to determine how that knowledge might affect our own behavior around dogs.

To get some perspective on this complex issue, it helps to look at how a variety of species relate to one another. A good place to start is with our own closest relatives, chimpanzees and bonobos. In chimpanzee society a lot of social energy is expended on rank, primarily by the males. Chimpanzee society is male-dominated, and high-status males have more social freedom than females. Alpha male chimpanzees get access to the best food and can have sex with the females when they are most likely to conceive.[3] High-ranking males get the most attention and the most grooming and are deferred to when they move around. They are greeted by lower-ranking members with displays of submission that we would all instantly recognize. The lower-ranking individual may hold out a hand, bow to the ground, crouch submissively with head down, or present his or her genitals.

Status in male chimpanzees is particularly interesting because it is based on the formation of coalitions, in which no single male can achieve and maintain power without a cadre of supporting males. The females can also play a role in these essentially male power shifts. In his book *Chimpanzee Politics,* Frans de Waal describes a newly risen male being harassed by others who had not yet fully accepted his leadership. The group turned on him (chimpanzees have huge teeth and can hurt one another badly), and he fled to the top of a tree, where he stayed, screaming and gri-

3. This distinction is not quite as simple as scientists used to think: recent studies suggest that a surprising number of young are actually the result of "sneak" copulations between a female and a lower-ranking but exceptionally quiet male. Pairs of females and low-ranking males have been known to hide behind a rock and copulate silently, and low-ranking males have been known to cover their erections when high-ranking males look their way!

macing in fear. The oldest and highest-ranking female climbed the tree, kissed him, and escorted him down, staying beside him to confer her acceptance of his position. He eventually took over the colony, but only with the backing of an active male coalition who supported him and further interventions from the elder female. Elder females in the colony play an extremely important role in mediating conflicts among the males. In many cases an elder female will facilitate a reconciliation between two rival males, calming one with kisses and grooming and then taking him by the hand to sit beside his rival, where she'll sit between them until tensions have calmed enough for her to leave and let them interact directly. This role of females in supporting certain males and encouraging reconciliations between rival males is common to chimp societies. (Sound familiar?)

Bonobos also focus a lot of energy on social status, but they differ from chimpanzees in two very important ways. Chimps often employ threat displays with lots of branch waving, screaming, pounding, and sometimes serious fighting as they act out their power struggles. Shakespeare would've loved chimps, but the Playboy Channel would prefer bonobos. You don't see as many nature shows on television about bonobos as you do about chimps, partly because bonobos are not considered suitable for American prime-time network television. Unlike chimpanzees, bonobos resolve conflicts with sex.[4] The "all-sex, all-the-time" species, bonobos have sexual intercourse with one another as freely as we shake hands (except, like us, they avoid incest). They have heterosexual sex, homosexual sex, frontal sex, oral sex, and sex in exchange for an apple. And that's before breakfast. Bonobos personify the "Make love, not war" motto, because they resolve social tension and conflicts with sex rather than threats and aggression. (In lighter moments, when I'm amazed by our own species—which I am most of the time—I wonder whether we exemplify the extremes of both chimps and bonobos: quick to be aggressive if we're threatened but obsessed with sex.) Like chimps, bonobos have

4. There are other reasons that bonobos are seldom seen on television: bonobos are endangered animals who live in remote areas, so it is very difficult to get footage of them in the wild. Human aggression in the form of civil war has made it even harder for researchers and photographers to study and film this fascinating species.

a strong sense of social hierarchy, but in bonobos the primary hierarchy is among the females, not the males.

This focus on social rank is not limited to primates.[5] It's found in a vast number of species in which there is the possibility of internal competition over resources. Wasps, hyenas, even my own small flock of sheep have an obvious leader and social hierarchy.[6] My Harriet is an old, wise ewe, who could be straight out of the movie *Babe,* and she makes all the decisions about when and where to move the flock. Cows, too, have a hierarchy, as many a novice dairyman has learned when he tried to force the cows into the barn in the "wrong" order. The cows themselves decide who goes first, and a wise farmer understands the importance of social conventions among his cows and lets them well enough alone. Sheep and cows pay so much attention to who's who that herding dogs can pick out the leader of a group in a matter of seconds, even if they've never seen that group of sheep before. When an experienced Border Collie is running in a wide circle to get behind the sheep, she'll turn her head every few seconds to look at the flock. Border Collie handlers (me included) believe that their dogs are checking on the sheep's response to their movement and looking to see which one is the leader. That's the one the dog needs to focus on when she starts stalking toward them, because that's the one with the power to decide when and where to move.

Some dogs will focus on the leader so intensely that they'll walk right through the rest of the flock. My eight-year-old Border Collie, Lassie, will still forget herself on occasion and let the stragglers drift off as she lasers in on the lead ewe. Since this results in her bringing me one sheep instead of thirty, I have to remind her that I actually need *all* the sheep. She stops, looks around, does what seems like a double take at the sheep behind her, and then turns back to the lead ewe. I don't know what she's thinking, but

5. I don't want to oversimplify here: social systems in primate species are highly variable. Some species, like rhesus monkeys, have strict, almost despotic hierarchies, and others, like muriquis and marmosets, are quite egalitarian.

6. Being the "leader" is often the role of a high-status female in hoofed animals, while the dominant male keeps the group together and "defends" them from other males. He's not necessarily defending them from danger—although he might do that, too—but you can count on him to defend his right to have them all to himself. The dominant male stallion can force the leader female to stay with the herd and run from another stallion, but he'll defer to her decisions about where to go to graze.

I imagine it to be something like "Yeah, yeah, I know, but *this* is the important one!"

"The important one" is a concept that we humans also intuitively understand, because of our awareness, whether conscious or not, of social status.

You Are What You Eat

Recently there's been some confusion in the world of dog training about the role that status and hierarchy have in dog behavior. Some people argue that wolflike pack hierarchies have no relevance to dogs, because our house dogs probably derived from scavenging village dogs who didn't live in packs like wolves. The image of historic dogs feeding on human garbage, as pigeons and rats do, may not be very romantic, but it's an excellent argument and deserves attention.[7] These village dogs, or "pariah" dogs, are found on the outskirts of settlements almost all over the world. They are smaller than wolves (they weigh in at 30 or 35 pounds), are less shy of novel things than wolves, and most important to our inquiry here, don't necessarily live in tight pack formations like wolves. The limited number of observations that we have on village dogs suggests that they live either alone or in small, loosely organized groups. Wolves primarily hunt large prey like elk and deer and depend on their cohesive pack system to coordinate their hunting as a group and to eliminate constant fighting over the spoils. Each individual wolf has his or her own social status relative to all the others.

Because the social relationships of scavenging village dogs appear to be different than the social structure of wolf packs, some dog trainers argue that social status and hierarchy are irrelevant to our own pet dogs. But that seems counterintuitive, given what we know about how our own dogs behave, and lacks an understanding of how behavior

7. See the book *Dogs,* by Raymond and Lorna Coppinger, for more on this interesting hypothesis, also proposed by Robert Wayne at UCLA.

and the environment interact. Although scientists have done remarkably little research on the social structure of domestic dogs,[8] we know a lot about the formation of social structure in wild animals, and we can use that knowledge to inform us about our own relationship with our dogs.

Like many inherently social species, canids exhibit tremendous flexibility in how they structure their interactions. For instance, coyotes in Wyoming live in packs during the winter, when they primarily feed on elk carcasses. At other times, when high-quality food isn't available in one handy location, the coyotes drift apart, living alone on small mammals, lizards, and berries. There's no advantage to living together when the meager food available is scattered far and wide. Similar changes in social structure occur in many species, primates included, when the distribution of food changes. Many species, called "facultatively social species," split up when food is scarce but return to living in groups as soon as possible when food availability allows it. The even distribution of a low-quality food (like lizards and berries for coyotes and garbage for village dogs) usually leads to a relatively loose social structure. There is no value in looking for food as a group in a garbage dump, and there's no point in fighting over discarded bones and empty soup cans if there is similar food scattered all around the environment. But if those same individuals leave that kind of food source and start living in an environment in which food is of high quality but less evenly distributed, they'll be more successful in a group, and the group needs some social mechanism to avoid serious conflicts over the spoils.

This fluid nature of sociality can explain why pet dogs behave as though a social hierarchy is important to them, even if they were derived from scavenging village dogs who might be less interested in keeping track of the social register. Scavenging dogs who live off garbage and waste are in a similar ecological niche as coyotes in summer. But take these same dogs and put them in a group living situation, where the food is extra tasty and comes from only one central location, then everything changes.

8. See the References for studies by Alan Beck and observations by Raymond and Lorna Coppinger.

I've met several "rescued" street dogs from Northern Africa and Central America, and after hanging out in their owners' air-conditioned houses and eating organic dog chow made from chicken and lamb, they didn't act like animals incapable of understanding a hierarchy. Unlike dogs with no alternative but to scavenge on empty food cartons and human feces, our house dogs are sitting on a veritable gold mine of resources, from gourmet food to free massages every night. If that's not worth competing for, I don't know what is.

A good hypothesis is that although social status is highly relevant to dogs, it's much less of an obsession with them than it is with wolves. Dogs are more like juvenile wolves than adult ones, and young wolves are less interested in social hierarchies than adults are. Erik Zimen's study of wolves (in *Wolves of the World*), showed that "rank differences are most prominent among the higher ranking wolves, less distinct among the lower ranks and younger wolves and non-existent among pups." Although, of course, it's much more complicated in humans, there's truth to that in our species, too. Very young children aren't status-conscious at all: we have to learn as we mature that some people are more equal than others.

Even within the category of American house dogs, I suspect that when we finally get around to doing some good, rigorous research on their social system, we'll find different levels of importance put on status depending on how the dogs live. I see much more status-related behavior problems with dogs who live in the house compared to dogs who live in kennels or in tie-out yards. So we need to be careful when we talk about the social behavior of "dogs," because the same dog can act differently depending on her environment.

The Truth About Dominance

Understanding social status is particularly important because misunderstanding what "dominance" means has led to appallingly abusive behavior. So much old-fashioned obedience training could be summarized as,

"Do it because I told you to, and if you don't, I'll hurt you." The assumption seemed to be that dogs should do what we say because we told them to: after all, we're the humans and they're the dogs, and surely humans have more social status than dogs. If a dog didn't obey, then he was challenging his owner's social status and needed to be forcibly discplined to be kept in his place. Regrettably the attitude that we must get dominance over our dogs with physical force works in some cases, especially with happy-go-lucky and relatively tough-skinned dogs like some hunting breeds. Bred for stamina and a "never-say-die" attitude, a lot of these dogs accept gruff corrections and "dominance displays" with equanimity. But this approach terrorizes many dogs and leads to dogs who are afraid of their owners or who become defensively aggressive because they perceive that they are under attack all the time.

Years ago I had two women as clients who reported that their dog, a Cattle Dog mix, was disobedient and very dominant. When I asked why they thought she was dominant, they said, "Because she's very resistant to an alpha rollover." I asked them to demonstrate so that I could watch the dog. One of the women, a seemingly kind and loving person, grabbed the dog by the scruff, swung her up into the air, and slammed her down on her back. As instructed by a local trainer, she then stood over her breathless, panicked dog and growled in her face. It all happened so fast that I couldn't stop it once it started. I can only imagine what the poor little dog thought. I was stunned myself, and I hadn't had the wind knocked out of me. Luckily the owners were thrilled to drop the "alpha rollover slam dunk" from their repertoire. They hated doing it but felt compelled to do what had been advised.

The hapless Cattle Dog is just one example of millions of dogs physically abused in the guise of training all over the world every year. Many humans equate "dominance" with "aggression" and quickly buy into using aggression to get what they want. The irony is that dominance is actually a social construct designed to decrease aggression, not to facilitate it. A hierarchical social system allows individuals to resolve conflicts *without* having to fight. Any individual who truly has a lot of social status has enough power that he or she doesn't need to use force. You could argue that force actually reflects the absence of real power, because if you have pure power, you don't need force. I could tell you to "sit and stay" in your chair, and if I had enough social status over you, my words alone would have the power to get you to comply. If I didn't have that much status-related power, I could threaten you with a gun or, worse, with having my four dogs shed all over your house for a week. In other words, if I found a way to exert enough force, I could get you to comply, but I'd only need it if I didn't have enough power in the first place.

"Status," "dominance," and "aggression" are completely different things, and it does our dogs no good when we confuse them. Status is a position or rank within a society, while dominance describes a relationship among individuals, with one having more status than others in a particular context. *Aggression is not a necessary component of dominance.* Aggression, as defined by biologists, is an action that intends to cause harm, while dominance is a position within a hierarchy. A bloody riot in which a monarch is killed is an example of human aggression, while the fact that there was a monarch at all is an example of a social hierarchy. That monarch or president or pack leader might have been selected without violence, perhaps through family relationships with past monarchs or an election. Thus, aggression and the threat of it can be used to achieve a higher social status, but it often isn't necessary.

My dog trainer friend Beth Miller calls my dog Luke a "natural alpha." Luke is a quiet, confident dog who is secure in his place in the world and seems to feel no need to prove himself. He greets visiting dogs with friendly confidence, tail up, ears forward, clearly Male Dog One on the farm.[9] Yet Luke has had plenty of opportunity to show aggression. He works dog-dog aggression cases for me on a weekly basis and has had innumerable occasions when other dogs have tried to start trouble with him. (I don't put him at risk of physical injury, don't worry.) But just because Luke is a dog with high social status, "dominant" over other dogs, doesn't mean that he is aggressive. If a dog barks and lunges at him, Luke simply

9. Elizabeth Marshall Thomas used the phrase "Female Dog One" in her book *The Social Life of Dogs*. I liked it so much, I used it here.

turns his head away, deflecting tension, and gives the other dog no energy to bounce off of. The only behavior that Luke won't tolerate is being mounted by another male. Unless a dog is in heat, mounting is a statement about social status, not about sex. If a dog starts to mount Luke, Luke will briefly growl or occasionally growl-lunge toward the other dog, making it clear that he can and will stand up for himself if challenged. Dogs accept his display of status and defer to him without incident.[10]

The Concept Formerly Referred to as Dominance

If dominance is not the same as aggression, then what is it? As first used in the study of animal behavior decades ago, the term *dominance* described a relationship between two animals. Dominance was defined as "priority access to preferred, limited resources"—nothing less, nothing more. It's about one bone on the ground, two individuals who want it, and who gets it. It's about which male gets to breed with the female chimpanzee when there are two who want to. It's priority access (I get it first) to preferred (I *really* want it), limited (there's not enough to share) resources (the best food, the best sleeping place, the best office, and so on, and so forth).

The aspect of dominance that's important to dog owners is the social freedom that comes with it. Some dogs will mug you relentlessly to get you to pet them but then growl at you later when you reach to pet them in their dog bed. Dogs who are status-seeking and who see themselves as high up in the social order feel the freedom to touch you and solicit petting when they feel like it but will warn you off for taking such social liberties yourself.[11] In the next chapter I'll talk about the practical implications of our status-related interactions with our dogs, but for now it's worthwhile to focus on the ethology of social hierarchies.

---

10. However, there are a few dogs who are willing to pay any price to establish a higher rank over another dog, and there are dogs who enjoy fighting for its own sake. I'm careful to prevent any of my dogs from interacting with either of those types of dogs.

11. Be careful about assuming that social status always explains such behavior. Some dogs behave the same way when they're in pain and can protect themselves when they initiate the contact but not if you reach out to them.

Sometimes people get confused about social status and dominance because it seems as though dogs are inconsistent: one dog will always get the bone first, but another will be first out the door. But dominance, or high social status, doesn't mean that one individual gets everything that he wants the second that he wants it every single time. Dominant individuals don't necessarily get first access to everything. Tulip is without question the highest-status dog on my farm. None of the Border Collies would even consider trying to take a real bone or a dead rabbit lying at her feet. But there are other things that just aren't that important to Tulip, so low-ranking Pip can sleep on the couch without disturbing the social order, because although Tulip likes to sleep on it, too, she doesn't care about the couch as much as she would a prize bone. Dominant individuals get to say what's important to them as part of the social freedom that they enjoy.

Social status isn't always just about the most powerful individual's taking charge, for hierarchies are more complicated than that. High-status individuals are often dependent on the support of others in the group and can't maintain their position without it. The dominant male chimpanzee holds his position only if he's backed by a coalition of supporters. Despotic dominant wolves can be overthrown by a group effort of the pack. As we all know, even high-status humans can forget themselves and lose their power by overreaching their boundaries.

It's also important to recognize that in animals with a social hierarchy, the group isn't composed of a "dominant" individual and then "the rest of the group." A typical social hierarchy consists of three main categories of individuals: the alpha, or dominant, individual; a "beta" group of individuals who are status seekers always looking for an opportunity to improve their position; and a third "omega" group of individuals who are simply out of the running. In wolves, for example, the omega group always includes the puppies and young juveniles but may also include mature adults who just aren't the type who want to be the leader. Being a leader, in any animal species, carries responsibilities and risk, just as it does in ours. All the evidence that we have so far suggests that individual animals of many species vary greatly in their desire to be "top dog."

Certainly all dogs do not want to be dominant, although some trainers assume that they do. It's true that many dogs, much like some people, are social climbers, always looking for a step up in how they are seen by others. Most of these dogs do what they can to improve their station in life and then accept where they end up in the pack. I have met a few dogs, however, who were obsessed with achieving complete social freedom. These dogs are rare, but they are very dangerous, because they are willing to pay any price to get what they want, and they couldn't care less if they hurt you or not.

Other individuals, whether human or canine, just don't seem to care. Not everyone wants to carry the weight of the group on his or her shoulders. We all know people who spend a lot of energy improving their station in life, and we all know people who seem more than happy to work from nine to five, enjoy their garden and their kids, and let others compete over the attention and power that status confers. There's nothing right or wrong about either perspective. Societies like ours probably need that variety in order to work smoothly. If every human desperately wanted to be the chair of the committee or the president of the company, it could get pretty messy, and that general principle is just as true with dogs as it is with people.

Don't be fooled, though, by dogs (or people) who sometimes exhibit extreme versions of submissive displays. Just because a dog is quick to signal submission to another dog doesn't mean that he or she is not a status-seeking dog. I've seen many dogs (females especially) who give extreme versions of submissive displays in some contexts, but then, as time moves on, or as the composition of the pack changes, they become the dog most likely to take over the top spot. Perhaps other dogs know perfectly well that these dogs are just biding their time, waiting for an opening, just as we often can tell social climbers even though they posture and grovel at our feet. Sometimes the people who make the most fuss to act submissive are the most status-conscious and the most interested in getting status for themselves. I had a student once at the university who all but kissed the hem of my skirt, praising every pearl of wisdom I had uttered that day.

While surrounding me with submissive words of appeasement, he moved closer and closer, demanding special attention that was far beyond what other students would dream of asking. (He wanted me to meet with him after each lecture and repeat the lecture to him word for word.) His behavior was such an amazing combination of appeasement and assertiveness that I coined a new phrase to describe it, *aggressively obsequious,* and now I use it to describe dogs, too.

I had a Border Collie bitch, Bess, who greeted new dogs to the farm in a classic high-status posture: her entire body, from her ears to her tail, was up and forward. She'd stand tall, as if stretching her body upward, and trot purposefully and assertively toward the newcomers. The arriving dogs immediately signaled their acceptance that they were visiting her territory and that she had rights that they didn't. They dropped their heads and tails, leaned their bodies backward rather than forward, and let Bess sniff them wherever she wanted to. But one day a big-boned Husky cross came to visit, and this time Bess met her match. As Bess trotted purposefully forward to greet the visitor, the Husky stood still and maintained her own tail-up/head-up posture. She exploded in a growl-bark when Bess went to sniff under her leg. In less than a quarter of a second, Bess had flattened herself on the ground, back legs spread in what's called an "inguinal presentation," forelegs cocked, head turned to the side. This time the visitor did the sniffing, and all the rest of that weekend, Bess treated the Husky like visiting royalty. They played and romped together, chased rabbits together, and slept side by side on the living room rug, but high-status Bess had instantly morphed into an obsequious groveler, constantly licking the lips of Queen Husky, bowing and scraping like the best of them. One morning I stood shoulder-to-shoulder with the other dogs, watching Bess grovel. After a few minutes of this, the dogs and I exchanged glances, just as you would with human friends. I can't begin to know what was in their heads, but I still wonder whether they were as amused as I was. If you'd only seen Bess around the Husky, you'd have described her as one of the most submissive dogs you'd ever seen. So remember Bess and the Husky, and don't assume that all dogs who give submissive displays want to be subordinate the rest of their lives, any more than aggressively obsequious people want to stay at the bottom of the social hierarchy.

Alpha Wanna-bes

Whether an individual is status-seeking is important to know, because the most aggression in social hierarchies in many species is among members of the beta group, the status-seeking individuals who have not achieved dominance but are jockeying for position. For example, dominant male wolves rarely join in when the pack's middle-ranking wolves attack the scapegoat of the group. This bullying is common in a wolf pack and is usually initiated by the "beta male," who is second in rank after the alpha. Researcher Erik Zimen reported that male wolves in the alpha position almost always "showed an unusual degree of tolerance." (He found that there was more than three times as much aggression from the beta males as from any other position in the pack.)

Aggression within the beta category of social status is common in many species with a social hierarchy, including humans. Any sociologist will tell you that the most tension and outright aggression in a corporation is in middle management, and primatologists who study apes and monkeys will tell you the same thing. Surely this makes intuitive sense when you think about the behavior of humans who are competing for power. Washington, D.C., isn't made up of the president and then a bunch of no-status followers. There's a large beta group of people constantly vying for power and position, and based on the news reports from our country's capital, it can get pretty toothy over there. Lots of people want to be at the top of the beta category, to be the one who has the dominant individual's ear—with free access to the throne, whether it's occupied by an alpha male or the president of the United States. I call it the Kissinger phenomenon, and I see it in dogs all the time.

The importance of status is also dependent on rankings of the individuals themselves. In wolves, for example, the rank differences are more pronounced among the high-status wolves and less distinct among the lower-ranking ones. In our own species, it seems that status becomes more important as an individual's social status increases. Which distinction is more important: the difference between winning the gold or the silver medal in the Olympics or coming in twenty-third or twenty-fourth in the same competition? If I won the gold and someone congratulated me on winning the silver, I'd correct her. But if the difference were between twenty-third or twenty-fourth, I'm not so sure that I would. The value of the resource matters, too. The same people whom I've seen graciously ignore discrepancies that lost them first place in a small herding dog trial don't hesitate to get loud if they feel they lost first place at a big, important competition.

Can Two Species Be in the Same Pack?

Given that rank is important to both humans and dogs, how does that affect our interactions with each other? It's not completely clear whether individuals of two different species, like humans and dogs, can merge into one social unit and hold different positions in a hierarchy. This question deserves a lot more attention from scientists, as well as from dog trainers and dog lovers. One night over cocktails, John Wright, another certified Applied Animal Behaviorist, and I thoroughly enjoyed debating each other over whether dogs envision humans as being part of their social hierarchy. He said no, I said yes, and by the second gin and tonic, we both thought that it mattered little who was right but that it was a great question. My own opinion is that dogs and humans can coexist within one social hierarchy because of the definitions of dominance and social status. If dominance is "priority access to resources" and confers more social freedom on one individual over the others, then it seems logical that individuals who live together in a house full of resources share the same problems as group-living animals anywhere. If you drop a pork chop between you and your dog, you are two individuals who both want the same thing that you don't want to share.

I commonly see dogs who challenge people in the family whom they probably perceive as lower-ranking (small, soft-voiced, nurturing females especially) but have never once challenged more authoritative family members. Additionally dogs greet humans with the same visual signals that they use when they greet members of their own species, heads down or up, tails stiff or wagging. Most dogs don't approach other species that way: they sniff them as objects of interest, play with them like toys (as Tulip does with lambs), or treat them like prey items. Of course, there are exceptions, but it's relatively rare for dogs to greet animals other than humans like social companions unless they live in the house with them. Dogs behave as though they see us as a part of their social circle, and it makes sense to me that they would. Even though we're of two different species, we live together, sleep together, eat together, and have conflicts over resources.

Although many of the serious cases that I see in which a dog has growled or bitten have little to do with dominance aggression, there are cases in which social status appears to be one of the factors that has led to trouble. The dog may not have been dominant, but that doesn't mean that social status was irrelevant. I suspect that a lot of the dogfights between dogs of the same household are about status, and I think that some of the bites that I see to owners are about conflicts over the social order. Dogfights within the home are most frequent and (and most injurious) between same-sex individuals (each sex often has its own rank order, as in wolves, sheep, horses, and many species of primates); fights commonly occur as an adolescent moves into maturity, when status becomes relevant; and fights often occur over resources like food, space, or attention. But the perception of social rank is complicated in a household that includes humans and dogs, because even the most spoiled of dogs has to wait for his human to open the door, get out the dog food, or get the leash. I suspect that most status-seeking dogs see themselves either as being high up in the beta category or as being in a complicated and fluid negotiation with their owner for the alpha position. If you have a dog like that, the next chapter will give you some ideas about how to be a benevolent leader while your dog learns to be patient and polite.

The Meek (and the Smart) Shall Inherit the Earth

There's one more aspect of social structure that needs to be understood by those of us who live with dogs, and Pip illustrates it well. Pip is without question the lowest on the social register at the farm and the one who's most afraid of conflict. She wouldn't challenge Tulip for a bone if she were starving. But last night, as all the dogs lay around me in the living room, Pip got the chew bone away from Tulip. While Tulip lay gnawing away in the center of the room, Pip lay 10 feet away and began to grin and thump her tail while she looked at Tulip. Keeping her head low and her lips pulled back submissively, she groveled her way across the floor, slowly and relentlessly getting closer and closer to Tulip. Eventually she ended up right beside her and began licking Tulip sloppily on the lips, her head still low, tail thumping. This kind of behavior, called active submission, is an appeasement display that inhibits aggression in polite dog society, so Tulip didn't growl at Pip, she just kept chewing on her bone and trying to ignore Pip's long, wet tongue. Pip kept it up, licking faster and faster, until Tulip finally shut her eyes and turned her head away. Tulip looked for all the world as we do when we want someone or something to just please go away. But just because Pip is submissive doesn't mean that she has no stamina. Pip kept it up, squirming and groveling and slopping her tongue all over Queen Tulip until Tulip finally got up and walked away. Victorious, Pip then settled down to a good, relaxed chew on the bone while I sat, jaw dropped, yet again amazed at Pip's ability to get what she wants in spite of her low rank in the hierarchy.

As Pip's success makes clear, social status isn't the only way to get what you want: stamina and appeasement work just as well sometimes. Pip's behavior is a good reminder of two important principles that all dog owners would do well to understand: First, social status is relevant in our relationship with dogs, but it's only one of many aspects of our interactions with them. With some dogs, especially the kind that aren't status-seeking, the attention that dominance has been given is out of proportion to its relevance. Second, for those dogs to whom social status is relevant, the last thing owners should be doing is using harsh, punishment-oriented training techniques. They are rarely necessary and should be considered unacceptable, just as it is no longer considered acceptable to beat wives or children. Keep in mind that there are basically three types of homes in which your dog can live: a home in which the humans use force and intimidation to get the dog to be obedient; a home in which your dog has all the social control and gets what he wants whenever he wants it; or a peaceful, harmonious household in which you are a wise, benevolent leader. You get to choose. Just remember, your dog can't.

8

PATIENT DOGS AND
WISE HUMANS

Your Dog Will Be Happier If You Teach Him
to Be Patient and Polite and If
You Behave Like a Benevolent Leader

Domino the Border Collie trotted into my office, politely came over to smell my hand, and then proceeded to sniff his way around the room. While he did, Beth and I talked about why she was here, although the purple-and-yellow bruises on her forearm were a clue. He had bitten her, not just once but repeatedly. Although the bites weren't deep, and her bruised arm was healing fast, the trust that she had once had in her dog was still severely injured.

Last week Domino wouldn't listen when Beth tried to call him away from barking at the window. His barking had become increasingly aggressive when people walked by the house with their own dogs. He was getting so agitated that Beth was afraid he would go through the window. (Her concern is not unreasonable; it's happened to two of my clients.) When Beth tried raising her voice to get Domino to stop bark-charging at the window, he paid no attention, so she took him by the collar and started to pull him away. In an instant he turned and bit her, not once but three times, and then went back to barking out the window. Beth was as shocked as she was hurt. She'd had dogs all her life and had never had one turn on her. Domino had been a delightful puppy and had been the love of her life for more than a year. Now he was maturing into a beautiful young dog, but she was growing increasingly afraid of him. Several times he'd turned and snapped at her when she took him by the collar, and now he'd bitten her. Last night he growled at her when she tried to push him over on the couch. Beth felt betrayed and scared by the behavior of the dog who used to be her best friend.

Just as we were concluding the interview part of our session, someone walked by the window to the office, a Bassett Hound schlumping alongside. Domino paused for an instant and then exploded at the window, his barks loud enough to hurt your ears. Beth visibly shrank back an inch or two. I said, "Oh, good!" because now I could see Domino in action. I walked over to him, careful to keep my hands to my side, and quietly observed him while he charged at the window. Beth hadn't been exaggerating: Domino really was "out of control." He wasn't just out of her control: he had worked himself up into such an aroused state that he was out of his own control. I have no doubt that if I had taken his collar, he would have whirled and bitten my arm just as he had Beth's the week before. His eyes were huge and round, and his pupils were fully dilated. His "hackles" were up (pilo-erected is the proper term) from his shoulders to his rump, a sure sign of high arousal in a dog. His mouth was open wide, his breathing short and fast, and his body seemed to be moving in at least three directions at once. It was ex-hausting just watching him. I let him be, curious to see how long it would take him to calm down after the passerby had moved away. It took him a full minute to stop barking and at least five minutes for his breathing to re-turn to normal.

Ask yourself, how would you describe Domino? Someone had told Beth that the bite to her arm was a clear example of "dominance aggression." But just because dogs bite doesn't mean that they're "dominant," as I hope was made clear in the last chapter. Another friend had suggested that Domino must have a serious aggression problem toward other dogs, since he only barked hysterically if there was a dog walking by the house. But Domino played well at the dog park and had lots of dog buddies in the neighborhood. Beth had never heard him growl at another dog unless he was at the window. Domino was the easiest dog to train that Beth had ever had and the star of obedience class. He seemed to adore Beth, following her everywhere, and was as affectionate as she was, as quick to lick her as she was to scratch him behind his ears. I needed more information to come to any conclusions, so I started working directly with Domino.

After Domino calmed down, I picked up a tennis ball, and Domino immediately crouched into the classic Border Collie stalking posture and played an intense game of fetch with me for a few minutes. I then purposefully hid the ball and turned my attention away from him and back to Beth. Domino, however, had no intention of quitting the game. He came over to me and nudged my arm. I studiously ignored him. He nudged again and followed it with a bark. I kept talking to Beth and told her to stay still and ignore Domino. Another bark, followed by another and another. Domino stood staring directly at me, barking one short bark over and over again, as dogs do when they are trying to get your attention. I let him continue because I wasn't training him, I was evaluating him, and I wanted to see what would happen if I didn't intervene. His barking got faster and lower-pitched, while he stared directly at me. I can't begin to say what is in the mind of a dog (or another person, for that matter), but at the moment Domino looked mad. Beth, on the other hand, looked nervous and kept asking me to throw the ball for him. Domino desperately wanted to play, and she desperately wanted Domino to be happy. She explained that the only way she could keep him exercised was to throw the ball in the house for him, something she could do while watching TV, working on the computer, or even talking on the phone. When he started barking at her to throw the ball, she couldn't get him to stop with her voice, but she'd learned that she could get peace and quiet by throwing the ball. As a result, ball play stopped at her house only when Domino got tired. Healthy one-year-old Border Collies don't understand the word tired very well, so Beth had an arm on her like a major league pitcher, and Domino got to play ball on demand, which was most of the evening.

Domino didn't just get ball play when he wanted it; he got petting when he pawed at Beth and treats when he barked at the kitchen cabinet. Domino reminded me of a child whining for dessert before dinner in a restaurant, whose beleaguered parents finally give in just to quiet him down. Domino had learned that demanding attention with rude, pushy behavior worked, *and if at first he didn't succeed, he could eventually get what he wanted if he just kept it up. As a result, Domino had grown up getting nearly everything he wanted, every time he wanted it.*

Kicking the Pop Machine

Any individual—human or canine—who grows up getting whatever he wants virtually every time that he wants it is going to mature into an individual who has no tolerance for frustration. After all, frustration derives from expectations. When we don't expect to get a reward each time that we try something, as at a slot machine, we don't get frustrated when our first efforts get no response. But if we expect a response, as when we put a dollar in the soda pop machine, we get frustrated if nothing happens. I read a news report a few years ago of someone who pulled out a handgun and shot a Coke machine because, after he put in his coins, the machine wouldn't produce a Coke. I've seen otherwise gentle people kicking pop machines, and I've been tempted to kick them myself on one or two occasions. (OK, OK, so I did it once myself.) Frustration is a recipe for aggression—just ask anyone who works with domestic abuse in families. Although most of us don't get violent as adults, frustration verging on aggression is a familiar emotion.

The same goes for Domino, whose hysterical barking out the window had as much to do with frustration as anything else. Domino didn't want to attack the other dogs when he first saw them out the window; he wanted to go outside to play with them. But he couldn't, so he started barking to get what he wanted. No matter how hard he barked, he still wasn't getting what he wanted, and he simply couldn't stand it. Domino was kicking the pop machine, and Beth had gotten in the way of his temper tantrum.

The acceptability of humans' and dogs' losing control of their emotions depends on their age. It's not alarming to see a two-year-old child screaming in a red-faced tantrum because her ice cream fell out of the cone onto the sidewalk. But as children mature, we expect them to learn to cope with the emotions of frustration and disappointment. If you saw a twelve-year-old boy having the same tantrum as a two-year-old, you'd pay a lot of attention, and if it were a thirty-year-old man, you'd clutch your children to your side and head for the car. We may feel like throwing a fit when we get frustrated, but most of us don't because we learned emotional control while we were growing up. If dogs are going to live as members of the family, they need to as well. Dogs who live independently from humans have no trouble learning to cope with not getting what they want: the difficulties of life take care of it for them. But for some of us, our love for our dogs results in their being so coddled that they never learn to tolerate frustration.

How a dog responds to our caretaking is based on his or her nature as an individual. Dogs, like people, are born with different personalities, and some dogs need to learn frustration tolerance more than others. Some dogs can be coddled all their lives and remain sweet and patient until they die. But then I'll see a wise, experienced dog owner who has never had a problem with a dog until she got Charlie, who has so little tolerance for frustration that he's making life miserable for everyone, including himself. So keep in mind that some dogs can be pampered without ever creating problems, but just as with people, most dogs need to learn how to cope with frustration.

Teaching dogs to tolerate disappointment is not always fun for owners, just as raising children is hard work. A lot of my clients have raised, or are busy raising, their own children, and they want their dogs to be the equivalent of grandchildren, sweet things to love and cherish without the hard work of setting boundaries and enforcing rules. It's extra difficult to say no to a begging dog, with those liquid brown eyes and that endearingly fluffy face. The primal feelings of nurturance that dogs elicit from us make it especially hard to deny a dog when she's begging for attention. Besides having all the visual characteristics that cue us to be nurturing, the dogs who live in our houses are dependent on us for their very lives and unable to use words to communicate. Like infants, they not only need constant care, but they also need us to figure out what it is that they need and provide it as best we can. But as our children get older, they don't need us to cater to them as much anymore, and neither do our dogs. But some people cater to their dog's every desire as if the dog remained infantile no matter what his age, with petting on demand, endless treats, and instant attention whenever the dog shows up to get it. Most of these people would never treat their children like that, carefully raising their kids to be polite members of the household. If you're not the kind of person who loves to cater to your dog, it might be tempting to laugh at people who do. But our tendency to be nurturing is not to be sneezed at; without it we'd be extinct. But as with everything else, if it's misplaced or excessive, it can create a problem.

It's a lot easier to stop catering to your dog when you're aware that, after about three years of age, she is a mature adult and perfectly capable of the emotional control that is necessary in all social animals. One client of mine was so appalled when I told her that the Lhasa Apso she'd been catering to for years was the equivalent of a thirty-five-year-old man sponging off her that she stood up in horror. Her fluffy, middle-aged friend, who'd been lounging on her lap in my office, tumbled indignantly (but harmlessly) to the floor. He had bitten his owner when she had taken his collar to pull him away from a food wrapper he'd found in the backyard. He was frustrated and had lost his temper when he couldn't get what he wanted. Dogs have their own ways of expressing frustration, lashing out with their mouths when they are overwhelmed with irritable emotions. Young children use their hands the same way that dogs use their mouths. Lucky for us adults that hands don't have any teeth in them.

It's simple to help your dog learn to cope with frustration and disappointment. Every time your dog comes over and begs for food or attention, just imagine a grown-up friend of yours walking up and saying, "*Yo! You!* Hey, Human, pet me, right *now!*" I'm not arguing that you shouldn't give your dog treats or attention when he wants it. I pet my dogs dozens of times a day when they come up for stroking. But don't do it because you feel that you have no choice. You do have a choice, and your dog needs you to exercise it on occasion. Think about what you had to learn growing up. Just because you wanted an ice cream cone didn't mean that you got it. Just because you'd enjoy a massage right now doesn't mean that your friend will drop what he or she is doing and rush to your side. So don't feel guilty if you don't feel like petting your dog right now. He can cope, honest. If he can't, then more petting is the last thing that he needs.

How you respond to your dog depends partly on his age. Just like people, younger dogs haven't yet learned how to control their emotions and desires, and it's up to us to help them. A lot of young dogs don't want petting or attention as much as they want activity, and they come up to their owners to get a game started. Of course, this is when many of us pet our dogs instead of going outside and playing with them. We're tired, and we finally got a chance to sit down, and we don't want to get up right then. So we pet our dog instead, gradually teaching her that although she can't get the exercise that she needs, at least she can mug us for a massage. The solution here is simple, although not necessarily easy. If you have a young, healthy dog, especially one who sleeps in a crate all day long, then either get yourself outside and exercise with your dog or find someone else to do it for you.

I say this because a large number of the behavioral problems that I see have their origin in boredom. Ironically the problem has gotten worse as we've taken more care of our dogs and stopped letting them run free. When I was growing up in the 1950s, we exercised our dog Fudge by opening the door in the morning. Fudge trotted over to the neighbors' house and collected a rough-coated Collie. The two of them joined up with a third dog and spent the morning supervising the children getting on the school bus, terrorizing the garbage men, chasing rabbits and lizards, and heaven knows what else. When Fudge came inside for the evening, there was no discussion about who was going to exercise the dog. She'd done it herself. Predictably there were dogfights and one tragic death of a dog killed by a car, so I would no more open the door in a suburb and let my dog wander now than I would a child. It's too dangerous for the dog and not respectful of other people and their property. But we can't expect dogs to be well behaved if they spend most of the day and all of the night in a crate, with a fifteen-minute-long leash walk as the highlight of their day.[1] So first things first. If you want your dog to stop pestering you, then give him what he needs *before* he has to pester you for it. But no matter how much exercise your dog needs, all dogs profit by learning how to cope with frustration. Here's an easy, benevolent way to help them learn some emotional control.

Enough Is Enough

All my dogs know "Enough," which means to stop whatever they're doing (like asking for petting or bugging me with the ball) and leave me in peace. It's easy to teach, and it's a wonderful way to let your dog know that as much as you love her, it's still your life. All you need to do is to say "Enough" in a low, quiet voice and then pat her briskly on the head two times. If she doesn't go away (which most dogs won't the first several times you do this), stand up and walk your dog away from the couch a few feet, using your body-blocking skills to back her away. Cross your arms and turn your head away to the side as you sit back down. If she comes right back as you sit down, "pat pat" on her head again and body-block her away a second time. When she returns, be sure to do a "look away" so that you're not making eye contact. (I'm always amused at how often we humans tell our dogs to go away and yet continue to make eye contact with them. Meanwhile, the dog is desperately looking at your face, trying to find the cue to what the heck it is that you're trying to communicate. If you turn your head away from your dog, you're saying that your interaction is over, and many dogs will seemingly understand and go away. If you

---

1. This would be a lot easier if the current interest in working and herding dogs as pets (Border Collies and Blue Heelers, to name a couple) would fade away. Border Collies, because of their medium size and their willingness to work as a team, have become increasingly popular pets, but they are as ill suited to most households as are mountain goats. They were bred to work the rough terrain of Scotland, running every day on expansive hillsides so green and round that they make your heart sing (and your legs ache). If you don't come home from work and put on jeans and go outside for a couple of hours where your dog can safely run free, don't get a Border Collie. Gardening in the yard while your Border Collie sniffs for rabbits doesn't count. To be sane, these dogs need to run for hours and use their capable brains to solve problems. I see a heartbreaking number of snarling, whirling, hysterical Border Collies in my office, and most of them would have been fine if they'd lived where they could exercise both their minds and their bodies as they were bred to do.

keep staring at him, using words to tell him to go away, he'll keep staring back at you, sure that you are trying to visually communicate something important and desperately trying to figure out what it is by looking at your face.)

These two little "pat pats" that I suggested are an important part of the signal. When visitors to my own home first found themselves with four large muzzles pressing into their lap, I wanted to find an action that I was sure that my company would readily use. I tried other ways for my guests to signal "Enough" (as in "Go away"), but none of them worked very well. The dogs learned the cues, but the visitors wouldn't use them, no matter how much they wanted the dogs to go away. I eventually learned that all my visitors were comfortable saying "Enough" and going "pat pat" on my dogs' heads when they were ready for a little less doggy breath in their face. Even dogs in training classes withdraw when their owners pat them on the head, although until they learn better techniques, the hapless owners are usually trying to praise the dog for doing something right.

This time there's a useful result to our primatelike tendency to pat dogs on top of their heads, so we might as well take advantage of it. It's the perfect situation: humans are quick to pat dogs on top of their heads, but dogs don't really like it (remember that patting is not the same as stroking: most dogs adore massagelike strokes just as we do). A wolf handler reinforced the usefulness of this technique when she told me that she and the other handlers got wolves to stop bugging them by patting them on the head two or three times. It's not aggressive or threatening, it's just mildly aversive, so both dogs and wolves decide to go elsewhere (probably to the person sitting next to you!).

My nieces call these pats "happy slappies." They coined the phrase after coming to watch a taping of "Petline," an animal behavior advice show on Animal Planet that I cohosted with my ex-husband Doug McConnell. They were visiting the set and watched in horror as a guest veterinarian swooped into the studio dressed like a Las Vegas showgirl. She deposited her tiny dog onto the rug, where he promptly urinated, defecated, and almost killed a visiting cockatiel while she changed into what became known as the "killer bee outfit." Clothed in yellow-and-black striped Lycra (the producer eventually forced her to change), she asked to borrow my Luke for a demonstration of brushing a dog's teeth. Luke is a trooper, so I said sure.

Luke had to sit and stay on top of a table while directors, four cameramen, and the usual herd of assistant producers swirled around getting ready to tape. Finally it was time to roll the cameras. Our guest veterinarian explained to the audience the importance of brushing a dog's teeth, and then, without so much as a word or a friendly touch, grabbed Luke's mouth and opened it as you'd open up your purse on a busy, hot day when you can't find your wallet. Luke's eyes got huge while I soundlessly mouthed "Good boy, good boy" and held out my hand in the universal "stay" signal behind the camera. After abusing Luke's mouth for a couple of minutes (I'd have bitten my own dentist if he'd been that rude), she turned to Luke and slapped him twice on top of the head to thank him. Little did she know that we had just taped a segment that explained how most dogs hate being slapped on top of their head in exactly the way that she had just illustrated. The entire crew burst into belly laughs, and we had to tape it again (minus the slaps). Poor Luke, bless his patient, benevolent heart.

The next day my creative nieces, Annie and Emily Piatt, wrote and acted out a satire of the show in which they devised a mechanical pancake turner that slaps your dog upside the head to praise him for obeying you. They called it the Happy Slappy, so I advise owners to use happy slappies to get a friendly dog to go away. It's the last thing you should do if you're around a dog that you don't know or that might be afraid of people—remember how scary it is for shy dogs to have people reach over their heads. But if you have a friendly goofball in your face and you'd like a little break, then say "Enough" in a low voice and give him a few happy slappies on top of his head. You may have to follow it up with a few body blocks and turning your head away, but it works better than anything else I've ever tried.

Please don't think I'm suggesting that you stop giving your dog attention. I slather attention on my four dogs like butter on hot corn. But I decide when to do it, and I don't reinforce rude and pushy behavior by mindlessly petting them when they jab their muzzles into my arm. It's not easy, because Luke is a pro at soliciting the attention that he adores. Luke's favorite events are banquets, where he gets to schmooze around the room, getting chicken and massages from every table because of his gentlemanly demeanor and his elegant mane of white fur ruffled around his chest. He looks something like Rhett Butler at a ball, and he fits in well at fancy banquet dinners. It didn't take him long to learn that he could keep massages going by nuzzling diners when they stopped petting him. If nuzzles didn't work, inserting his muzzle under an arm and pushing up quickly did, since this technique tends to spill drinks or send silverware flying. It's hard to eat when your utensils are launched skyward, so diners would give up on their rubber chicken and stroke Luke again instead.

Luke tried to bring this technique home, but it's the last thing that I want to encourage. Luke is eleven years old now, a grown-up, mature male who has no business acting like a puppy. But it'd be a lot easier if I weren't a human—a primate who is hardwired to groom others endlessly and to seek out touch as moths do light. Like a lot of people, I love petting my dogs. Not only am I a primate, I'm an especially cuddly one at that. I go to sleep petting my cat Ayla, who's purring on my chest. I get on the floor in the evening and spoon with all of my dogs, making contact with as much of their bodies as I can. I love holding hands at the movies. But I don't need a dog who gets what he wants for being pushy. Nor do I need to treat Luke like a fragile infant, who truly requires attention on demand. So I don't pet Luke if he nudges me. I am careful to pet him when he's being polite instead of pushy. Sometimes when he mugs me for massages, I turn my head away, careful to keep my nose up like a valley girl so that I look dismissive rather than coy. When I really want to pet him but he's being a pest, I ask him to do something, like "sit" or "bow," so that I can pet him as a reinforcement for good behavior rather than bad.

You can also help your dog learn to stop pestering you and entertain himself by giving him a hollow toy stuffed with food after he goes to settle down. Don't leap up and give him a chew toy the instant that he comes over to beg. That's just teaching him that begging is even more productive than he thought. Rather, say "Enough" when he scratches at your leg (or whatever his version of making demands is) and body-block him away. Once he lies down and settles himself, get up (stay quiet, no need to talk) and give him the toy stuffed with treats that you efficiently have stored in the kitchen for just this very moment. Put it down right where he had settled, even if he's gotten up to follow you out of the room. Now your dog has learned that it pays to settle down on the floor instead of working you like a slot machine. This is especially helpful for young dogs who can barely contain themselves, the equivalent of giving young children something to do with their hands while you finish your meal in a restaurant. Smart parents don't wait for trouble; they head it off at the pass by giving their children something appropriate to do rather than waiting for them to get attention by doing something wrong. You can do the same for your dog and have more time to relax.

Mind Your Manners at the Door

You'd be appalled if you visited a home where the children knocked you over while running out the door, yet many of us let our dogs do just that. It's not that I don't love exuberance, I do. But just as we teach our children that there's a time and a place for everything, it makes sense that we should expect that of our dogs, too. If dogs are going to be part of our "family," then we have to raise them to be polite.[2] Just because they're dogs instead of children is no reason to think that their going into a frenzy is cute. If they're going to live with us, dogs need to learn impulse control and some good, old-fashioned patience. In the wild their own family would teach

2. Teaching manners to dogs at the door has become controversial in the world of dog training. Who goes out the door first is significant in human social interactions, and some people think that it is for dogs, too, while other trainers and behaviorists don't. We do know that doorways are significant to humans: we tend to let those whom we hold in high regard go through them first. My own guess, having heard hundreds of clients describe dogfights at doorways, is that there *is* some social relevance to dogs. What I am sure about is that doorways are another situation in which dogs can either learn to manage their excitement or let their emotions get the best of them.

them manners, so don't abdicate your responsibility as an elder and encourage your dog to act like a baby when he's become a grown-up.

Keep in mind, though, that the importance of this exercise depends a lot on the personality of your dog. Some mellow or extremely submissive dogs would never dream of barging out the door in front of you. If your dog is like that, put this book down for a minute and go tell him how special he is. All dogs are not like him, honest. Other dogs enjoy illustrating why clipping is illegal in football: many of my clients have been badly hurt after their dog upended them while charging out the door. (I think the count is three knee surgeries, two sets of broken bones, and one concussion.) I've had more cases in which dogs have gotten into horrible fights at the door, like overly excited fans at a ball game. I know of dozens of dogs who bolted out the doorway and disappeared for hours or days. Some of these dogs ended up being killed by cars or being the subject of nasty lawsuits, so good manners at the door isn't a trivial issue for dogs or the humans who love them.

It's relatively easy to teach dogs to be polite at the door. One of the reasons why I suspect that doorways have some special significance to dogs is that they seem to catch on quickly how to behave at the door, while exercises like heeling take months of work. (There's nothing relevant to a dog about heeling. My own translation of *heel* from a canine perspective is: "Walk slowly at the pace of death by your owner's knee while ignoring all interesting things.") You don't need to use food or toys for this training, because access to the great outdoors is its own reward. If Fido behaves politely, he gets to go outside, which is what he wanted in the first place. If he doesn't, he doesn't. Simple enough, and simple is always good when both humans and dogs are learning something new.

Start by deciding what signal you're going to use to ask your dog to pause at the doorway. We use "Wait" in our training classes, but I use "Mind" myself (short for "Mind your manners") because "Wait" sounds too much like one of my herding signals. Just pick a word that doesn't sound like the other signals that you use and be consistent with it. Remember to use a quiet but low voice and to say the word as if it were a statement rather than a question. ("Wait?" said like a question translates to something like: "Would you consider waiting? Are you going to listen this time, huh? Maybe? Please?")

For safety's sake, if the door that you're going to use for training goes to an unfenced area, be sure to have your dog on a leash. Don't, however, use the leash to pull your dog back from the door, because doing so will cause your dog to pull toward the door even harder. The muscles of all mammals work against opposing forces, so whenever you pull on a dog, you cause him automatically to pull back. If you pull steadily back on the leash, you aren't training your dog to stop pulling forward, you're encouraging it. So keep the leash loose while you're doing your training at the door, although I'll be the first to warn you that it's not always easy. It's so tempting for us to pull on a leash when it's in our hand that it works better to have someone else hold the leash while you work on "wait" at the door. You can also tie the leash to a railing or to your belt if it's a small dog, so that you won't use it to try pulling your dog away from the door. It should be your body that keeps the dog from rushing out the door, not the leash.

Once you get to the door, move yourself in front of your dog, so that you're between the door and your dog. Stand facing your dog, with your back to the door, so that you can see what she's doing and respond to it. If she's crowded up against the door (which most dogs will be), back her away by moving directly toward her, herding her with body blocks away from the door. Do this quietly and gently, moving forward with small, quiet steps so that she has no choice but to back up. If she tries to dart around you, move quickly to the right or left to block her with your body. Just keep imagining yourself as a goalie whose job is to keep the ball from entering the goal. Once you have quietly and gently moved her back about 3 to 4 feet from the door, back yourself up toward the door and give a signal like "Mind" or "Wait" in a low, even-toned voice, and then partly open the door.

What you do next depends on your dog's behavior. Most dogs dart forward when they see the door open (or even when you move back toward the door), so be ready to use your body to block the path to the door. Concentrate on not repeating your verbal signal (not surprisingly, this takes some practice at first) and just using your body to impede her forward progress. Some people prefer to close the door before a dog can get through it rather than using their body to stop the dog. This teaches the dog that if she tries to charge through, the door will shut before she gets there, but if she sits and waits patiently, it opens. If you use this method, be sure not to slam the door on your dog. I've seen it happen, so my preference is to use my body to block the doorway, but both methods work. Once your dog has paused (either simply stopping her forward movement or, ideally, stopping and looking up at you), even just for a microsecond, say "OK" and let her out the door. Timing is everything here. It's critical to reinforce your dog when she first takes the pressure off the door, so watch her carefully and be ready to open the door when she first pauses even just the littlest bit. As time goes on, you can expect her to do a better and better job of being patient, but in the beginning help her win by being observant and being ready to release her as soon as she does anything even approaching what you want.

While you are working on this, resist the oh-so-human urge to drape yourself over the doorway to protect it. You want your dog to learn to make a choice for herself: she needs to learn the consequences of waiting or trying to make a break for it. Leave the path through the doorway clear, but stand right beside it and be ready to move into it if you need to. If your dog chooses to wait (good girl!), be ready to release her by saying her name in a lilting, singsong tone of voice or using your usual release word like "OK" or "Free." If she tries to bolt through, use your body to block her and then give her another chance to pause. Most dogs catch on incredibly fast, because they learn that if they wait politely, they get to go outside, and if they try to charge through, they get stopped.

Let me warn you now about the most common mistakes that people make so that you can work to avoid them:

- Repeating the verbal signal over and over again (think chimp). Concentrate on saying it just once and then letting your body do the rest.
- Using the leash to stop the dog rather than your body (again, another very human thing to do: it's almost impossible not to do something with a leash in our hand). Use your body, not the leash.

- Walking or leaning forward toward your dog when he has already stopped moving toward the door. Remember that body blocks are very powerful visual signals, and the microsecond that your dog stops leaning forward and putting pressure toward the door (you can feel it even if you're not touching the dog), you should respond instantly by stopping your own forward motion. Continuing to move or lean forward puts too much pressure on your dog and will create its own problems.

Don't confuse your use of "Wait" with "Stay." "Stay" means that your dog needs to remain in one exact location until being released, while "Wait" means that your dog can't move *forward* until released. If you say "Wait" and your dog turns away from the door entirely, that is absolutely fine. "Wait" basically means "Don't proceed *forward* without further instructions." You can certainly use "Stay" at the door if you'd like, and it is another good way to stop your dog from barging out the door, but it's a different concept ("Don't move until I tell you"). I prefer teaching "Wait" in this context, because I think it's good for dogs to figure out how to inhibit their impulses for themselves rather than letting us make all their decisions for them.

Oh, He's Just So Friendly!

You don't have to let your dog dance all over your head, honest. If you like it when your dog jumps up to greet you, that's fine, but there's no reason that your dog should be so disrespectful of you that he knocks you over. Other dogs would never permit such rude behavior, and you shouldn't either. One of the first dogs that I ever worked with was Duke, a huge, floppy-eared Doberman Pinscher that his elderly owner, Edith, had gotten for protection. Duke grew up the first year of his life with a lot of love but no boundaries, and when I met him at the front door, he rose up and slapped his huge paws onto my shoulders. After almost knocking me over (Duke had flattened several of Edith's elderly friends), Duke proceeded to race around the living room, leaping over tables and chairs, knocking down lamps and books in an excited frenzy until he finally settled on my lap on the couch, paws again on my shoulders while he slurped his tongue across my face. Meanwhile, Edith laughed until she cried and told me how much she loved Duke's friendliness. But if Duke had pulled that greeting routine with dogs at the dog park, he would've been a social pariah within seconds. Silly young puppies are taught by their elders that it's not polite to leap onto another's head and be oblivious of his personal space. There's no reason that dogs shouldn't learn to be respectful of your personal space, too.

I wouldn't want to see a dog forced to do a sit/stay every time he greeted a human any more than I want to see children curtsy when adults enter the room. But social animals all have an awareness of the personal space around others, and as they mature, they learn to be polite about not barging into others' faces, even when they're excited. It's actually very easy to teach dogs to be polite when they greet you or when they want to come cuddle up on the couch. You just have to stop acting like a human and learn to move like a dog. Rather than backing up when a friendly but rude dog lunges toward you, use the body blocks that we talked about in Chapter 2 to protect the personal space around you. Say you're seated on a chair and Duke is moving across the room at the speed of light. It's clear that in three strides he's going to launch himself into your lap. Instead of doing what comes naturally, which is to lean backward to avoid the furry missile (which creates a space for the dog to move into), lean forward with your chest and shoulders and meet him more than halfway. Avert your face, keep your hands tucked into your belly, and use your shoulders and torso to block the dog from entering the circle of space around you.

Once he's stopped trying to climb into your lap, reinforce him with petting, praise, treats, or play when all four of his paws are on the ground. You usually have to repeat the body blocks a few times before all four paws will actually stay on the floor, but it's amazing how many dogs drop leaping up at you from their repertoire. Some people feel guilty about stopping their dogs from leaping all over them. They shouldn't, unless they allow grown-up humans to sail onto their head and shoulders whenever they feel like it. If you like it when your dog jumps up to greet you, go ahead, let her do it, but don't let your dog behave as though she can barrel into humans with no consideration for their safety or personal space. That's not friendly; it's just rude.[3]

The Sound of Silence

Another thing that we can all do to help our dogs behave like polite members of our family involves virtually no dog training whatsoever. If you're like most of us, you might have to teach *yourself* something, though, and as all trainers know, people are harder to train than dogs. It is truly simple, however, and it is this: shut up.

OK, maybe that's a little blunt, but the fact is that we tend to talk so much to our dogs that we not only confuse them, we overstimulate them and sometimes scare them. Lest you think I'm being rude, please know that I include myself in the category of people who would profit by being quieter around their dogs. We humans are relentlessly verbal primates, and there are times when I chatter like an idiot to my dogs. Worse, I sometimes raise my voice, getting louder and louder if my dogs aren't doing what I want them to, until I get hold of myself and start acting like a good dog trainer. Certainly every year I get better about using a quiet voice with my dogs, and it's rare now that I raise my voice when I shouldn't. But it still happens on occasion, because it's very human to get loud when we get frustrated, and as we saw in Chapter 1, it seems to be a trait that we share with our relatives the chimps. But although Mike the chimpanzee may have risen to dominance on a dramatic crescendo of clanging metal tins, getting loud isn't going to teach your dog much about being patient and polite.

We talked earlier about the value of staying quiet but using a low pitch

3. Lots of dog trainers confess sheepishly to one another that they let their own dogs jump up on them—it's so much easier than bending down to pet them. Most of us teach our clients not to allow it because it's harder to teach a dog that she can jump up at some times but not others. My own dogs will stand up to say hi and rest their paws on you if you say "Be bad," but not unless you ask them. I think that's ideal, but it takes some serious training.

when you want your dog to respond, but here I want to talk about what effect yelling has on your dog's perception of you. Getting loud may get your dog's attention, just as it would get the attention of students in a classroom, but what message does yelling convey about you? Yelling makes you look scary and out of control. It might get your dog's attention, but it doesn't make you look like a calm, collected leader, and it doesn't model the behavior that you'd like to see from him. It can make your dog worse in the short run and cause him to lose faith in you in the long run. I speak from experience. As I mentioned earlier, when I first started working herding dogs on sheep, I was quick to get anxious when things started to feel out of control. That was about 95 percent of the time. That high-pitched, nervous voice was like pouring gasoline on a fire, and Drift, my first Border Collie, would clench his teeth and run at the sheep even harder. I spent an entire summer teaching myself to use a quiet, calm voice in times of sheepherding excitement. I can do it now about 90 percent of the time, maybe a little more, but some handlers can speak calmly to dogs even when the sheep are thundering out of control, the dog looks as if he's about to leap up and eat one, and the entire fracas is taking place beside a busy highway. These people are like gods to me, and I try to spend as much time as possible beside them in the hope that it rubs off.

Dogs seem to love people who are quiet, cool, and collected and prefer sitting beside them over sitting beside others. We humans, too, are attracted to those rare individuals who have a dignified and quiet sense of power about them. One of the people I know with that aura is Julie Simpson, the first woman to win the Supreme Championships of the International Sheep Dog Society in Great Britain. She doesn't say much to a dog, and when she does, it's usually softly spoken, but she radiates a sense of inner peace and confidence. The dogs in the training clinic that she gave listened to her when she was a hundred yards away and speaking quietly. You may not be able to generate the kind of respect that Julie can, but you can get your dog to pay more attention to you if you radiate quiet confidence rather than using a loud voice all the time.

Be thoughtful about what you say to your dog and teach yourself to go closer to your dog to get his attention rather than raising your voice from a distance away. Think about Ghandi and the Dalai Lama. Breathe. Smile. Be comfortable setting boundaries, as all good teachers are. Having a dog who respects you as a quiet, confident leader that he can count on is a wonderful feeling, every bit as good as having a dog who loves you. Lucky us, we can have both at the same time, and part of it is learning to simply say less rather than more.

Benevolent Leadership

Leader is another loaded term in dog training. The concept of dominance has been so misused and misunderstood that even the word *leadership* has fallen out of favor in some circles. That's a shame, because most social animals profit from the wisdom of a wise leader. Teaching dogs to be patient and polite while acting like a loving, benevolent leader has helped hundreds of my clients who were having trouble with their dogs. I don't know whether the problems between some of my clients and their dogs were because of their social relationships or because the dogs had no frustration tolerance, but the suggestions presented in this chapter can positively affect both. Perhaps the owner starts to act more like a benevolent leader and, as with troubled adolescent boys who finally find a wise, older mentor, that action itself results in better behavior. Or perhaps the dogs learn that they can get what they want by being patient and polite rather than rude and pushy and learn to deal with frustration without becoming aggressive or out of control.

I'd argue that it depends on the dog. Every dog is different: some are truly status-seeking and do better when their owners provide leadership; others can't regulate their own emotions and have no impulse control and need to learn patience. The most problematic dogs that I see are a combination of both—easily aroused dogs with no emotional control who are reactive to any perceived challenge to their own social position. On the other hand, some dogs are so benign—"peopleproof," I call them—that we couldn't mess them up if we tried. If you have one of those, read the rest of this chapter as an interesting intellectual exercise and smile be-musedly over the rest of us, who own normal dogs.

Whose House Is It, Anyway?

Even though dog trainers have overplayed the importance of social status in the past, it is still relevant in some cases. I've had clients whose dogs controlled all the social interactions: they barked when the owners were on the phone; demanded attention if another dog came up to say hi; de-cided when to play, when to get petted, and when to get fed. How and when your dog gets attention is not always just about learning patience and a tolerance for frustration. It's also an important aspect of social rela-tionships, because who can get attention on demand depends on their rank in the social hierarchy. High-status chimps, bonobos, humans, and wolves, to name a few species, are always the center of visual attention of the group. High-ranking individuals get to decide whether to accept a subordinate's solicitation of social contact or not. Subordinates may initi-ate contact more often, but the one with the higher rank gets to decide when and if to interact. Low-ranking Pip continually tries to get Queen Tulip's attention by licking her muzzle and groveling at her feet. Most of the time Tulip looks away, refusing to give Pip the canine equivalent of the time of day. (My friend Beth Miller reminded me of how the same scenario is acted out on playgrounds around the country, with the "cool" kids snubbing the "losers" at recess.) Think about how these asymmetri-cal social interactions play out at your house. If your dog gets all the at-tention and controls all the interactions, then it's possible that she interprets your behavior as supportive of her as a high-status member of the group. Some dogs insist on controlling who touches whom and when. Some of these dogs show no respect for the personal space of their own-ers, leaping onto their laps and getting "in their face" whenever they feel like it. They also often decide when and where they can be touched and may growl at their owners if the owners initiate contact. Look again at grooming interactions in a variety of species. In most social species, the lower-status animals groom the higher-status one, not vice versa. If your dog can demand that you drop everything you're doing and pet him on demand, then in his mind you've no business taking away the pork chop that you drop later that night.

Status-seeking dogs might take possession of all the objects in the house, including the bed, it being one of the prize objects in a household to both humans and dogs. Until I started working as an Applied Animal Behaviorist, I had no idea how many people couldn't get back into bed after going to the bathroom. Who would've guessed that the country is full of men wandering around the house at night because their wife's dog won't let them back in bed after they got up to pee? It's sort of amusing in a stand-up-comic kind of way, but not so funny when those threats turn into bites. (Some people still think it's funny. I'll never forget the look on one husband's face as his wife guffawed over the last bite he'd received from her Lhasa Apso. She thought it was hysterical, even though his arm looked like fresh hamburger. He and I were not so amused. My first suggestion involved a marriage counselor.)

Even though I think dominance aggression is usually an incorrect description of what's going on with a dog, there are cases in which social status is relevant. Some of the problems that I see are not so much about dogs who are "dominant" as about dogs who simply live in a state of confusion about who's who. Sometimes they seem to have the most social freedom, while other times the humans do. If this is true, if in some households there's no clear leader, then there is value in clarifying the social relationship between human and dog. If dogs live in a world in which they perceive themselves as high in status but in that tension-filled "beta" category, then, based on what we know about social hierarchies, they are more likely to obsess about status and try to move up in the world.

My favorite way to work with status-seeking dogs is to teach them that social status isn't all that important at their house, because they can get what they want by being patient and polite rather than pushy and status-conscious. If owners can remember that neither humans nor dogs need to have social status to feel loved, then they can create a more harmonious household in which their dogs feel cherished but aren't trying to improve their position in the hierarchy. It's stressful in middle management, so do dogs like this a favor and don't confuse them with mixed messages. Keep in mind that this only applies to dogs who are status-seeking and that a large number of dogs wouldn't try to move up on the social register if you soaked it in liver juice. If you pay attention to the suggestions in this chapter and expect your dog to learn to be patient and polite as he matures, you'll avoid many of the problems that status-seeking dogs can create.

Spare the Rod and Have a Better Dog

You don't need to use physical force to impress your dog. If you do, you're sending the message that you have no real power and no alternative but force and intimidation. It's sad that it is taking us so long to drop the threat of physical injury from our training repertoire, no matter what the species. You may get obedience out of a dog by threatening him, but mostly you're going to get a dog who is afraid of you. Far too often, you'll get a dog who learns to defend himself by getting aggressive back. Aggression leads to more aggression, and many of the dog bites that I see were made in self-defense. However, there are other dogs who love a good fight and can't wait for you to "make their day." You may win the battle with these dogs, but you're not going to win the war, and who wants a battlefield in their living room, anyway?

It's bad enough that we use unnecessary amounts of violence in training, but it's especially problematic because our dogs don't perceive it as discipline. Dogs are disciplined by their elders with a swift, inhibited bite across their muzzle, a behavior I strongly suggest that you do *not* replicate. Trust me: you could never do it fast enough, you probably wouldn't be able to do it with the intensity that another dog would, and you would end up getting bitten yourself. Almost as bad, you'll get a mouthful of dog hair. Dogs do not discipline other dogs by biting at the scruff of their neck: bites to that area are about challenges to the hierarchy or are the equivalent of barroom brawls. Some dogs can be effectively corrected with scruff shakes, but that doesn't mean that you should do them yourself. When and where to use a physical punishment on a dog is one of the hardest things to learn in dog training, and it's the last thing that people who haven't had a lot of training themselves ought to try.

Many people use force because of the myth about "getting dominance" over their dogs. But yelling at a dog, reaching for her collar, and shaking her is a very primate kind of thing to do, not something that she will inherently understand. It might make her afraid of you, and it might make her pay a lot of attention to you, but it won't teach her what you'd like her to do. Giving a dog a hard jerk on her collar is like rapping a child's hand in school when she gets the wrong answer. It may make the child afraid of making a mistake, but it doesn't do anything to teach her the right answer. Because aggression does work on some dogs in some cases, some people use those successes to justify harsh treatment of all dogs under all circumstances. But just because something that is wrong and cruel is sometimes successful is no reason to advocate it. You can torture and intimidate people to get them to do what you want, and if you use enough force and control, it will work. That doesn't make it acceptable.

Correcting Your Dog

In my experience people usually get physical with their dogs when the dogs do something "wrong." Most of my clients who hit or shook their dogs honestly didn't know what else to do. It's no good to tell people not to get rough with their dogs and then give them no alternative, so here's an alternative that works for almost all dogs and almost all people.[4]

If your dog is doing something that you don't want her to do, your job is to do two things. First, stop her from doing what she's doing by startling her. You don't have to hurt her or terrorize her, just interrupt her by

---

4. There is virtually no piece of advice that I can think of that works for every dog ever born. The best anyone who gives advice in limited space can ever do is play the odds by giving advice that works in the most cases, most of the time.

making a noise that evokes what is called the mammalian startle response. If you slap the wall or the table, drop a paperback book, or toss an empty pop can with a few pennies in it on the floor, she should momentarily look up to see what the noise was about. Like lightning, you're going to take advantage of her attention and redirect it onto doing what you *want* her to do. Say, for example, that your eight-month-old Labrador is chewing on the coffee table. Your job is to interrupt that behavior and instantly redirect her to doing something appropriate, like gnawing on the chew toy that you spent a fortune on last night. Say "No" in a low, *quiet* voice and immediately make a sound to startle her. In the microsecond that she looks up, say "Good girl" to praise her for stopping what she was doing, smooch or click your tongue to keep her attention on you, and then redirect her attention to something more appropriate.

The key is to be prepared to take advantage of that half a second (or less) of attention that you're going to get when she looks up. It won't last long, and most beginners lose the moment by staring back at their dog while deciding what to do next. Their dogs figure that there's nothing interesting going on, so why not go back to chewing on the table leg? Be ready to act the microsecond that your dog looks up, and you'll find this working like a charm. It sounds simple, but as with all dog training, it takes some practice, because the timing of your responses needs to be in sync with your dog's behavior. Work on responding to your dog's actions as quickly as you can. Even if your timing isn't Olympian yet, you're going to be way ahead of the game if you remember the basics: interrupt the problem behavior and *immediately* redirect it to something else.

However, if your dog is absolutely committed to what she's doing—say, barking out the window at the neighbor's mutt who loves to taunt her—then there's probably no sound you can make that's going to get her attention. In cases like that, give up trying to get louder and louder from across the room and go over closer to her. I like to lure dogs away from contexts like that with a treat held right up to their nose, like luring a donkey with a carrot, and then ask them to do something else when they're away from all the excitement. In some cases dogs are so excited that it helps to quietly put their leash on and use that and food lures to help them move away from the focus of their attention. Then ask your dog to "Sit pretty" or "Go get your big ball" or "Go upstairs and wake up _____" (fill in the name of that other person in the house who always lets you get up to take the dog out). Once she learns that your voice is a predictor of something even more fun than what she's doing, you can drop out the food lure as your dog improves.

These suggestions are not substitutes for a complete dog training manual or good video, or better yet, a good dog training class where you'll have a coach to help you out. But if you can get into the habit of interrupting your dog from doing what you *don't* want and simply redirecting him to what you *do* want him to do, both you and your dog will be much happier. It seems very human to stay fixated on the negative: "No!" seems to come out of our mouths as easily as breathing. But saying no doesn't teach a dog what *to* do, and it keeps the attention focused on it and nothing else. If I said, "Stop thinking about red. Now, I mean it, *don't think about red!*" how easy would it be? But if I said, "Don't think about red; think about blue—beautiful, cool blue. Think blue!" wouldn't it be easier to stop thinking about . . . What was that other color again? There are an infinite number of things that your dog can do wrong but only a few that he can do right. Why don't you make life easy and teach your dog what right is rather than continually saying no to yet one more thing that is wrong?!

So when your dog is doing something wrong, say "No" quietly, use another sound to startle him to get his attention, and then redirect him on to doing something that he should be doing. Don't think about physically punishing him; think about teaching him. Replace the hot, red aggression of old-fashioned dog training with the calm, cool benevolence of sky blue. It's a lovely color.

9

PERSONALITIES

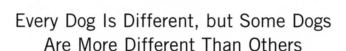

Every Dog Is Different, but Some Dogs Are More Different Than Others

I am writing this ten minutes after Luke almost died. I'm overwhelmed with the agony of what almost happened and the relief that it didn't. I can barely type right now; my fingers are stiff, and I'm starting to shake. I cannot bear the thought of Luke's dying, and the knowledge that he nearly died a tragic death just a few minutes ago has stunned me as if I'd been slammed into a wall.

My neighbors brought Luke home after finding him in the road about a quarter of a mile away from the farm, walking in the center of the right lane of the county highway that runs by my farm. He was on top of a steep hill that comes right after a sharp curve. The speed limit is 55, but people are people, and many of my neighbors go a lot faster. Visibility is poor on this section of the road, and four or five times a year people hit deer there and then knock on my door at two in the morning to call the sheriff, while I peer out the window behind the deep barks of Luke and Tulip. On this particular morning, the road was especially busy, the usual morning traffic dodging a parade of gravel trucks that roared back and forth to a construction site.

Luke is eleven years old. Neither he nor any of my other Border Collies has ever been in the road in his life. I could leave Luke, Lassie, or Pip outside loose for hours (although I don't), and they would curl up on the porch. They've been carefully trained to stay away from the road, and because of their train-

ing and their personalities, they haven't set a paw in it. Deer can rush out of my garden and tear across the road with their white tails flashing, and even if the dogs are in hot pursuit, they'll stop at the road. They ignore bicyclists, joggers, and cars, although they barked big-eyed once when a horse and rider went by. Even Tulip will stay away from the road. It admittedly took me years to train her: she is a Great Pyrenees designed to work independently, and a particularly headstrong one at that, but as long as I'm out with her, Tulip will stop at the edge of the road, even if she's chasing a deer. But I'd never leave Tulip loose outside alone, because she would eventually go on a wander, and it's simply not worth the risk.

Unlike Great Pyrenees, Border Collies come from a long line of farm dogs who stay by the farmhouse waiting to do the chores—until this morning, when, as best as I can tell, Luke ran away from home. As usual, Luke and the other Border Collies had been outside, where I let them out every morning to potty before we go down to the barn to tend to the sheep. I was on the phone to the office, when a crew of workers drove up to complete the job of ripping off my roof and replacing it with a new one. It's a horrible project, dirty and noisy, and all of us were suffering from it. Listening to eight hours of pounding every day is bad enough, but it's particularly disorienting when it comes from the very cover over your den. To make matters worse, we were having a hateful heat wave, with the temperature and humidity both in the high 90s. It was so bad that one of my lambs had died of the heat, so I couldn't possibly have left the dogs in the car or in the barn. With few alternatives I decided to try to work at home and see if we could all manage.

When the pounding started, I threw the ball for the dogs to jolly them up and gave them toys stuffed with treats. They clearly didn't like the noise, but they seemed less concerned than I thought they'd be. Luke and Pip were perhaps a bit clingier and a little quicker to alert to sounds at night, but during the daytime onslaught, they'd settle down by my feet. I thought Luke was managing. I was wrong, and it almost killed him.

Luke must have left the yard when the roofers arrived to resume their pounding. I had gotten on the phone when my neighbors, John and Connie

Mudore, appeared with Luke a few minutes later. It's a miracle that he wasn't killed. I've never seen the road so busy.

I love all my dogs so much that it hurts sometimes. But as much as I love each of them, it is different with Luke. I fell in love with Luke right after I got him and am still hopelessly in love with him now. Luke is that one-in-a-million dog that most people never get, even dog trainers and breeders who've known hundreds of dogs. Every once in a while, someone will come up to me in a seminar and start talking about their Luke-equivalent, a dog who is so special that they can't talk about him without getting tears in their eyes. Maybe you had one once, too, a dog full of such goodness that your heart swells within your chest when you think of him. Maybe you have one now. I hope so—lucky us.

Luke is as handsome a dog as I've ever met, but I've worked with too many dogs who were gorgeous but troublesome to care much about looks anymore. Luke looks like handsome Rhett Butler in Gone with the Wind, *but he acts like Ashley—good, kind, ethical Ashley, the one whom Scarlett would've married if she'd had an IQ larger than her waist size. Luke is noble, pure and simple. He adores people, but rather than barreling them over with his enthusiasm, he goes over and sits beside them, as if respectfully pleased to be in their company. Luke is Zen-dog, always in the present, always exuding what seems like a spiritual kind of peace, the Dalai Lama of dogs.*

Luke is gracious to other dogs and unfailingly polite to children. He's a brilliant sheepherding dog, athletic, dedicated, and smart. He has great "sheep sense," and he knows far better than I what the sheep are about to do, long before they do it. It's Luke whom I count on to get the market lambs into the truck. It's Luke whom I always took with me when I went into the pasture where the aggressive ram lived. And it's Luke who risked his own life one day and in the process might have saved mine.

I had gotten trapped in the corner of the barn by Colleen, a crazed, horned ewe who seemed hell-bent on killing me. A grumpy Scottish blackface ewe,[1] Colleen had just delivered a lamb, and I'd gone in to give her grain and

---

1. In this breed even the females have horns.

fresh water. But her maternal protectiveness turned into a red-eyed rage, and she lowered her head and tried repeatedly to ram me into the cement wall, like some huge, wooly Green Bay Packer. With each charge I'd dodge to the side, and she'd slam into the wall, instead of into me. With each impact the barn shook, pieces of paint drifting down from the rafters. I grabbed a loose board and slammed it across her head and horns when she came for me the next time, hoping to back her off so that I could make it to the gate. It broke across her thick, bony skull, sending shock waves up into my shoulders. She didn't seem to notice. I don't think there's much she would've noticed. This was not a calculated attack. Colleen had lost it: she was in the same version of rage that I see in aggressive dogs who are completely out of control.

Wild-eyed, Colleen continued ramming toward me and slamming into the wall, paint chips flying, me dodging left, then right. My irritation changed to fear as my legs got tired and my knees began to shake. It seemed absurd that I couldn't get out. I work with aggressive dogs, big ones and little ones, dogs who have hurt people and who want to hurt me. I've had dogs of every description go after me in my office, teeth bared, eyes round and hard. I've had sheep for years, including a ram I'd named Beavis (but should've named Butthead), who was so aggressive that he sent a 6-foot-3-inch friend 10 feet through the air. But this was different. I couldn't get an edge in this game, and I couldn't get out of it. Colleen, armed with her full set of horns, had me trapped in the corner, tired and alone on a farm in the middle of nowhere. It was Saturday morning, and I wasn't due back to work until Monday morning. It'd be a long time waiting for help if I was badly hurt. I was supposed to spend the morning enjoying the chores and smiling at lambs, not trapped with some crazed ewe from hell who was trying to kill me. She finally got me, a hard, painful rip into my right thigh.

I remember the entire incident as being strangely silent, except for the thudding impact of each of Colleen's blows. Perhaps that is why the sound of Luke's paws hitting the top of the wooden stall are as clear in my mind today as if I had just heard it. Thwapp. Luke's front paws slapped on top of the wooden walls of the stall, and before I could think, he darted between me and Colleen, a blurry streak of black and white, headed like a bullet toward her head. Colleen turned toward him, nose still tucked toward her tail, so that her whole head faced backward, and only the bony area between her horns faced toward him. Now she was trying to smash Luke into the wall instead of me. Luke weighs 48 pounds, and if she'd got-ten him against the cement wall, she could've killed him in one blow. But Luke is lightning fast, and far more capable of handling an aggressive animal than I could ever be, and soon he and I both maneuvered across the pen to the gate, where we fled to safety.

We collapsed together in the straw of the barn, both of us panting and gulping air. Luke's sides heaved, the corners of his mouth grimaced from a lack of oxygen. Blood was pouring from his mouth where two of his teeth had bro-ken off at the gum line. It began to dawn on me then that by jumping into the pen, Luke had risked his life. I am sure that he knew the danger of what he did. Luke had had years of experience with sheep, and herding dogs learn fast what situations are and aren't dangerous. Luke has been rolled under pounding hooves and pressed against walls enough times to understand the physics of sheepherding. He has never once acted in a way that suggested that he was afraid of being hurt. That's not because he's a Border Collie; it's because he's Luke.

Pip is a Border Collie, too, but Pip wouldn't have taken on Colleen, not in exchange for steak dinners for the rest of her life. She's terrified of physical pain and considers having her nails trimmed to be the ultimate in heroism. Luke's daughter Lassie would've taken on Colleen, although I think she'd have been truly scared, and I doubt that she could've generated the force and determination that her father showed that morning. If Tulip had been there, she'd have charged in like an angry mama bear. I'm sure of that, because she did once, when Beavis the ram had me smashed between the ground and a fence and wouldn't stop even while Luke repeatedly attacked his head.[2] Tulip roared in like a train, bark-growling, teeth flashing, and the ram reared back like a frightened horse and trot-ted away. Gentle as she is, Tulip won't let anything attack anything else, and she can switch into full warrior mode faster than you can blink. But even given Tulip's peacekeeping tendencies and Lassie's desire to do what's right, I don't think that any of my dogs except Luke would've taken it upon themselves to scramble

---

2. One might think from reading this that my sheep are exceptionally aggressive, some mutant flock of crazed, dangerous wooly beasts. But the dramatic incidents that I described stand out in my mind for the very reason that they are so rare. I've had sheep for about sixteen years now, and for most of that time, they've been placid, peaceful animals who are a joy to be around.

over a 4½-foot-high wooden wall to jump into the fray. Luke isn't perfect, but you can almost hear the sound of the cavalry when he thinks you need help.

Maybe that's why I love him so much, because I feel as if I can count on him to take care of me. Maybe not; maybe that's just the kind of explanation that we make up after the fact to try to make sense of our feelings. In some ways it doesn't really matter why I love Luke in a way that I've never loved another dog. I just do, and since the incident in the barn years ago, my love for him has continued to grow. He's my soul mate dog, and if you asked me today to list my three best friends in the whole world, his name is on the list. I'll be grateful for the rest of my life that he didn't die needlessly on the road this morning, when I was reminded once again how every dog is unique and how deep the love can be between a human and a dog.

Every Dog Is Different

My love for each of my dogs is different, because each dog is different. Every one of my dogs has a unique set of strengths and weaknesses, just like every one of my two-legged friends. We call it personality, meaning the suite of psychological and behavioral characteristics that uniquely defines each of us. But ascribing personalities to nonhuman animals is radical to some, who still cling to a mechanistic vision of animals as stimulus/response machines. I was appalled to receive an E-mail last year from a university student who said that her philosophy professor had told the class that animals were incapable of feeling, thinking, and learning. He suggested that individual animals could no more have their own personalities than could clocks. It's one thing to read that from a long-dead, seventeenth-century philosopher like Descartes, but the thought that an educated professor at a university would teach that to his students in the year 2001 is nothing less than amazing. I'll grant that questions relating to "nonhuman animal thinking" are convoluted and complex, but our understanding of the basic principles of how humans learn originated with studies on rats and mice. Single-celled organisms can learn, for heaven's sake, and arguing that animals can't learn is patently absurd. It's equally absurd to deny the obvious differences in behavior among individuals of a complex species like dogs or cats.

Pet owners know that their dogs have their own personalities, and many objective scientists report the same phenomenon in wild animals. Even though most animal behavior research is looking for general trends that are only confounded by individual differences (Do male and female red-winged blackbirds differ in their responses to territorial intruders? Are older Japanese macaques more or less likely than juveniles to try out new foods?), researchers often comment on compelling individual differences in behavior within many species. Shirley Strum, a well-respected scientist who's been observing olive baboons for several decades, describes one high-status female, Peggy, as "a strong, calm, social animal, self-assured yet not pushy, forceful yet not tyrannical." A little later in her book *Almost Human,* she describes Peggy's daughter, Thea: "Thea, was, in fact, a bitch. Her status in the troop was second only to her mother's, and she used it tyrannically; she was unprovokedly aggressive, intimidating other females in situations where Peggy would have calmly quelled the whole matter with a rebuking glance or approached and waited for what she wanted."[3]

Steve Suomi is a primatologist who doesn't hesitate to ascribe different personalities to rhesus macaques. It's been the focus of his research for decades. He and his colleagues have found that in these monkeys stable differences in personality can be seen as early as one month of age. Many of the personality differences that he describes in his monkeys conform closely to personality differences in humans and dogs. Some macaques, just like some people and some dogs, are shy in unfamiliar situations or around novel objects, while others can only be described as irritable and quick to fly off the handle. What makes these traits so interesting, and so similar to what the research on human personality has found, is that while they can appear early in life and remain relatively stable as the animal matures, experiences in early development have a profound effect on how each animal behaves later in life.

3. More evidence, by the way, of the ubiquitous nature of "benevolent leaders" and "alpha wanna-bes."

Shyness, for example, is common in people and dogs, as well as rhesus macaques, and it appears to have both a genetic and an environmental component to it. We've known for many years that shy dogs tend to have a high percentage of shy puppies: John Paul Scott and John L. Fuller's classic research on the genetic basis of dog behavior found that shyness was one of the behavioral traits most affected by genetics. Good breeders know that breeding two shy parents can result in puppies who are extremely shy, although it's rarely as simple as that. More likely, the litter will be a mixed bag of some very shy puppies, some moderately so, and perhaps one or two who aren't shy at all.

Researchers have conducted studies on shyness in humans that adroitly separated out genetics and the environment by looking at adopted babies. They found a correlation between shy infants and shy biological mothers, even when the babies were raised by nonshy adoptive parents. The evidence that shyness is partly mediated by genetics in other species is overwhelming. According to Steve Suomi, about 15 to 20 percent of the populations of several species of primates react more fearfully than others to unfamiliar things. Shyness appears to be what biologists call a "conservative" trait, meaning that the trait tends to stay in a population and continue to be passed on at similar frequencies. That makes sense, since Suomi also found that shy rhesus macaques are more successful than their bolder peers in some contexts. For example, young male macaques have to leave their natal troop at early maturity and emigrate to another troop. It's a dangerous time for a monkey, and up to half of the males die in the process. The most successful males are the ones who are the largest, and because shy males are more cautious, they strike out on their own at a later age than their peers. Because they are older when they leave, they tend to be larger and are, ironically, more successful than their bolder peers.

But researchers have also found strong evidence of environmental influences. Scott and Fuller found that if puppies weren't exposed to humans during their early period of socialization, they grew into adults who were always nervous around new people. Researchers on cat behavior found that kittens from bold parents would react shyly to newcomers if they hadn't interacted with humans when they were young, the most important early interactions being between weeks three and seven. Suomi has found that the young of shy rhesus macaque mothers, who are genetically predisposed to be shy themselves, can nonetheless be relatively outgoing if they are fostered with adoptive females who are highly nurturing and who provide their young with security while encouraging them to interact with others.

The evidence is overwhelming that in all complex animals, an individual's personality is the result of the interaction between his or her genetics and the environment. So in this very important sense, too, we are very much like our dogs, and our dogs are very much like us. Asking if the behavior of either one of us is "genetic" or "environmental" is like asking if bread is formed by the ingredients or by the process by which you put them together. If you cooked the eggs before you mixed them with the flour, you wouldn't have what you'd call a loaf of bread, even if you did use all the right ingredients.

No matter what influences a dog's and a human's personality, the two can mesh together in sweet harmony or scrape against each other like fingernails on a blackboard. So much of whether a human and a dog get along, and whether the dog is perceived as being "obedient," is based on how their individual natures combine. All relationships are driven by the alchemy of the personalities within it, and that makes just as much sense in relationships between us and our dogs as it does in relationships between us and other people. Most people and most dogs fit into general categories of personality types, from outgoing to reserved, trusting to suspicious, moody to sanguine, active to passive.

Most of what seems to make dog lovers happy is to have a dog that has the personality that they cherish, whether it's a slaphappy social butterfly, a feisty fido who takes on the world with relish, or a quiet, passive, couch-potato dog who likes curling up in the study and watching old movies as much as you do. What follows are some thoughts about personalities in dogs and some advice about how to look for the dog that you will be happy with and that will be happy with you.

I Didn't Think Golden Retrievers Could Bite!

Every dog owner whom I know will argue that his or her own dog has a distinct personality, but paradoxically many people seem to think of all dogs within a breed as behavioral clones. Some people tend to think of a breed designation as if it were a prescription drug, with each dog like a pill in a bottle, each guaranteed to have the same amount of ingredients. I learned how prevalent this belief was when I started seeing aggression cases. "What is that dog doing here? I didn't think Golden Retrievers could bite!" I've heard sentences like that a hundred times, just substitute *Labrador* or *mutt* or *Cocker Spaniel* for the "breed" that wasn't supposed to have behavioral problems. Dogs can bite if they can open and shut their mouths, and I've seen plenty of individual dogs of "docile" breeds that have gotten into a lot of trouble with their teeth. Most Golden Retrievers may be sweet and willing to please, but some individuals within the breed are as hardheaded as hammers.

Luke, Pip, and Lassie are all Border Collies, yet they are as different from one another as I am from other humans with similar genetic backgrounds. Pip is my sleeper Border Collie, looking a little goofy, a little like Larry Labrador, when in fact she's from pristine sheepdog lineage. Pip's sweet nature has allowed her to rehabilitate almost a hundred dogs who were aggressively afraid of other dogs. Time and time again, Pip would lie down 20 feet from barking, snarling dogs and spend as long as she needed to convince them that she meant no harm. She'd ignore their defensive snarls, and eventually they'd stop, calm down, and make friends. I've had dozens of owners who got tears in their eyes when they watched their dog play with Pip—the first time in their lives that they'd seen their previously aggressive dog play with another.

And then there's Lassie, Luke's daughter, the dog that many people foolishly expect to get, not realizing how rare dogs like her really are.

From the day I got her, Lassie has always done everything I've ever asked. Lassie came to me the first time that I called, while she was streaking after a group of dogs at a dead run. That level of obedience usually takes years of training, but with Lassie, it just happened. From day one she has been one of those remarkable dogs who always knows what you want and, more amazingly, is happy to do it. Dogs like Lassie make dog trainers like me look brilliant, when all along we've barely done a thing. That's why I named her Lassie, after the miraculous television dog who always knew what to do when she heard commands like: "Lassie, run down the road into town and get the sheriff and bring him back to the old well about a mile north of here!" Lassie is intense, emotional, status-seeking with dogs but not people, clingy to me, and relentlessly obedient. Pip is mellow, submissive, smart, and afraid of conflict or putting herself at risk. She can surprise people by being headstrong. Luke has a noble demeanor, is physically fearless, submissive to people, and a natural leader around dogs, intensely focused but a team player. They are all Border Collies, and they share a great deal. They are all athletic, they all quickly learned to run around to the back of sheep and bring them to me, and they all can focus their attention like lasers. Yet they are vastly different from one another, just as you are from others who share your genetic and cultural background.

Last week two of my clients brought in a dog they'd long identified as a mutt. The vet thought maybe a Dachshund/terrier cross, but the dog was a stellar example of what's affectionately known in this country as a PBGV, or a Petit Basset Griffon Vendéen. Although it mattered little in the long run to them, it was fun to show them photos of the rather expensive and rare breed that their former "mutt" represented. When they learned of his true breed identity, they said, "Well, then, next time we get another dog, we're getting a PBGV, because he's such a great little dog." I winced internally, because although many PBGVs are indeed delightful dogs, what they adored about this particular dog is his docility and his willingness to learn. That's what they need to look for next. It may well be that certain breeds have a higher proportion of individuals who are like that than others, but it's always smart to focus on the central personality traits that are important as well as just the breed itself. I've seen many disappointed clients in my office who came because the dog they had didn't fit what they expected. When their own dog died, they got another dog of the same breed, expecting to get the same sweet, loving dog that they had before. But while their first dog was docile, the next one was irritable, or while dog number one was exuberant, dog number two was phlegmatic. Their experience is a good reminder that although choosing the right breed will increase your odds of getting what you want, looking directly at the personality of each dog as an individual will up them even more.

The need to pay attention to personality doesn't negate the relevance of the behavioral characteristics of each breed. As a group, each breed has its own characteristic traits, both physical and behavioral. After all, a breed is a group of dogs selected from a small subset of all possible dog genes—genes that provide the blueprint for both the physical and behavioral makeup of a dog. Right now, selection for most breeds is based primarily on skeletal structure, movement, and coat, which results in a tendency for each individual to look a lot like others of the breed. But most breeds were originally bred for function, and there are generalizations you can make about how the dogs within them are going to behave. Most retrievers love to play ball, and most Beagles want to put their heads down and sniff out rabbits. So while keeping an appreciation for the unique nature of individuals, it's important to know the behavioral predispositions of the breed of dog that you're considering. If the odds say that eight out of ten Beagle puppies are going to obsess about tracking rabbits, then you'd better be prepared for a dog that's hard to keep in your backyard without a fence.

For example, Border Collies are terrible pets for most families. Having a typical Border Collie as a pet is like having a brainy sports car that revs its own engine in the garage if you don't drive it enough. Border Collies are smarter than some people, and if they were sports cars, they'd figure out how to open the garage door and drive into your living room to get your attention. You might read the stories about mine, look at the pictures, and think, "That's the perfect dog for me!" They are—if you're willing to buy your dog a sheep farm instead of a cheaper toy, if you think it's fun to go on long walks in blizzard conditions, and if you're planning on becoming a professional dog trainer. Most Border Collies don't just need physical exercise, they need mental exercise as well, so if you're too busy to bring a new child into your household, don't get a Border Collie.

The idea of a smart dog like a Border Collie is attractive to a lot of people, but when people tell me that their dog is especially smart, I usually say, "What a shame." Smart dogs learn how to get in the garbage, how to play you off against your husband, and how to open the cabinet door that you thought you'd padlocked. They are also enthusiastic ("*Hi!* Wow! It's morning! Isn't that great? Hey, . . . Did the cows get out? What? It's five in the morning? I know, I know, it's *late!*"). Of course, as I said earlier in the section, every Border Collie is different. Luke and his daughter are far more enthusiastic than their cousin Pip, who is the most mellow Border Collie I've ever known, but people would do well to carefully research the typical behavior of the breed in which they're interested before they bring a dog of that breed into their home. A dear friend of mine wanted a dog that would stay around her house in the country and not bother her chickens. Before I knew it, she had adopted two Husky puppies from the same litter. The pups are only five months old now, and the chicken population, I'm sorry to say, is declining at an alarming rate.

Dogs Don't Read the Books

Both personality and general breed characteristics are important when deciding on a dog, but there's a vital caveat to keep in mind when you're reading about breed characteristics. Dogs don't read the written breed descriptions. The world is full of Border Collies that won't herd, Doberman Pinschers that hide behind your skirts, and pushy, status-seeking retrievers. Every dog is different, because each dog's behavior is the result of a unique combination of genes and the environment. There'll never be another Luke, just as there'll never be another you. That's the benefit of sexual reproduction: sex causes all kinds of problems (not just to us humans), but it guarantees that the genes of two individuals are mixed and matched such that each of the offspring is unique. That's why even the best of breeders can't predict how their puppies will turn out. With each breeding a breeder is playing the odds that a particular mating will produce the desired breed characteristics and personality. But as we all know, good odds aren't guarantees about how any one event will turn out. If you look at one hundred dogs of a given breed—say, one hundred Standard Poodles—most of them will be about the same size and height and will be athletic, brilliant, and joyful. But some of them, a smaller number, will be shorter or taller, or maybe not quite so smart, or perhaps clingy and submissive. It's like the odds in horse racing: good odds mean that if your horse ran ten races, he might win seven of them, but it doesn't tell you whether the next race will be one of the seven that he wins or one of the three that he loses.

The Right Stuff

Besides being aware of the behavioral tendencies of the breed in which you're interested, you'll also want to know the specific qualities the breeder admires. The traits that you want in a dog might not be the same ones that a breeder wants. Right now, most breeders get rewarded for breeding dogs that win conformation shows or field trials, not for breeding sweet, docile dogs that you can trust with your family. The blue ribbons and the attention in the dog world are mostly focused on physical traits like coat condition or the right shoulder angle and behavioral traits like "confidence" and "drive." Conformation judges favor dogs that "show well," meaning that the dogs are confident and assertive and stride around the ring as if they owned it. Breeders who compete with their hunting dogs in field trials need dogs with phenomenal drive and stamina who aren't stopped by freezing water or thornbushes. People who need great working livestock dogs need dogs who are capable of working a twelve-hour day in a snowstorm. But none of those qualities is what most pet owners need in their family dog. Confident, assertive dogs may look great in the show ring, but they can be too much to handle in a house with three kids under the age of seven. Retrievers who won't give up, no matter what, will use their drive and stamina to find yet another way to get at the garbage. Herding dogs who are capable of working twelve hours a day turn into maniacs when their daily exercise consists of a half-hour leash walk.

Although a lot of breeders care deeply about disposition, the fact of the matter is that they get little tangible reinforcement for breeding sweet, docile dogs. They get money, ribbons, and public recognition for breeding dogs who match the written breed standard, who sail around show rings, or who can perform hunting, retriever, or herding tasks, but not for breeding dogs who are easy to train and good with children. "Pet-quality" dogs are often sold for less money than "show-quality" dogs, as if somehow a dog who is going to make a family's life either heaven or hell is of less value than one who wins some blue ribbons at a competition. Pet-quality dogs are usually just as healthy as show-quality dogs, but their coat isn't the right color or their muzzle is too snippy to win blue ribbons, so they are sold as family pets.

What matters most, I think, to those of us who have dogs living in our homes as companions, is that our dogs are healthy and that they don't hurt anybody. Some breeders argue that their dogs could never compete in dog shows if they weren't well tempered, but sad to say, I've seen lots of dogs with long dog show histories who may be polite at dog shows but aren't polite at home. Still, there are many breeders out there for whom a good disposition is their most important breeding criterion, but they don't get a lot of support or credit for it, even though we know that docility can be influenced by careful breeding (remember the experiment on docility in foxes?). I know breeders of herding dogs who breed for useful farm dogs who can bite a bull on the nose when they need to but who would turn inside out before they snapped at a child. I know conformation breeders who want to win Westminster but who would never breed a dog they wouldn't trust with their grandchildren. They don't get blue ribbons or prize money or acknowledgment on national TV for it: that's reserved for dogs with a balanced stride and a good body. Maybe someday we'll have a star-studded night of glitz and glamour that celebrates breeders who produce sweet, docile dogs, but for now prospective dog owners have to use criteria other than dog shows and competitions to be sure that they're getting a good family pet.

Of course, a dog's behavior is only partly influenced by her genetics: the environment in which she grows up and lives has a profound effect on whether or not a dog will bite. Almost all dogs can be made to bite, and I've seen some pathetic cases of truly good dogs who were given no other alternative. But I've seen just as many dogs given good starts in life who lived with good people and yet still terrorized the family with their teeth. My office has seen at least thirty puppies who snarled and bit at your face when they were just eight or nine weeks old. I'm not talking about puppies who didn't know how to be polite with their mouths and got a little nippy in play. I'm talking about puppies whose eyes go hard while they stare straight at you and who bring the corners of their mouth forward in an offensive pucker just before they try to hurt you. It's chilling when you see an animal that young act with such intensity, and although some of these dogs can be handled so that they grow up to be safe in some contexts, they're hardly the dog that most people want to bring home.

No matter what you as a breeder or a puppy buyer do, you can't guarantee that the dog that you bred or bought (or have now) will never bite. It's just not possible. A dog's behavior is such a complicated interplay of so many things[4] that it's impossible to make solid predictions. What you *can* do, however, is get the odds on your side. I've seen scores of people in my office who said, "I don't know what the disposition of my dog's mother or father was. I couldn't get near them because they were barking and snarling." Oh, dear. May I suggest that the barking and snarling might provide a clue? Puppy buyers need to pay careful attention to the behavior of the parents and avoid getting a puppy from parent dogs who aren't polite. The behavior of the parents will tell you a lot more about the eventual disposition of a puppy than the behavior of a seven-week-old puppy will. If you can't pet the mother, the sweet little pup that you're about to take

---

4. Including genetics, hormonal physiology, brain chemistry, the effects of early development, and learning, to name a few.

home may not let your visitors in the house once she's an adult. Of course, as I said earlier, there's no guarantee that the pups will act like their parents or grandparents, but why not get the odds on your side?

One of the ways to do that is to ask the breeder very specific questions about the behavior of the pups' parents and grandparents.[5] What would the father of the pups do if someone barged into the house at night? (You may like the idea of a protective dog, but don't forget that the person barging in may be a firefighter trying to rescue your child.) What if a young child tried to take a real bone away from the pup's mother? Many breeders won't know what would happen in that context, because they wouldn't allow that situation to occur, but how they answer the question can say a lot about what level of docility they expect from a dog. Some breeders will tell you that they would never expect a dog to tolerate such a violation, while others will answer that their dogs wouldn't even blink and that their five-year-old nephew did that very thing last night and Queenie responded by licking his face.

When you are talking to either the breeder of the puppies or the former owner of the adult dog, there are a lot more questions to ask. Does the dog allow people to pull burrs out of her tail? If you're looking at a little puppy, do the dam and the sire allow grooming and handling? How about trimming their nails? Taking away their favorite toys? How are they at the vet's? How about with other dogs, both familiar and unfamiliar ones? Do they bark out the window for a few seconds when visitors arrive, or do they bark nonstop for ten minutes? Have they ever growled, shown their teeth, snapped, nipped, or bitten anyone, for any reason? Is the dog different with unfamiliar people than he is with familiar people?

It's important to ask very specific questions, not general ones like "Are the parents friendly?" *Friendly* can mean a lot of things. I've met hundreds of dogs that people described as the sweetest, most loving dogs you could imagine. All of these dogs may have bitten numerous times, but they still had wonderful dispositions, according to the owners. And that was true in one sense, because the dog might have been wonderful with the fam-

---

5. Even better, if there's another litter of the same breeding, talk to the owners of those dogs.

ily, cuddling on the couch each night with the teenage daughter. But let a stranger try to enter the house, even a welcome guest, and watch out. So in this case, the dog was "friendly" to familiar people but not to unfamiliar ones. That's why the questions need to be so specific. Just as with people, the behavior of dogs varies depending on the context, and you need to ask about a dog's behavior in as many different situations as you can imagine to get a clear idea of who he really is. After all, Jeffrey Dahmer was nice all day long at the chocolate factory.

If you're asking about a young dog, remember that age has an important effect on behavior. Just like humans, most dogs behave differently when they're mature than when they're younger. Just because an adolescent dog hides behind your legs when visitors come doesn't mean that he will when he's three years old. By then he might have gotten over his fears, or he might be more inclined to act on them and go after your guests with his teeth.

How about exercise? Again, be sure to be specific, because *exercise* means different things to different people. Two short leash walks a day don't even get a Welsh Corgi warmed up. A year-old Labrador Retriever can barely think until he's had a good long session of running two or three times a day. Young Australian Cattle Dogs can no more sit still for hours than a five-year-old boy can.

The list of questions goes on and on. Develop your own list based on what is important to you. If you're sound-sensitive, you probably don't want a dog that barks a lot, while other people wouldn't mind at all. Some dogs require extensive grooming, and for some people that's a problem. I can barely keep my own hair brushed, so I'd be a disastrous owner for a Lhasa Apso. So if you're looking for a dog, be thoughtful about what you want. There's great value in writing it down, because it focuses your attention on what's important. And for those of us who already have a dog or dogs, it's useful to ask the same questions and get a clear evaluation of whom you're living with. Be a field researcher in your own living room and write down an objective description of your dog as an individual. You might be surprised at what you come up with.

Pretty Is as Pretty Does

A few years ago I got a call from a dairy farmer who wanted a good working dog and had heard that I bred Border Collies. "Ya got any dogs with a brown spot on their ear?" I did have a litter of puppies from good working parents, so I asked him what he was looking for. "I don't need any fancy dog. I just need a dog who'll do the chores, sort out the heifers, back off the bull, protect the farm when we're gone, and be real good and gentle with my grandchildren. I had a good dog like that before, but he died. He had a brown spot on his ear, so I'm looking for another one just like him." This is the place in a Dave Barry column where he'd say, "I am not making this up." Try as I might, I couldn't convince the caller that although my puppies had no brown spots on their ears, they had the potential of being fine working dogs who were also good with kids. Apparently the caller had had a wonderful dog, the only one he'd ever had with a brown spot on his ear, and he figured that the brown spot was the key to his good disposition. Lest you start feeling a bit smug about the beliefs of an old, seemingly ignorant farmer, keep in mind that many of the people whom I see, including Ph.D.s and physicians, put a tremendous value on what a dog looks like.

For years I asked all the dog owners who came into my office why it was that they picked the pup that they did, when they had an entire litter from which to choose. The first criterion was sex, with most people strongly wanting one or the other. But after sorting out which sex they wanted, about 85 percent of them picked their dog based on looks rather than behavior. They liked the one with more white on him or the one marked most like their previous dog. They didn't want the pup with one blue eye, or they *only* wanted the one with one blue eye. They liked long hair rather than short or short hair rather than long, droopy ears rather than prick ears, or black noses instead of pink ones. Some physical features are universally attractive (symmetry, for example), but each of us has our own special reaction to the looks of different dogs. A survey of the people at the central office of Dog's Best Friend, Ltd., illustrates the tendency of all of us to be attracted to different kinds of dogs. Aimee Moore, the training director, is a sucker for fluffy dogs, especially white ones. The office manager, Denise Swedlund, may think white and fluffy is cute, but cream-colored Golden Retrievers melt her heart. Jackie Boland, office assistant, can't resist shorthaired Labrador Retrievers, and Karen London, Ph.D., Applied Animal Behaviorist, likes dogs who look playful and youthful. We all may favor different types of looks, but looks play no small role in our attraction to dogs.

Our obsession with looks is not surprising, I suppose, when you consider what a visual species we are and that looks are staggeringly important in our interactions with people. Attractive people are more likely to be hired, are more likely to get raises, are more likely to get away with shoplifting, and are judged to be more intelligent than those who are less attractive. With a legacy like that, no wonder we care so much about what our dogs look like. But being seduced by good looks can get puppy buyers in trouble, just as it gets people in trouble when they are shopping for a prospective mate. Pretty figures and handsome faces may have a powerful effect on us in the beginning of a relationship, but they don't keep us happy in the long term. When you have to take a bone out of your dog's mouth, you're not going to care much if her ears are cute. "Pretty is as pretty does" applies just as readily to our dogs as it does to people. Remember when that good-looking date turned out to be a jerk? Picking the prettiest puppy can have the same result, so look more carefully at the plain black dog that everyone else ignores—he just might be the best one.

But He Never Does That at Home!

For some reason we humans are surprised when our dogs act differently in one context than another. "Gosh, he's always been so good with dogs," says the owner of the spaniel/Akita mix that got into a dogfight at her neighbor's house. But it turns out that the dog has only been around dogs that he knows, not ones that he's never met before. Meeting a new, unfamiliar dog at the neighbor's is going to bring out a different dog than the one sharing the rug with the Cocker Spaniel with which he grew up. Just as with humans, changes in the environment affect how your dog behaves. A dog who's hot and frustrated at the pet food store isn't going to react the same as a dog who's contented and relaxed in the backyard. We all know that people behave differently in different environments: you may be one person on a cool walk in the spring countryside and an altogether different one on a hot, humid day in a traffic jam. But for some reason we don't transfer this knowledge to our dogs. Different environments bring out different aspects of your dog, and you don't really know your dog until you've seen her in a variety of situations.

This explains why different members of the family will disagree with one another in my office about how their dog behaves. "He does *not!*" a woman will say, frustrated that her husband is describing something that her dog has never done in his life. Ah, but her dog probably *has* done it, no matter what "it" is, just not in her presence. Just as you and I have done things in one context that we'd never do in another, it's common for dogs to behave differently in different places and with different people. Rocky might growl at home to his female human but not to his male human. Ginger may retrieve tennis balls in the living room but not in the backyard. Duke may be a sweetie at the vet clinic but rude and demanding at home. So don't get in a fight with your spouse about her bogus descriptions of your dog's behavior. She just might be describing something that happens when you're not there to see it.

Dog trainers and veterinarians would also do well to give their fellow humans more credit. I see an amazing number of frustrated dog owners who plaintively say, "No one will believe me, but honest, I swear to you, he looks right in my eyes and growls at me!" I've had clients, usually women, who showed me their scars and bruises, all the results of dog bites, with a kind of victorious relief—because finally they had evidence of what they'd been complaining about for months. Meanwhile, in my office, their dog is doing a brilliant impersonation of a "perfect" pet, but I always make it clear to them that dogs behave differently in different places and that I have no trouble imagining the dog who's a big, goofy lover boy in my office being different at home.[6]

Dogs not only behave differently in dissimilar environments, but they behave differently in the same environment at different times of the day. This, too, seems inexplicable to many dog owners: "How could he be so good this morning and so grumpy last night?" Probably for the same reason that you too are sweet one minute and grumpy the next. Few of us react exactly the same to each of life's irritations. Last week, happy and relaxed from a lovely weekend, I broke one of my favorite bowls and shrugged it off in an instant. A few days later, exhausted from a tiring and stress-filled week, I dropped a glass that I care little about and yelled an epithet so loudly that my dogs left the room. It's so common for us to have good days and bad days that humans who are always patient and benevolent stand out like saints. That kind of consistency is as rare among dogs as it is among people. Just like us, dogs can get tired, frustrated, hungry, or irritated, and just like us, they don't respond the same from minute to minute. The behavior of complex mammals is influenced by a daunting number of factors—from blood sugar levels to serotonin and dopamine re-uptake mechanisms in the brain to conditioned responses to stressful encounters with others—so do your dog a favor and don't get confused by her flexibility of responses. She'll be much better off if you spend your energy asking yourself what it was, specifically, that caused her to act in a way that surprised or disappointed you rather than being perplexed that her behavior varies.

This natural tendency to react differently at different times and in different places explains a tremendous amount of what looks like "disobedience." Just as actors tend to forget lines when they first put on their costumes, our dogs forget their lessons when we ask them to do things in new contexts. That's why professional dog trainers spend so much time "proofing" their dogs—ensuring that the dog is comfortable in a new environment before they put too much pressure on her to perform. Your

---

6. That's why good Applied Animal Behaviorists and trainers always prefer to see you in your own home, even though it's more trouble for us and more expensive for you.

dog will be grateful if you follow their lead. "Sit" in the kitchen before dinner isn't the same as "Sit" at the front door with visitors outside. "Sit pretty" in the TV room doesn't automatically transfer to "Sit pretty" in the vet's office, so expect your dog to need help in new environments and give her the same permission that you give yourself—to need time to adapt to new environments and to practice a skill in the context in which you'll be using it. Your dog will thank you for it, I promise.

Perhaps one of the kindest things that you can do for your dog is to understand that, just like us humans, every dog has both a unique nature and a bevy of characteristics that he shares with others and that this bedrock foundation of "personality" is influenced each second by internal and external factors that impinge upon him throughout the day. Every dog is indeed special, and he deserves a human who gives him permission to be who he is, whether it's sweet and shy or bold and cocky. It's not fair to expect him to be perfect, although like us, some may be a lot closer than others.

I don't want you to get the impression that Luke is perfect, because he's not. In his youth he was too pushy with sheep, lacking the finesse that he's gained through experience and maturity. He has been known to lose his temper with sheep, as he did when we were in the lead in a big herding dog trial. We were at the end of the best run of our lives and had all the sheep but one in the pen. If we could just get them all inside and I could close the gate within the next two minutes, we'd win the trial. My heart was beating so loudly I could hear it, but the crowd was stone quiet in anticipation of what would happen next. Four times in a row, a balky ewe leaped away from the pen just when it appeared she was about to go in. The crowd groaned in shared disappointment each time that she bolted, and each time my hot, tired dog gathered her up and herded her back to the mouth of the pen. Again, she dashed away, but this time Luke pinned back his ears and bit her. It was not an appropriate nip to round her back up; it was an irritated cheater bite to her back leg. He nipped once and let go immediately, but he'd clearly had it with her foolishness. Anyone who'd ever seriously worked a dog on sheep knew that Luke was just frustrated. The judge certainly knew and said, appropriately enough, "Thank you," which is herding trial lingo for: "Please leave the course now— you and your dog are disqualified."

I could've been mad at Luke, I suppose, because if he hadn't lost his temper, we could've won the trial. But all of us who raise sheep understood how he felt: we've all had our patience stretched thin trying to move sheep in the heat of the summer and the stinging cold of winter, running out of time, desperate now to get the sheep out of the alfalfa, where they'll die of bloat, or away from the ram who jumped the fence. But you don't need to raise sheep to understand losing your temper. Luke is good and noble and brave, but on occasion he can lose his temper around sheep. I would like to be good and noble and brave, too, but that's not for me to say. I can lose my temper, though. Maybe that's another reason Luke and I get along so well.

10

LOVE AND LOSS

When Your Dog Needs Another Home and When You Need a Hug

Katherine sat crumpled in my office, crying as if her heart would break. You could feel the hurt across the room, and I soon let my own tears stream down my cheeks. Her soft-eyed German Shepherd, Tasha, licked her face, while we talked about how difficult it can be to stop some female dogs from feuding. Her two female dogs, Tasha and Cinqa, were both buttery sweet to people, but they had hated each other for years. Their fights had become life-threatening. The last fight took ten horrifying minutes to break up after the family's third dog, a huge female Newfoundland, joined in. Figuring out how to intervene in a dogfight is no small problem for any of us: Where do you grab? How can you get in the middle without getting hurt? Imagine trying to pull apart three huge, fighting dogs, when two of them are determined to kill each other.

In the last fight Tasha had been seriously injured, and so had Katherine. Katherine had already tried for more than a year to resolve the problem, with little success. Sometimes you can fix spats between two females in the same household, but in the wild either Tasha and Cinqa would've killed each other or one would've left for another territory. It was time to relocate one of the dogs, but the thought of splitting up the family was agonizing to Katherine. She loved them both, but she couldn't live knowing that another terrible fight, possibly a fatal one, was just around the corner.

Tasha eventually did go to another home; Cinqa stayed with Katherine.

Like most psychologically healthy dogs who go to good homes, Tasha slid easily from one pack to another. She was a bit restless that first day with her new family, but she played ball, luxuriated in belly rubs, and ate her dinner as usual. Katherine, the human part of this mixed-species family, grieved Tasha's absence like a death. It took her days to be able to eat normally. She cried off and on for weeks. She's a perfectly normal, well-adjusted woman, but sending Tasha to a new home felt as if she were betraying her own child.

It's been about two years since Tasha moved, and she's clearly doing well, basking in the love of her new family. Katherine knows she made the right choice. Tasha is happy in her new home, Katherine's remaining dogs get along well, and both she and her dogs are enjoying the peace that comes with a good decision. And yet, even years later, knowing that she made a good choice, Katherine has moments when the pain comes back, thinking of the day that her dog slipped so neatly into a new pack, when she herself felt as if her own had shattered.

Greater Love Hath No Owner

Some of the hardest cases that I see involve a loving, responsible dog owner who has little choice but to find another home for his dog. I sat in my office one afternoon listening to a fireman sob because his dog had bitten his son, and it seemed clear that he and his wife had no choice but to rehome the dog. There sat this huge, brave man, someone who runs into burning buildings that the rest of us would flee in a panic, crying as if his heart would break. His little black dog licked the tears off his face. After they left, I slowly closed my office door behind them, laid my head down on the desk, and cried like a baby. I would have given anything to have been able to give them the tools to solve their problem, but I couldn't. Their dog had the worst personality possible around young children. He was nervous, hyper-reactive, and quick to use his mouth. He was terrified of anyone under the age of twelve. The chance that their six-year-old son would be badly injured again was extremely high. All I could do was tell it to them straight: that many behavioral problems can be successfully managed and sometimes truly cured, but "alpha wanna-be" dogs with no bite inhibition (the child had had over a hundred stitches) are not the kind of dogs that you can "cure" in a family with young children.

I had been warned when I started as an Applied Animal Behaviorist that most of the cases that I was going to see would be about serious aggression. I was prepared to hear about growls and bites and to work at a job that entailed some physical risk to myself. But I wasn't prepared for the emotional pain of helping people make decisions that broke their hearts. It wasn't a surprise to me how much people love their dogs. I grew up in a family of dog lovers, and I was raised by a mother who to this day loves dogs almost as much as life itself. So I wasn't surprised at how deep the love could be between people and dogs. After all, if people didn't love their dogs so much, they wouldn't come to see me to solve their behavioral problems. But even after fourteen years, I am still overwhelmed at times by the raw pain that comes when my clients decide that they have to send their dog away.

I can't take away the grief that comes when clients say good-bye to a dear friend. But I can say something that has helped scores of people in this situation, and it is this: *Rehoming your dog into a situation where he will be safe and happy is not a betrayal.* And yet, I've seen owner after owner who might have been sad in anticipation of losing their friend, but whose unbearable pain came from feeling that placing their dog in another home would be betraying a trust. But I don't think dogs interpret it that way.

Luke's daughter, Lassie, is a good example. She was sold by the dam's owner to a single woman with three young kids who lived in Milwaukee. It was a good place for a Border Collie to go bad. Smart, high-energy, but underemployed dogs always find something to do—it's just usually not what you want. True to form, Lassie drove her owner crazy by digging, barking nonstop, and recycling the kids' toys. Like most Border Collies, she was a terrible pet for a busy family with young children. The breeder agreed to take her back, and I agreed to foster Lassie while the breeder went on her honeymoon. When she returned, we'd both look for a good home for Lassie where she'd get the mental and physical exercise that she needed.

Lassie came to the farm at eleven o'clock at night, too late to do much, so I leashed her to the bed beside me and lay all night with my hand touching her soft back. In the morning I took her outside with the rest of the dogs. Pip heard a rabbit up the hill behind the house, and the pack took off like some cartoon race of dominoes, black and white streaking through the golden brush of a Wisconsin fall. I don't know why I bothered to call Lassie's name: a test, I guess, although what could be the odds of stopping a full-out charge from a dog you've barely met? She turned around in midair. I remember a black-and-white U suspended for an instant, and then she hit the ground running to me. She stopped just before she ran into my legs, launched herself yet one more time to flip-spin herself beside me, and looked up, grinning.

That first morning she seemed a bit restless. She'd lie down and then get up, pad over to the window and look for who knows what, then come back and lie down again beside me. There was no question that she was a bit unsettled. But this was not a dog in extreme distress. She romped and played and licked my face. She ate voraciously, fell in some doggy version of love with her father, and took to herding sheep as if she'd been doing it all her short life. By the end of her first day, she felt like "my dog." I liked her so much, I called the breeder that very afternoon and asked her if I could keep her. Lassie seemed to like me, too, acting as if I was "her human" within a few hours of her arrival. By the third day, you wouldn't have known that she hadn't lived here all her life. Lassie loves me dearly now, I am sure of that. I am equally sure that if something happened to me, Lassie could be happy with someone else who communicated clearly to her, who rubbed her belly at night, and who had sheep for her to work.

I am *not* saying it's acceptable to pass dogs around like an old paperback book. What I'm saying is that, although Lassie needs someone who loves her, love isn't always enough. Every dog is different, and that means that, just as with people, every dog needs an environment that brings out the best in her. At eleven months Lassie came to the kind of place that she was bred to be in, and her problem behaviors melted away. She neither barks nor chews inappropriately nor digs where she shouldn't. Lassie came home, thanks to an owner who was wise enough to see that her city home and busy life couldn't do justice to an active, bright little dog who was hungry to put her skills to work.

Lassie's story is like that of hundreds of other dogs who accepted a new home with the same philosophical peace with which dogs seem to accept much of life. My own belief is that dogs are like humans in that they can form incredibly strong emotional attachments to others. As I said earlier, I have no problem calling that love. But unlike humans, dogs can switch attachments, if it doesn't happen too often, relatively easily. I imagine that it's part of living more in the present than we humans do; perhaps it's an advantage of the very different intellectual state of dogs versus humans.

If you think about it, there's no reason why dogs would interpret a change in circumstances as a betrayal by the humans whom they loved. Wolf packs can be quite fluid, their changes dependent on food availability and breeding seasons. Some individuals are driven out of the pack, while others choose to leave voluntarily. Even many species of primates leave their first home and move on to another when they mature. In chimpanzees and gorillas, the females are more likely to leave home for a new group, while baboon and macaque males usually do the traveling. Besides, as my associate Karen London notes, our own children leave home and form their own families eventually, too. It's not always easy in the short run, either for the one who's leaving or for the ones who are left, but it's ultimately for the best. I've come to believe that when an animal comes into our lives, our responsibility is to use our resources and intelligence to provide him with as good a life as possible. The trick is to learn enough about the dog to know what he needs to be really happy and to get our own ego out of the way.

Years ago it took me longer than it should have to realize that my Border Collie Scott would be better off at another home. I'm a professional dog trainer who's truly good to her dogs, I live in the country, and I have sheep to herd, so what could have been better for a Border Collie?

Besides, I loved Scott dearly. But he had to share herding chores for a small flock of sheep with three other Border Collies, and it wasn't anywhere near the level of work that he really needed. Scott wanted to work so badly that he herded the cat in the house all night long. It drove all three of us—me, Scott, and the beleaguered cat—equally crazy. Additionally Scott was shy and hated new things, and yet I travel a lot, and my dogs are constantly exposed to new places, new people, and new dogs. He was stressed on trips and didn't enjoy visits from clients and friends at the farm. I eventually found Scott a home with two hundred sheep that needed moving every day, few visitors, and two adult humans who adored him. I won't pretend it was easy. It wasn't. But two days after I drove away (with tears falling so thick and fast, I had to pull over to the side of the road), I felt 50 pounds lighter after a phone call confirmed that his new owners excused his quirks without a blink and raved about his herding ability and his sweet disposition. Scott was in heaven, my poor cat got a break, and I glowed with relief and contentment.

Scott was a bit disoriented the first day on his new farm, as all animals (including humans) are when they're in a new place with new social partners. But also like humans, once things become more familiar, dogs settle into their new routine, far better than we humans at peacefully accepting what's happening around us.

If a dog truly needs a new home, either for his own sake or for the sake of others, what's important is to find the right home for him. It amazes me how many wonderful people there are out there who are not just willing but happy to help out a needy pet. I had a friend who was moving out of the country, and he was devastated because he thought he'd have to euthanize his fifteen-year-old cat. He'd just learned that she had diabetes, and she needed a lot of medical care, including injections from the owner two times a day. He was sure no one would adopt her and that he'd have to put down his dear old friend. I encouraged him to have faith and advertise, and he finally did. He ended up choosing among five wonderful families who wanted to adopt her. No doubt some dogs are harder to find good homes for than others, and it's certainly not responsible to pass on a serious behavioral problem to an unsuspecting owner. Neither do I want to see people use this as an excuse to pass around a dog like a fruitcake. There's a limit to how often a dog can adapt to a new home, and it's important to try to find the right place on your first try. But if you find yourself unable to provide a dog with what she needs, you won't be betraying a trust if you find a way for her to get it. You'd be betraying her if you didn't.

I see far too many underemployed dogs who are driving their owners crazy, always chewing, barking, never settling down. Some of them have physiological problems, but many of them simply need a purpose in life, and not going potty in the house isn't enough to inspire them. Other dogs do well with some people and not others. Perhaps you have a dog who is absolutely wonderful with adults but is terrified of children, and you're expecting a baby in six months. This is a dog who, if anything, would be grateful if you found him a home where he didn't have to cope with the stress of a toddler. That's not a betrayal; it's an act of love.

Of course, it *is* possible to betray a dog. People do it all the time. They abandon them on quiet country roads or tie them to stakes and drive away forever, with no intention of coming back. They dump them at humane societies just because they are sick and old, with little regard for what might happen to them. The ease with which some people abuse their dogs is a painful reminder of the dark side of human behavior. But I think that dogs can also be betrayed by the people who love them—by owners who want a dog themselves so badly that they're unable to consider what the dog actually needs. Even the best of owners can't provide the right environment for every dog. It's cruel to cast off a dog like an old sweater, but it can be responsible and loving to acknowledge that no matter how much you love a particular dog, you can't give her what she needs. Dogs don't get to decide to leave the pack if it's in their best interests. Greater love hath no owner if you're willing to place that bored, unexercised little Golden Retriever in a home where she'll truly be happy, even if it does break your heart.[1]

---

1. If you do rehome a dog, never give her away for free. If people can't afford $75 to buy a dog, then they can't afford to take care of her well either. If they *can* afford it, but they're not willing to pay it, then they've told you that the dog isn't very important to them, and they don't deserve her. Always screen people first on the phone, and before you give them the dog, insist on going to their home. You'll get a great idea of what the prospective owners are like by visiting and can decide for yourself if you think she'd be happy there.

Grieving

I learned that my dog Misty was sick Thursday night. By Tuesday night she was dead. Although she was a fine-boned little Border Collie, she was tough as nails, and I had always imagined her living to age sixteen. But at twelve and a half, she started losing weight and began to eat her food gingerly. I thought perhaps a tooth was bothering her. My vet suspected something serious from the beginning but allowed me the luxury of a few hours of ignorance. "Let's just X-ray her to be sure," he said. "Why don't you come back in a few hours?" When I returned to pick her up, my mind fussing with my own client's concerns and the next day's lecture at the university, Dr. John's face stopped me in my tracks. It had the quiet stillness you see on the face of a kind person who is searching for a way to tell you something painful. She had hemorrhagic sarcoma, a hideous cancer that had turned her liver into Swiss cheese and had filled her body with bloody tumors.

The next day the internist at the University of Wisconsin vet school said that Misty could last weeks or die in five minutes. She started bleeding out that weekend, internal hemorrhages that couldn't be stopped. I spent the weekend rubbing her belly, feeding her chicken, and crying bittersweet tears of love and sorrow. Gradually her belly swelled with blood, and by Tuesday morning I saw that she couldn't rest comfortably anymore. She shifted position constantly, trying to find comfort in the middle of the dining room, a place she'd never lain in the entire twelve and a half years of her life. Dr. John came to the house that night, and while I held her and cried, Misty died.

I let her body lie in the middle of the living room, where we had put her down. Pip, her granddaughter, was the first dog to come over to her body. Pip was the dog that Mist liked best. For that matter, Pip was the only dog that Mist liked at all. Misty loved people, but other dogs were the bane of her existence. Pip's submissiveness was a balm to Misty, who was the ultimate "alpha wanna-be." Insecure, afraid of getting hurt, Misty nonetheless wanted to rule the farm, and she coexisted with the other two female dogs only because she had to. Lassie and Tulip aren't as submissive as Pip and had no intention of sucking up to the bully that Misty could be. Aware of the tension, I carefully rewarded polite behavior and continually kept an eye out for signs of trouble. Every few months Mist would laser a hard-eyed look toward Lassie or Tulip, and I had learned to respond immediately. Mist would find herself on a "down/stay" for an hour, and I'd tighten up the rules at the farm for a few weeks.

Pip circled Mist's body for the longest time, staying a foot or so away, never leaning in to sniff or smell her. After continually pacing around her body, Pip finally settled down with a loud sigh right beside her, face impassive. She stayed there for more than an hour. Lassie, whose face is more expressive than that of most humans, looked appalled. She hid behind my legs, occasionally peering out from behind my knees, sneaking looks at Mist and then instantly turning her head away until curiosity overwhelmed her and she peeked again. She stayed farther away from Mist than she had when Mist was alive. I have no idea what was in her head, but she looked terrified. Lassie behaved as a dog would if she couldn't understand what Mist was doing, and while a predictable Mist was trouble enough, an unpredictable Mist was downright terrifying. Luke, on the other hand, didn't visibly acknowledge Mist's presence. He didn't look toward her or go to sniff her, but neither did he go out of his way to avoid her. She simply seemed not to be there at all. He looked for his toys, sat beside me practicing his noble Collie look, and waited for another chance to do the chores.

Mist lay "in state" all night. Three times that night, I padded downstairs and stroked her soft black fur, sometimes crying, sometimes not, trying to bridge the gap between life with Mist and life without her. When dawn came, the dogs awoke to find me sitting beside Mist yet again. Pip had by now sniffed her all over, off and on all through the night, and perhaps found no reason to come over yet again. Lassie still darted back and forth, like a filly thoroughbred who'd seen her first freight train, round-eyed and snorting. Luke continued to look oblivious, until I finally called him over, patting Mist's flank with those little, short taps that get a dog's attention. Luke bent his head down to sniff and then threw it up as if shocked. His eyes rounded like pancakes, he looked straight up into my eyes with an expression of pure amazement, and then sniffed every inch of Misty's body. He nuzzled her, pushed her with his nose, whined, licked—all alternated with looking at me, straight into my eyes, as though asking a question.

It's been three years now since Mist died. I still miss her delicate little muzzle, her Don Quixote obsession with herding pigeons, her sweetness to people.

I've been crying a bit while I wrote this, Mist's death being close enough and her life big enough to have these memories still swell my heart. Luke is lying in the middle of the living room, right where Misty lay that long, black night. If there were ever a time when I was allowed to learn what a dog is thinking, I would ask him what he thinks happened to Mist, where he thinks that Mist is now, and whether he misses her.

It will be a long time before we understand what's going on in the mind of dogs when one of their social circle dies. I've had clients whose dogs seemed to grieve just like humans. One dog waited at the window for more than six months for a little boy who never came home. The child had been killed in a car accident, and his Golden Retriever buddy still waited every afternoon by the door for his return. After waiting several hours, Goldie would sigh deeply, lie down dejectedly, and refuse to play or go for a walk. Her owner called me because the dog was barely eating enough to stay alive.

We simply don't know if dogs have a concept of death. As Marc Hauser correctly reminds us in the book *Wild Minds*, it's perfectly possible that animals are distressed at the strange behavior of another or suffering because they have lost the social interaction of a companion without actually understanding the concept of death. The pain of a loss and an understanding of death are two very separate issues, and given that humans don't understand the concept of death until they are around eight or ten years of age, it's a reasonable question to ask. Certainly there are some amazing anecdotes about animals' behaving in ways that suggest a grieving process. Elephant researchers like Cynthia Moss have observed individuals desperately trying to rouse a dying member of the herd by getting her up on her feet, even trying to get her to eat by stuffing grass in her mouth. Elephants are famous, and accurately so, for not leaving the carcass of a dead family member for days or longer, fondling the body with their feet and trunk repeatedly. Chimpanzees and gorillas have been known to carry the dead body of an infant for days, even though the body itself is starting to rot. A research assistant at the Monterey Bay bottle-nosed dolphin project observed a group of familiar dolphins swimming in an atypical formation one day. They were swimming so slowly and in such a coordinated way that the observers described it as a "procession." In the center of the group was a mother dolphin with a dead neonatal calf on her "nose" (rostrum), being conveyed slowly through the water in the middle of the group. The human observers were so moved that, out of respect, they stopped following them.

Andy Beck, an ethologist at the White Horse Farm in New Zealand, relates an amazing story about a "group bereavement" he observed in a herd of horses. Three foals died within seventy-two hours, and for three days afterward, the entire herd of horses stood in a circle and faced the foals. They left only to get a drink of water from a nearby stream and then returned to take up their same position. He's never seen anything like it before or since.

But Beck emphasizes that he has found no consistent reaction to death in the farm's horses, even in mares after the death of their own foal. One mare who had delivered malformed (and dead) twin foals showed no reaction at all, while others have shown signs of true distress when their dead foal was removed. Beck speculates that one factor that may explain the different reactions is the actual biological impact of the death: looking at it biologically rather than emotionally, a young mare has lost little when her first attempt at reproduction dies. An older mare, however, with no live progeny and few chances remaining to pass on her genes, might react quite differently. It's an interesting hypothesis and perhaps one that will help us someday understand what is going on in the minds and emotions of other animals when there is a death.

The same range of responses that Beck sees in horses is evident in dogs reacting to the death of a human or another dog. Some dogs seem to suffer greatly, while many (if not most) act as though nothing had happened. When my first Border Collie, Drift, died at fifteen and a half, he was euthanized in the house and carried away by the vet. There was no change in behavior in any of the dogs that I could observe after he left. I don't know if it's relevant that Drift was almost blind and deaf when he died and not a very active part of the group of younger dogs. Even so, they constantly attempted to gain his attention. He basically ignored them, unless it was to grump at them if they inadvertently bumped into him in the doorway, and perhaps that affected their reaction (or lack of it) to his death.

But some animals do show signs of depression and behave in ways very similar to the ways that grieving humans behave. I've had clients whose dogs seemed to pine away for weeks after the death of a doggie friend. In my Ph.D. studies one of my brood bitches killed her puppies when they were ten days old.[2] After we took the pathetic little bodies away as soon as the deaths were discovered, the mother spent three days howling and searching everywhere, as if looking for her puppies.

What we do know is that in some cases it seems to help to let the living animals spend time with the body of the deceased one. I first heard about this practice in horses. White Horse Farm had always taken the bodies of deceased foals away from the mothers as soon as possible, because of concerns about cleanliness and disease prevention. Usually the mares reacted with extreme distress, neighing wildly and thrashing around their stalls in a frenzy. However, one day a foal died when no one was there, and it was many hours before they could remove the body. When they did, the mare paid no attention and continued eating her oats. It seemed that the hours she had spent with her foal's body allowed her to accept its removal a little later. Because of that observation, the farm purposely leaves a dead foal with the mare for several hours and has found that the mares appear calm when the bodies are removed. I was thinking of that story when my own Mist died and left her in state in case it would be helpful for my other dogs.

I didn't realize, though, how helpful having Mist's body stay in my home overnight would be for me. It was comforting for me to spend time with her body, feeling it with my hand. I hadn't even known she was sick until a few days earlier, and even though I'd had the weekend to adapt, having her drop out of my life seemed unbearable. I shouldn't be surprised at how valuable being with her body was, since we know from human experience that finding the body of a loved one is an important

2. She'd had a C-section, and I suspect that the vigorous nursing around her incision was irritating her, although I'm just guessing.

part of the grieving process. We go to great lengths to find the bodies of people who die, in the knowledge that it is much harder to resolve grief if no body has been recovered. Perhaps, in other species as well as humans, the body acts as a bridge between life with our loved ones and life without them, which allows us all to move into the future.

Keeping the body of a deceased dog, even just for a few hours, is not for everyone. Some people are put off by the thought of it, and if that's the case, don't even consider it. One of the things that we know about grieving is how very personal it is. Each of us needs to do what feels right and not what other people think we should do. But if you find that you have to euthanize a dear old friend and you're concerned about how your other dogs might react, consider bringing them to the vet's to sniff the body before it's sent away. If the vet comes to your home, think about keeping the body for a few hours so that you and your other dogs can pay your respects.

There's something else you can do for yourself that your dogs can't, which is enfold yourself in the support of your friends. We all know how important the love of our friends is when we're grieving. I can't think of a time when family, friends, and community are more important than when someone we love dies. But it's different when a dog dies. People's reactions vary, depending on their own relationship with dogs. Some people understand how profound our love for a dog can be and that the sense of grief and loss can be overwhelming. Others will shrug: "Gosh, sorry about your dog, hey-do-you-wanna-go-to-that-party-tonight?" This remarkable continuum of concern from our friends, from tears of sympathy to the barest of acknowledgments, can make a healthy grieving process difficult. Psychological studies have shown that people go through the same stages of grieving for a pet that they do for a loved human. The progression and resolution may be faster, but pet lovers go through denial, anger, sadness, and eventual resolution, just as we do when grieving for a human family member.

As horrible as losing a human is, there is a solid support system for people who have lost close family members. When my father died, a network of people allowed me to stop my life to attend to his death and my grief. Someone showed up at the house to take care of the dogs and the sheep.

The university where I was teaching said, "Take as long as you need. We'll cover you." I would never compare the death of a parent to that of a dog, but still, those first few days after Misty's death were agony. When she died, I was blessed with lots of sympathy, but the possibility that I wouldn't go teach the next day was never considered. I think it's important to give yourself some time to stop your life, if you can, and acknowledge the passing of a dear friend. Because I have to help my clients deal with loss so often (specializing in serious aggression is like being a cancer specialist: by the time I see them, many cases just can't be cured), when Misty died, I knew there was much that I could do to help myself move through the grieving process. I made a photo collage of her life that first night; I wrote her a letter on another. I still have her ashes, waiting for just the right day to throw a riproaring wake at which my buddies and I can tell stories about her, celebrate her life, and probably end up howling with our dogs at the moon.

It's important not to let others demean your love for your dog. Like many people, I used to be embarrassed if I got emotional about my dogs or my cat, anticipating at least the thought, if not the comment, "Geezzz, it's just a pet; get hold of yourself." I'm over that now, because although I adore logic and rigorous analysis, I treasure honest emotion just as highly. The scientist in me is perfectly comfortable with the animal lover in me, and we are both happy to celebrate together the miracle of our relationship with dogs.

AFTERWORD

Luke placed the damp, sandy thing in my hand as if it were a precious egg. He'd never done that before and has never done it since. "Keep away" is his favorite game, and although he reliably drops his toys to a quiet word, you can tell that it goes against his nature. Luke hogs the ball every second that he can and had to learn not to mug Pip if she should get it first. But this time he eased the object into my hands with a kind of serious nobility and then backed up and sat quietly before me. At first I didn't even know what it was, just a wet handful of brown. Gradually I began to distinguish tiny paws and a tail. My hands held a half-drowned chipmunk, chest pumping with shallow breaths, eyes screwed shut, tiny paws clenched. It had just rained 5 inches in twelve hours. There was white water in my front yard, a waterfall by the garage. The chipmunk must have gotten caught in the flooding that overtook the farm in the drama of a summer thunderstorm.

Chipmunks are generally bad guests on Wisconsin farms, chewing holes in sacks of grain and nesting in boxes of old photographs in the attic. But this gasping little mammal found her way into my heart, so I cleaned her off and warmed her up. In half an hour she was warm and dry and not at all pleased to be in a box on my kitchen counter. Luke and I watched her skitter across the garage when I let her out.

I will never know why Luke picked her up and handed her to me, ever so gently. He was not being predatory, nor was he being playful. You can't miss his intense play-stalk when we play ball: his head and tail drop while he crouches in anticipation of the chase. But this time he didn't look playful or predatory. He was quiet and serious, but soft-eyed, moving as if he were in slow motion. What was he thinking when he eased her into his jaws and presented her to me like a newborn baby at a hospital? Was he saving her life? The idea seems foolish to me: my other Border Collies hunt ground-dwelling mammals with a passion. But then, Luke pays little attention to mice and baby rabbits, and is always gentle with baby lambs. Luke has risked his own life to save mine, although I'll never know if he was purposefully saving me from danger or just getting in on the action. Perhaps he found the chipmunk confusing, out of place, and was handing her to me to get things back to normal. I don't know.

You already know that Luke is one of my best friends. After a hard morning loading sheep onto the truck, Luke and I sit together with a closeness born of hard work, mutual respect, and some undefinable connection that he and I have always had. But I'll never know what was on his mind when he picked up that soggy chipmunk. It's just not the kind of thing that dogs and humans can discuss.

We are so much like our dogs in so many ways—sharing the joys of a playful frolic on the spring grass, cuddling up for naps together on sleepy Sunday afternoons, equally excited about a walk in the cool fall woods. And yet we are a cosmos apart, separated by individual and species differences too vast ever to bridge. As Henry Beston said in *The Outermost House:*

> For the animal shall not be measured by man. In a world older and more complete than ours, they move finished and complete, gifted with the extension of the senses we have lost or never attained, living by voices we shall never hear. They are not brethren, they are not underlings: they are other nations, caught with ourselves in the net of

life and time, fellow prisoners of the splendour and travail of the earth.

The miracle is that, in one sense, it doesn't matter if I ever understand what Luke was doing. Love is not the same thing as understanding. Everyone who's been perplexed by his or her spouse or child knows that.

Of course, it matters greatly that people who love dogs understand enough about them to provide a good environment for them. That understanding allows them to help their dogs to be healthy, happy, and polite rather than inadvertently hindering them. The first thing that every dog trainer learns is that most of the problems people have with their dogs, and dogs have with their people, are due to misunderstandings that could have been prevented. Indeed, the goal of this book has been to promote an increased level of understanding of human and dog behavior, in the hope that it improves the relationships between people and their dogs.

But there are different levels of understanding, and perhaps there's a level of understanding that's not necessary between us and our dogs. Perhaps there's value in a relationship that strives to share what it can and that accepts, deeply and peacefully, its limitations.

I like that Luke is not a small, furry, four-legged human. I am blessed with many human friends and I don't need dogs as substitutes. Some of what I get from my dogs is similar to what I get from my human relationships. But just as I can't discuss world peace with Tulip, there's something that I get from my connection to her that I can't get from my other, human friends. I'm not even sure what it is, but it's deep and primal and good. It has something to do with staying connected to the earth and to sharing the planet with other living things. We humans are in such a strange position—we are still animals whose behavior reflects that of our ancestors, yet we are unique—unlike any other animal on earth. Our distinctiveness separates us and makes it easy to forget where we came from. Perhaps dogs help us remember the depth of our roots, reminding us—the animals at the other end of the leash—that we may be special, but we are not alone. No wonder we call them our best friends.

REFERENCES

Introduction

An excellent source of well-written and accessible information on the comparative behavior of chimpanzees, bonobos, and humans are the books of ethologist Frans de Waal, including *Chimpanzee Politics, Peacemaking Among Primates, Good Natured: The Origins of Right and Wrong in Humans and Other Animals,* and *The Ape and The Sushi Master.* An exquisite book of text and photographs on the bonobo, which includes pictures of bonobos so humanlike that it's disconcerting, is *Bonobo: The Forgotten Ape* by Frans de Waal and Frans Lanting. For a riveting account of gorilla behavior (and the real-life drama of the battle to conserve them), read *In the Kingdom of Gorillas* by Bill Weber and Amy Vedder.

Details on those books, and other books that were used as sources for this section, or were mentioned within it are:

Coppinger, R. and L. Coppinger. 2001. *Dogs: A Startling New Understanding of Canine Origin, Behavior and Evolution.* New York: Scribner.

Delson, E. et al., eds. 2000. *Encyclopedia of Human Evolution and Prehistory.* 2d ed. New York: Garland Publishing.

de Waal, Frans. 1989. *Peacemaking Among Primates.* Cambridge, Mass.: Harvard University Press.

de Waal, Frans. 1996. *Good Natured: The Origins of Right and Wrong in Humans and Other Animals.* Cambridge, Mass.: Harvard University Press.

de Waal, Frans. 1998. *Chimpanzee Politics, Power and Sex Among Apes.* Baltimore: Johns Hopkins University Press.

Diamond, Jared. 1992. *The Third Chimpanzee: The Evolution and Future of the Human Animal.* New York: Harpers.

Gibson, Kathleen R. and Tim Ingold. 1993. *Tools, Language and Cognition in Human Evolution.* New York: Cambridge University Press.

Harrington, Fred H. and Paul C. Paquet, eds. 1992. *Wolves of the World: Perspectives of Behavior, Ecology and Conservation.* Park Ridge, NJ: Noyes Publications.

Ingold, Tim, ed. 1994. *Companion Encyclopedia of Anthropology: Humanity, Culture and Social Life.* New York: Routledge.

Jolly, Alison. 1985. *The Evolution of Primate Behavior.* 2d ed. New York: Macmillan Publishing Co.

Morris, Desmond. 1967. *The Naked Ape.* New York: McGraw-Hill Book Co.

Peoples, J. and G. Bailey. 1997. *Humanity: An Introduction to Cultural Anthropology.* Belmont, Calif.: West/Wadsworth.

Serpell, James, ed. 1995. *The Domestic Dog: Its Evolution, Behaviour and Interactions with People.* New York: Cambridge University Press.

Weber, Bill and Amy Vedder. 2001. *In the Kingdom of Gorillas.* New York: Simon and Schuster.

Wills, Jo and Ian Robinson. 2000. *Bond for Life: Emotions Shared by People and Their Pets.* Minoequa, Wis.: Willow Creek Press.

Chapter 1: Monkey See, Monkey Do

The literature on primate behavior is massive, and I encourage readers to learn more about the primate-based behavior of humans through readings, videos, or web searches. One of the best resources in the country for information on primate behavior is the Primate Center Library of the University of Wisconsin–Madison. It's Web site is: www.primate.wisc.edu. Two good introductory texts on ethology are *Animal Behavior: Mechanisms, Ecology and Evolution* by Drickamer, Vessey, and Miekle, and *Perspectives on Animal Behavior* by Goodenough, McGuire, and Wallace. Anyone who is seriously interested in learning more about the behavior of dogs and their humans will profit by getting a solid foundation in the study of behavior itself through the often unheralded science of ethology.

Those books, and other good sources for descriptions of the visual signals of primates and canids are:

Abrantes, Roger. 1997. *Dog Language.* USA: Wakan Tanka Publishers.

Darwin, Charles. 1872/1998. *The Expression of Emotions in Man and Animals.* Definitive edition, with commentary by Paul Ekma. New York: Oxford University Press.

de Waal, Frans. 1989. *Peacemaking Among Primates.* Cambridge, Mass.: Harvard University Press.

de Waal, Frans. 1996. *Good Natured: The Origins of Right and Wrong in Humans and Other Animals.* Cambridge, Mass.: Harvard University Press.

Drickamer, Lee C., Stephen H. Vessey, and Douglas Miekle. 1995. *Animal Behavior: Mechanisms, Ecology and Evolution.* New York: McGraw Hill.

Fox, Michael W. 1978. *The Dog: Its Domestication and Behavior.* New York: Garland STMP Press.

Goodall, Jane van Lawick. 1971. *In the Shadow of Man.* Boston: Houghton Mifflin Company.

Goodenough, Judith, Betty McGuire, and Robert A. Wallace. 2000. *Perspectives on Animal Behavior.* New York: John Wiley & Sons.

Jolly, Alison. 1985. *The Evolution of Primate Behavior.* 2d ed. New York: Macmillan Publishing Co.

Kummer, Hans. 1995. *In Quest of the Sacred Baboon: A Scientist's Journey.* Princeton, NJ: Princeton University Press.

Mech, David. 1970. *The Wolf: The Ecology and Behavior of an Endangered Species.* Minneapolis, Minn.: University of Minnesota Press.

Snowdon, Charles T. In Press. "Expression of Emotion in Nonhuman Animals." In *Handbook of Affective Science.* edited by R. J. Davidson, H. H. Goldsmith, and K. Scherer. New York: Oxford University Press.

Strum, Shirley C. 1987. *Almost Human.* New York: Random House.

Zimen, Erik. 1982. "A Wolf Pack Sociogram." In *Wolves of the World: Perspectives of Behavior, Ecology and Conservation.* edited by Fred H. Harrington and Paul C. Paquet. Park Ridge, NJ: Noyes Publications.

Readers who are interested in learning more about using classical counter conditioning to treat dogs who are fearful of approaching strangers, as briefly described in this chapter with the dog Mitsy, are cautioned not to proceed without learning to master the process. The method is described in detail in a booklet that I wrote for my clients, *The Cautious Canine: How to Help Dogs Conquer Their Fears*, but owners of profoundly shy or potentially aggressive dogs are encouraged to seek experienced help before they proceed, since doing conditioning incorrectly can make the problem worse, instead of better. Listed below are several good sources describing the process and/or the uses of classical counter conditioning.

Campbell, William. 1975. *Behavior Problems in Dogs.* Santa Barbara, Calif.: American Veterinary Publications.

Campbell, William E. 1995. *Owner's Guide to Better Behavior in Dogs.* 2d ed. Loveland, Col.: Alpine Blue Ribbon Books.

Dodman, Nicholas. 1996. *The Dog Who Loved Too Much.* New York: Bantam Books.

Hetts, Suzanne. 1999. *Pet Behavior Protocols*. Lakewood, Col.: AAHA Press.

McConnell, Patricia B. 1998. *The Cautious Canine: How to Help Dogs Conquer Their Fears*. Black Earth, Wis.: Dog's Best Friend Training, Ltd.

Overall, Karen. 1997. *Clinical Behavioral Medicine for Small Animals*. St. Louis, MO: Mosby.

Ryan, Terry. 1998. *The Toolbox for Remodeling Your Problem Dog*. New York: Howell Book House.

Some wonderful books with delightful stories about herding dogs are:

Billingham, Viv. 1984. *One Woman and Her Dog*. Cambridge, U.K.: Patrick Stephens.

Halsall, Eric. 1980. *Sheepdogs: My Faithful Friends*. Cambridge, U.K.: Patrick Stephens.

McCaig, Donald. 1998. *Eminent Dogs, Dangerous Men*. New York: Lyons Press.

Chapter 2: Translating Primate to Canine

Chapters 2 and 3 are about how we can communicate most effectively with our dogs, and effective communication is the key to having the well-behaved dog that most of us want. Listed in the references below are some of my favorite training books—I'd suggest getting more than one, and paying particular attention to the points that all the authors agree upon. There are a lot of different methods of dog training, as anyone who has started reading training books can attest, but there are some universals that everyone agrees upon as critical to making learning easy and fun for both humans and their dogs. Stay away from manuals that suggest physical corrections as a primary way of communicating with your dog (that includes "leash pops"). It is true that on rare occasions I will physically correct a dog, but I do it only in very special cases, and knowing when and how to use a physical correction is an advanced skill that shouldn't be attempted by novices. In almost all cases, using positive reinforcement is much more successful, and much more fun for humans and dogs.

If readers are interested in contacting a professional animal behaviorist or dog trainer, they can contact the Animal Behavior Society at www.animal behavior.org., the American Veterinary Society of Animal Behavior through the American Veterinary Medical Association or the Association of Pet Dog Trainers at www.apdt.com.

Many of the books below are also excellent sources for canine visual signals that owners are wise to learn to recognize.

Booth, Sheila. 1998. *Purely Positive Training: Companion to Competition.* Ridgefield, Conn.: Podium Publications.

Coren, Stanley. 2000. *How to Speak Dog.* New York: Free Press.

Donaldson, Jean. 1996. *The Culture Clash.* Berkeley, Calif.: James and Kenneth Publishers.

Dunbar, Ian. 1998. *How to Teach a New Dog Old Tricks.* Berkeley, Calif.: James and Kenneth Publishers.

Kilcommons, Brian. 1992. *Good Owners, Great Dogs: A Training Manual for Humans and Their Canine Companions.* New York: Warner Books.

McAuliff, Claudeen E. 2001. *Lucy Won't Sit: How to Use Your Body, Mind and Voice for a Well-Behaved Dog.* Neosho, Wis.: Kindness K-9 Dog Behavior and Training

McConnell, Patricia B. 1996. *Beginning Family Dog Training.* Black Earth, Wis.: Dog's Best Friend, Ltd.

Milani, Myrna. 1986. *The Body Language and Emotion of Dogs.* New York: Quill.

Reid, Pamela. 1996. *Excel-erated Learning: Explaining in Plain English How Dogs Learn and How Best to Teach Them.* Oakland, Calif.: James and Kenneth Publishers.

Rogerson, John. 1991. *Understanding Your Dog.* London: Popular Dogs Publishing Co.

Rugas, Turid. 1997. *On Talking Terms with Dogs: Calming Signals.* Kula, Hawaii: Legacy By Mail.

Ryan, Terry. 1998. *The Toolbox for Remodeling Your Problem Dog.* New York: Howell Book House.

Weston, David. 1990. *Dog Training: The Gentle Modern Method.* New York: Howell Book House.

The books below were important sources for this chapter on visual signals of primates.

de Waal, Frans. 1996. *Good Natured: The Origins of Right and Wrong in Humans and Other Animals.* Cambridge, Mass.: Harvard University Press.

de Waal, Frans. 1998. *Chimpanzee Politics, Power and Sex Among Apes.* Baltimore, Md.: Johns Hopkins University Press.

Goodall, Jane van Lawick. 1971. *In the Shadow of Man.* Boston: Houghton Mifflin Company.

Snowdon, Charles T. In Press. "Expression of Emotion in Nonhuman Animals." In *Handbook of Affective Science.* edited by R. J. Davidson, H. H. Goldsmith, and K. Scherer. New York: Oxford University Press.

Strum, Shirley C. 1987. *Almost Human.* New York: Random House.

Chapter 3: Talking to Each Other

The training books listed under Chapter 2 contain important information about how best to use your voice. If readers would like more details about the use of sound by professional animal handlers in my dissertation research, they can consult an academic source: *Animal Behavior* or *Perspectives in Ethology* (listed below) or a popular article: "The Whistle Heard Round the World" in *Natural History*.

The sources listed below barely scratch the surface of the extensive literature on the vocal behavior of animals. A particularly interesting book for general readers about the use of sound in primates is *How Monkeys See The World* by Dorothy Cheney and Robert Seyfarth.

Readers who are interested in pursuing the topic in depth might enjoy looking up the journal of the Animal Behavior Society, *Animal Behaviour.* Almost every issue contains fascinating articles about the vocal behavior of selected species, from insects to primates. (Readers are forewarned that this is an academic journal and it is written in a scholarly fashion.) To see examples of articles, go to the Web site of the society, www.animalbehavior.org, and click on Animal Behaviour, or look up the journal in your local college or university biology library.

Barfield, R. J., P. Auerback, L. A. Geyer, and T. K. McIntosh. "Ultra-sonic Vocalizations in Rat Sexual Behavior." *American Zoologist* 19.

Berger, C. R. and P. de Battista, 1993. "Communication and Plan Adaptation: If at First You Don't Succeed, Say It Louder and Slower." *Communication Monographs* 60: 220–238.

Booth, Sheila. 1998. *Purely Positive Training: Companion to Competition.* Ridgefield, Conn.: Podium Publications.

Cheney, Dorothy and Robert Seyfarth. 1990. *How Monkeys See the World.* Chicago: University of Chicago Press.

Frost, April. 1998. *Beyond Obedience: Training with Awareness for You and Your Dog.* New York: Harmony Books.

Gibson, Kathleen R. and Tim Ingold. 1993. *Tools, Language and Cognition in Human Evolution.* Cambridge, U.K.: Cambridge University Press.

Goodall, Jane van Lawick. 1971. *In the Shadow of Man.* Boston: Houghton Mifflin Company.

Hirsh-Pasek, K. 1981. "Doggerel: Motherese in a New Context." *Journal of Child Language,* 9.

Harrington, F. H. and L. D. Mech., 1978. "Wolf Vocalization." In *Wolf and Man: Evolution in Parallel.* edited by R. L. Hall and H. S. Sharp. New York: Academic Press.

Marler, P., A. Dufty, and R. Pickett. 1986. "Vocal Communication in the Domestic Chicken: II. Is a Sender Sensitive to the Presence and Nature of a Receiver?" *Animal Behaviour* 43: 188–193.

McAuliffe, Claudeen E. 2001. *Lucy Won't Sit: How to Use Your Voice, Body, Mind and Voice for a Well-Behaved Dog.* Neosho, Wis.: Kindness K-9 Dog Behavior and Training.

McConnell, Patricia B. 1988. "The Effect of Acoustic Features on Receiver Response in Mammalian Communication." Dissertation: Madison, Wis.: University of Wisconsin–Madison.

McConnell, Patricia B. 1990. "Acoustic Structure and Receiver Response In *Canis Familiaris.*" *Animal Behaviour* 39: 897–904.

McConnell, Patricia B. 1991. "Lessons from Animal Trainers: The Effect of Acoustic Structure on an Animal's Response." In *Perspectives in Ethology.* Vol. 9. edited by P. P. G. Bateson and Peter H. Klopfer. New York: Plenum Press.

McConnell, Patricia B. 1992. "The Whistle Heard Round the World." *Natural History* 101, no. 10: 50–59.

McConnell, Patricia B. 1992. "Louder than Words." *AKC Gazette* 109 (May) no. 5: 38–43.

McConnell, Patricia B. and Charles T. Snowdon. 1986. "Vocal Interactions Between Unfamiliar Groups of Cotton-top Tamarins (*Saguinus oedipus oedipus*)." *Behavior* 97-3/4: 273–296.

Mitani, J. C. 1996. "African Ape Vocal Behavior." In *Great Ape Societies.* edited by William McGrew, Linda Marchant, and Toshissanda Nishido. New York: Cambridge University Press.

Morton, E. S. 1977. "On the Occurrence of Motivation-Structural Rules in Some Birds and Mammals Sounds. *American Naturalist* 3: 981.

Snowdon, Charles T. In Press. "Expression of Emotion in Nonhuman Animals." In *Handbook of Affective Science.* edited by R. J. Davidson, H. H. Goldsmith, and K. Scherer. New York: Oxford University Press

Chapter 4: Planet Smell

My favorite discussion of the sense of smell in humans is in Diane Ackerman's exquisite book *A Natural History of the Senses*. You'll never take your nose for granted after reading her chapter on scent. Stanley Coren has a great chapter on smell in his book, *How to Speak Dog*. See Roy Hunter's delightful book *Fun Nosework for Dogs* to get inspired about all the ways your dog can amaze you and your friends with her nose.

Ackerman, Diane. 1990. *A Natural History of the Senses*. New York: Vintage Books.

Bownds, M. Deric. 1999. *The Biology of Mind*. Bethesda, Md.: Fitzgerald Science Press.

Budiansky, Stephen. 2000. *The Truth About Dogs*. New York: Viking Press.

Coren, Stanley. 2000. *How to Speak Dog*. New York: Free Press.

Ganz, Sandy and Susan Boyd. 1990. *Tracking from the Ground Up*. St. Louis, MO.: Show-Me Publications.

Gilling, Dick and Robin Brightwell. 1982. *The Human Brain*. London: Orbis Publishing.

Hunter, Roy. 1995. *Fun Nosework for Dogs*. Eliot, Me: Howln Moon Press.

Johnson, Glen R. 1977. *Tracking Dog Theory and Methods*. Rome, NY: Arner Publications.

Laska, M., A. Seibt, and A. Weber. 2000. "'Microsomatic' Primates Revisited: Olfactory Sensitivity in the Squirrel Monkey." *Chemical Senses* 25: 47–53.

MacKenzie, S. A. and J. A. Schultz. 1987. "Frequency of Back-tacking in the Tracking Dog." *Applied Animal Behavior Science* 17: 353–359.

Sanders, William. 1998. *Enthusiastic Tracking*. Stanwood, Wash.: Rime Publications.

Scott, John Paul and John L. Fuller. 1965. *Genetics and the Social Behavior of the Dog*. Chicago: University of Chicago Press.

Steen, J.B. and E. Wilsson. 1990. "How Do Dogs Determine the Direction of Tracks?" *Acta Physiologica Scandinavica* 139: 531–534.

Washabaug, Kate and Charles Snowdon. 1998. "Chemical Communication of Reproductive Status in Female Cotton-top Tamarins (*Saguinus oedipus oedipus*)." *American Journal of Primatology* 45:337–349.

Chapter 5: Fun and Play

Besides my own observations, the primary sources for the comparisons of play in dogs and humans are two excellent, academic books: *Play and Exploration in Children and Animals* by Thomas G. Power, and *Animal Play: Evolutionary, Comparative and Ecological Perspectives* edited by Marc Bekoff and John Byers. Listed below are those books and other sources for this chapter.

Bekoff, Marc and John A. Byers. 1998. *Animal Play: Evolutionary, Comparative and Ecological Perspectives*. New York: Cambridge University Press.

Bolhuis, Johan J. and Jerry A Hogan. 1999. *The Development of Animal Behavior*. Oxford, U.K.: Blackwell Publishers.

Budiansky, Stephen. 1999. *Covenant of the Wild*. New Haven, Conn.: Yale University Press.

Coppinger, R. and L. Coppinger. 2001. *Dogs: A Startling New Understanding of Canine Origin, Behavior and Evolution*. New York: Scribner.

Fiske, A. 1884. *The Destiny of Man Viewed in Light of His Origin*. Boston: Houghton-Mifflin.

Hunter, Roy. 1995. *Fun Nosework for Dogs*. Eliot, Maine: Howln Moon Press.

Itani, J. and A. Nishimura. 1973. "The Study of Infrahuman Culture in Japan: A Review." In *Precultural Primate Behavior*. edited by E. W. Menzel. Basel: Karger.

Power, Thomas G. 2000. *Play and Exploration in Children and Animals*. Mahwah, NJ: Lawrence Erlbaum Associates.

Chapters 6 and 7: Packmates, and The Truth About Dominance

I've combined the notes for these two chapters because much of the scholarly information about their contents are in the same books. There is a vast range of approaches to the social nature of humans, other primates, dogs, and other canids, from beautiful stories to technical research results. One of my favorite literary books is the exquisitely written *Pack of Two: The Intricate Bond Between People and Dogs* by Caroline Knapp. Elizabeth Marshall Thomas writes beautiful stories about her dogs, including *The Social Life of Dogs: The Grace of Canine Company*. A fascinating book about the historical relationship between people and dogs is *Dogs: A Historical Journey* by Lloyd Wendt.

For scholarly information about social systems in primates, I recommend *The Evolution of Primate Behavior* by Alison Jolly and *Primate Social Conflict* by

William Mason and Sally Mendoza. Some of the many excellent popular books on primate behavior include those written by Frans de Waal, Shirley Strum, Jane van Lawick Goodall, Bill Weber, and Amy Vedder. I encourage dog lovers to read about the behavior of *any* species that interests them, because there is great value in looking at the behavior of any individual animal within a larger perspective, just as one can't truly understand a tree without understanding the forest within which it grows.

The problem in recommending books on primate behavior is in choosing from literally thousands of sources. I regret that the problem of recommending good, scientifically based books on the social behavior of dogs is the opposite. Apparently, familiarity really does breed contempt, because good academic research on dog behavior is amazingly rare. (For example, there has been very little work done on analyzing the vocalizations of domestic dogs, while the vocalizations of Red-winged Blackbirds are discussed in over one thousand published studies.) I'm happy to say that this trend is starting to reverse. Just in the last few years there has been some solid research on the behavior of the domestic dog. At present, the best science-based book on the behavior of dogs is James Serpell's *The Domestic Dog: Its Evolution, Behaviour and Interactions with People.* Stephen Budiansky wrote an interesting book about our relationship with dogs, *The Truth About Dogs: An Inquiry into the Ancestry, Social Conventions, Mental Habits, and Moral Fiber of* Canis Familiaris.

There is a lovely book of quotes and photographs, *Bond for Life: Emotions Shared by People and Their Pets,* which has graced my living room since I received it and that I highly recommend. There are, of course, many, many more, some of which are listed below along with sources for information in the chapters.

There are several books that present strongly expressed opinions about the consequences of human selection criteria on dogs. Two of the most recent ones are Mark Derr's *Dog's Best Friend: Annals of the Dog-Human Relationship* and Raymond and Lorna Coppingers' *Dogs: A Startling New Understanding of Canine Origin, Behavior and Evolution.* For a completely different perspective, go to the American Kennel Club Web site at www.akc.org.

The Web site of Wolf Park, in Indiana, can be accessed at www.wolfpark.org.

Beck, Alan M. 1973. *The Ecology of Stray Dogs: A Study of Free-Ranging Urban Animals.* Baltimore, Maryland.: York Press.

Beck, Alan and Aaron Katcher. 1983. *Between Pets and People: The Importance of Animal Companionship.* New York: G. P. Putnam's Sons.

Beckoff, Marc, ed. 1978. *Coyote Biology, Behavior and Management*. New York Academic Press.

Bolhuis, Johan H. and Jerry A. Hogan, eds. 1999. *The Development of Animal Behavior*. Oxford, U.K.: Blackwell Publishers.

Brazleton, T. Berry. 1983. *Infants and Mothers: Differences in Development*. New York: Delacorte Press.

Campbell, William E. 1995. *Owner's Guide to Better Behavior in Dogs.*, 2d ed. Loveland, Col.: Alpine Blue Ribbon Books.

Delson, Eric, Ian Tatersall, John A. Van Couvering, and Alison S. Brooks. eds. 2000. *Encyclopedia of Human Evolution and Prehistory*. New York: Garland Publishing.

de Waal, Frans. 1989. *Peacemaking Among Primates*. Cambridge, Mass.: Harvard University Press.

de Waal, Frans. 1996. *Good Natured: The Origins of Right and Wrong in Humans and Other Animals*. Cambridge, Mass.: Harvard University Press.

de Waal, Frans. 1998. *Chimpanzee Politics, Power and Sex Among Apes*. Baltimore, Md: Johns Hopkins University Press.

Dodman, Nicholas H. 1996. *The Dog Who Loved Too Much*. New York: Bantam Books.

Goodall, Jane van Lawick. 1971. *In the Shadow of Man*. Boston: Houghton Mifflin Company.

Gould, Stephen Jay. 1979. "Mickey Mouse Meets Konrad Lorenz." *Natural History* 88. no. 5: 30–36.

Gould, Stephen Jay. 1982. "A Biographical Homage to Mickey Mouse." Pp. 95–107 in *The Panda's Thumb*. New York: W. W. Norton.

Harlow, Harry F. and Margaret K. Harlow. 1962. "Social Deprivation in Monkeys." *Scientific American* 207(5): 136–46.

Ingold. Tim, ed. 1994. *Companion Encyclopedia of Anthropology: Humanity, Culture and Social Life*. New York: Routledge.

Jolly, Allison. 1985. *The Evolution of Primate Behavior*. 2d ed. New York: Macmillan Publishing, Co.

Knapp, Caroline. 1995. *Pack of Two: The Intricate Bond Between People and Dogs*. New York: Dial Press.

Llewellyn, Karl, and E. Adamson Hoebel. 1941. *The Cheyenne Way*. Norman, Okla.: University of Oklahoma Press.

Mason, William A. and Sally P. Mendoza, eds. 1993. *Primate Social Conflict*. Albany, NY: State University of New York Press.

McConnell, Patricia B. 1998. *The Cautious Canine: How to Help Dogs Conquer Their Fears*. Black Earth, Wis.: Dog's Best Friend, Ltd.

McGrew, William C., Linda F. Marchant, and Toshisada Nishida, eds. 1996. *Great Ape Societies*. New York: Cambridge University Press.

Monks of New Skete. 1978. *How to Be Your Dog's Best Friend*. Boston: Little, Brown and Company.

Patterson, Francine. 1985. *Koko's Kitten*. New York: Scholastic.

Peoples, James and Garrick Bailey. 1997. *Humanity: An Introduction to Cultural Anthropology*. 4th ed. Belmont, Calif.: Wadsworth Publishing Co.

Ryan, Terry. 1998. *The Toolbox for Remodeling Your Problem Dog*. New York: Howell Book House.

Scott, John Paul and John L. Fuller. 1965. *Genetics and the Social Behavior of the Dog*. Chicago: University of Chicago Press.

Serpell, James, ed. 1995. *The Domestic Dog: Its Evolution, Behaviour and Interactions with People*. New York: Cambridge University Press.

Strum, Shirley C. 1987. *Almost Human: A Journey into the World of Baboons*. New York: Random House.

Thomas, Elizabeth Marshall. 2000. *The Social Lives of Dogs: The Grace of Canine Company*. New York: Pocket Books.

Walker, Peter. 1995. *Baby Massage: A Practical Guide to Massage and Movement for Babies and Infants*. New York: St. Martin's Griffin.

Wendt, Lloyd M. 1996. *Dogs: A Historical Journey*. New York: Howell Book House.

Wills, Jo and Ian Robinson. 2000. *Bond for Life: Emotions Shared by People and Their Pets*. Minoequa, Wis.: Willow Creek Press.

Zimen, Erik. 1982. "A Wolf Pack Sociogram." Pp. 282–322 in *Wolves of the World*. edited by Fred H. Harrington and Paul C. Paquet. Park Ridge, NJ: Noyes Publications.

Chapter 8: Patient Dogs and Wise Humans

You can find a range of opinions about the role of "dominance" or social status in relation to behavioral problems with your dog in the following books:

Dodman, Nicholas. 1996. *The Dog Who Loved Too Much*. New York: Bantam Books.

Donaldson, Jean. 1996. *The Culture Clash*. Berkeley, Calif.: James and Kenneth Publishers.

Dunbar, Ian. 1998. *How to Teach a New Dog Old Tricks*. Berkeley, Calif.: James and Kenneth Publishers.

Hetts, Suzanne. 1999. *Pet Behavior Protocols*. Lakewood, Col.: AAHA Press.

London, Karen L. and Patricia B. McConnell. 2001. *Feeling Outnumbered? How to Manage and Enjoy Your Multi-Dog Household.* Black Earth, Wis.: Dog's Best Friend, Ltd.

McConnell, Patricia B. 1996. *Beginning Family Dog Training.* Black Earth, Wis.: Dog's Best Friend, Ltd.

McConnell, Patricia B. 1996. *How to be Leader of the Pack and Have Your Dog Love You for It.* Black Earth, Wis.: Dog's Best Friend, Ltd.

Overall, Karen. 1997. *Clinical Behavioral Medicine for Small Animals.* St.Louis, MO: Mosby.

Wright, John C. and Judi Wright Lashnits. 1999. *The Dog Who Would Be King.* Emmaus, Penn.: Rodale Press.

Chapter 9: Personalities

Anyone looking for a dog would be well served by finding an experienced dog trainer or behaviorist to help them evaluate the personality of their potential new dog. A little bit of experience can go a long way when trying to make predictions about what a dog from one enviroment is going to do in another environment. A knowledge of the general characteristics of a breed can help if you're looking at a "purebred," but there are millions of great dogs who aren't purebreds, and as mentioned in the chapter, the dogs don't all read the books anyway.

Although most of the standards for purebred dogs registered through the American Kennel Club are about physical traits, reading through the standards of the breed clubs can sometimes tell you about the generic personality of many individuals of the breed. (Keep in mind that the American Kennel Club is one of many registries that keep track of canine genealogy. It is without question the biggest registry, but AKC "papers," just like the papers from other registries, are simply a list of a dog's forebearers, they are not a guarantee of quality.) Breed standards and descriptions always need to be taken with a grain of salt. They are usually written by the people who love the breed most, and are often written as though every individual within the breed is a clone of every other. Nonetheless, when a breed standard or breed description says "aloof around strangers," pay attention. This just might not be the best breed for someone who has a lot of visitors, unless you find one of those individual dogs who hasn't read the breed description.

The book that best describes dog breeds is by Bonnie Wilcox and Chris Walkowicz, *The Atlas of Dog Breeds of the World.* It's been updated recently and contains the most in-depth description of a myriad of dog breeds, along with helpful information about the breed's origin. Pay careful attention to the origin of a breed—selecting a Tibetan Mastiff, who was bred to work in complete isolation from humans and to be inherently suspicious of all other dogs, may not be the best choice for your son's 4-H obedience project. If you're looking for help finding first the right breed, and then the right individual dog for you, your best bet is to start with books and web searches, and move quickly to face-to-face meetings with as many dogs and their humans as you can manage.

Don't neglect to seriously consider a "mutt." Just because a dog doesn't have "papers" doesn't mean that she's not a good dog. Whatever you do, do it thoughtfully, and avoid the impulse buying that causes so much pain and suffering for both people and dogs.

Cambell, William. 1975. *Behavior Problems in Dogs.* Santa Barbara, Calif.: American Veterinary Publications.

de Waal, Frans. 1998. *Chimpanzee Politics, Power and Sex Among Apes.* Baltimore, Md.: Johns Hopkins University Press.

Etcoff, Nancy. 2000. *Survival of the Prettiest: The Science of Beauty.* New York: Anchor Books.

Karsh, Eileen B. and Dennis C. Turner. 1990. "The Human-Cat Relationship." In *The Domestic Cat: The Biology of Its Behavior.* edited by Dennis C. Turner and Patrick Bateson. Cambridge, U.K.: Cambridge University Press.

Scott, John Paul and John L. Fuller. 1965. *Genetics and the Social Behavior of the Dog: The Class Study.* Chicago: University of Chicago Press.

Strum, Shirley C. 1987. *Almost Human.* New York: Random House.

Suomi, Stephen J. 1998. *Genetic and Environmental Factors Influencing Serotonergic Functioning and the Expression of Impulsive Aggression in Rhesus Monkeys.* Plenary Lecture: Italian Congress of Biological Psychiatry, Naples, Italy.

Suomi, Stephen J. 2001. *How Gene-Environment Interactions Can Shape the Development of Socioemotional Regulation in Rhesus Monkeys.* Round Table: Socioemotional Regulation, Dimensions, Developmental Trends and Influences, Johnson and Johnson Pediatric Round Table, Palm Beach, Fl.

Wilcox, Bonnie and Chris Walkowicz. 1989. *The Atlas of Dog Breeds of the World.* Neptune City, NJ: T.F.H Publications.

Zimbardo, Philip G. 1977. *Shyness: What It Is, What to Do About It.* Reading, Mass.: Addison-Wesley.

Chapter 10: Love and Loss

Marc Hauser has an interesting discussion about animals experiencing the loss of a social companion in *Wild Minds: What Animals Really Think,* and I found it useful when I was working on this chapter. It's a well-written book that does a good job summarizing much of the research on cognition for animal lovers who are not themselves scientists.

The Web site of White Horse Farm, from where Andy Beck reported the strange "group bereavement" behavior in a herd of horses, is www.equine-behavior.com.

A particularly good book on coping with the death of your pet is *Crossing the Rubicon* by Julie Kaufman. Also see *It's OK to Cry*, a book of stories by pet owners who have lost a beloved animal. The authors recommend reading only a few stories at a time, and it's good advice, because if you're anything like me, you'll be crying after just a few pages.

Details on these and other references in this chapter are:

Beston, Henry. 1992. *The Outermost House: A Year of Life on the Great Beach of Cape Cod.* New York: Henry Holt.

Harrington, Fred H. and Paul C. Paquet, eds. 1992. *Wolves of the World: Perspectives of Behavior, Ecology and Conservation.* Park Ridge, NJ: Noyes Publications.

Hauser, Marc D. 2000. *Wild Minds: What Animals Really Think.* New York: Henry Holt and Company.

Kaufman, Julie. 1999. *Crossing the Rubicon: Celebrating the Human-Animal Bond in Life and Death.* Cottage Grove, Wis.: Xenophon Publications.

Kay, William J. et al. 1984. *Pet Loss and Human Bereavement.* Ames, Iowa: Iowa State University Press.

Quintana, Maria Luz, Shari L. Veleba, and Harley King. 1998. *It's OK to Cry.* Perrysburg, Oh.: K & K Communications.

INDEX